Life and Half Life

George Dureau, 83
1930–2014

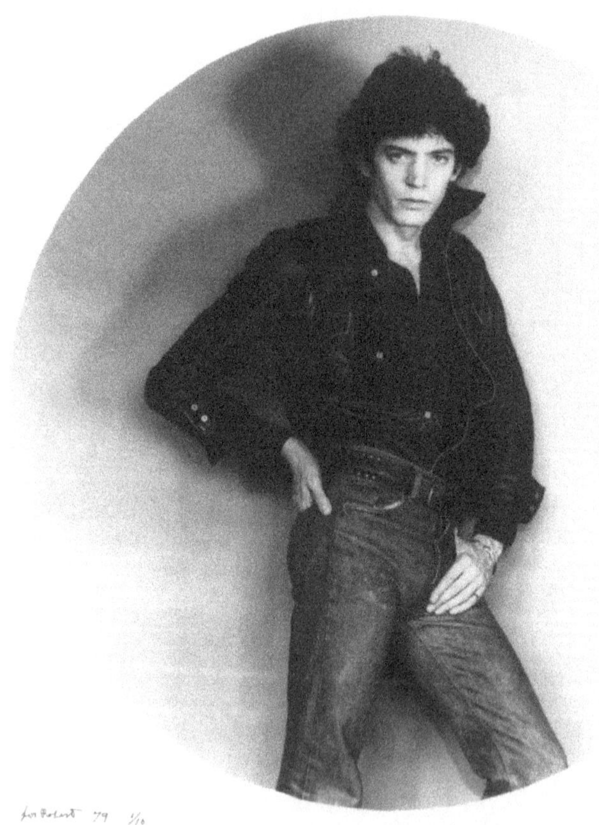

Robert Mapplethorpe, 42
1946–1989

"Robert Mapplethorpe" by George Dureau from the cover of
Jack Fritscher's 1994 memoir *Mapplethorpe: Assault with a Deadly Camera*

"This book is essential art history giving a sense of time, place, and context while illuminating two Titans—one remembered, one nearly forgotten—at the end of the 1980s.

These lively historic transcripts of legendary New Orleans artist George Dureau in conversation with gay historian Jack Fritscher act as a lens through which we're able to peer into one of 20th-century art's great questions of influence and mentorship: George Dureau and Robert Mapplethorpe.

The author who knew both men for years leads us Virgil-like through these sessions recorded at long-distance on landlines—and up close on video cameras on Dureau's French Quarter balcony from 1989 to 1991. George is fit and on top fifteen years before Hurricane Katrina and Alzheimer's took their toll.

Fritscher's release of this archival material is a great gift and an act of love for Dureau and Mapplethorpe and the models."
—Jarret Lofstead, writer/filmmaker, *George Dureau: New Orleans Artist*

"In 2018, when my gallery hosted the first exhibit hanging Mapplethorpe and Dureau side by side, reviewer John d'Addario noted that going beyond mentorship, the joint pairing revealed both men were working 'in the same vernacular' creating 'a kind of dialogue through their images.' Having represented George since 1988, I couldn't agree more with d'Addario that 'the full story of Mapplethorpe and Dureau is still one that needs to be told.' And here in *Dueling Photographers* that story begins."
—Arthur Roger, Arthur Roger Gallery, New Orleans

"*Dueling Photographers* is a biographical history and indispensable archive giving George Dureau his due as a singular photographer of non-normativity. Suitably adjacent to queer and disability studies, this unique book takes on the important task of revealing this artist whose compassionate camera presents the beauty of the disabled human body in all its wondrous diversity."
—Robert McRuer, PhD, author of *Crip Theory: Cultural Signs of Queerness and Disability*

"*Dueling Photographers* is my 'black bible' reminding me, chapter and verse, how my longtime friend George Dureau inspired me, a Puerto Rican New York photographer, about body, soul, and spirit in my own multiracial shoots and books. I deeply appreciate Fritscher's candid and authentic portrait of George mentoring Mapplethorpe on the aesthetics, boundaries, and courtesies of interracial photography. Back in the day, I knew both George and Robert, so it's lovely to hear George speaking for himself in the telephone calls and in-depth interviews that deliver great insight to his life and work which are both compelling and now historic."
—Michael Alago, author, photographer, music executive, *Polaroid Encounters 1998-2009*

"Fritscher takes us deep into George Dureau's world where George speaks for himself mentoring Robert Mapplethorpe about photography and race.

As close witness and part-enabler to Mapplethorpe's trajectory, Fritscher who was friends with George and lovers with Mapplethorpe cross-stitches the two great artists to explicate both from his unique perspective.

For Dureau, who called himself Big Daddy, another southern Big Daddy appears in Tennessee Williams who is, at a slight distance, omnipresent in the French Quarter context whilst the other Big Daddy Sam Wagstaff in New York pours fuel on Mapplethorpe's fire with notions of what parts of a Dureau picture work best for his boy Robert to slice off—distilling the concepts of form and deformity in the robustly humanistic portraits of George Dureau into his own stylised New York masks and mirrors.

Whilst one can't ignore their dueling personalities, Fritscher takes pains to reassure the reader that neither Robert nor George was a villain. So I've discarded notions of which of the two rivals is better. I'm entranced by Fritscher's eyewitness research in this richly detailed memoir of fresh scholarship documenting two artists and the eternal visions they left us."
—A M Hanson, artist/photographer, London

DUELING PHOTOGRAPHERS

GEORGE DUREAU
and
ROBERT MAPPLETHORPE

Jack Fritscher, PhD

PROFILES IN GAY COURAGE
Volume 2

Archival Edition
Jack Fritscher-Mark Hemry Archives

Palm Drive Publishing™

For author history and for historical research https://JackFritscher.com

Cover photo: *George Dureau and Brian Reeves* (front studio, second floor, 1707 Esplanade Avenue, New Orleans) by ©1984 Jonathan Webb

Cover and book design by Mark Hemry

Published by Palm Drive Publishing, Sebastopol CA
www.PalmDrivePublishing.com
Email: publisher@PalmDrivePublishing.com

Library of Congress Control Number: 2024936757
Fritscher, Jack 1939-
Dueling Photographers: George Dureau and Robert Mapplethorpe. Profiles in Gay Courage: Volume 2 / Jack Fritscher
p.cm

ISBN 978-1-890834-69-2 Print
ISBN 978-1-890834-70-8 eBook

1. Fine Arts. 2. Visual Arts. 3. Photography. 4. Gay Photography. 5. Art History. 6. Gay Art History. 7. Biography. 8. George Dureau. 9. Robert Mapplethorpe. 10. Black Men. 11. Racism. 12. Homosexuality. 13. Disability. 14. New Orleans History

First Printing 2024
10 9 8 7 6 5 4 3 2
PalmDrivePublishing™.com

Special dedication and thanks
to my stoic editor and husband Mark Hemry
without whose remarkable diligence
for nearly fifty years
this material would have been
impossible to collect, analyze, and present

"A portrait is not made in the camera,
but on either side of it." —Edward Steichen

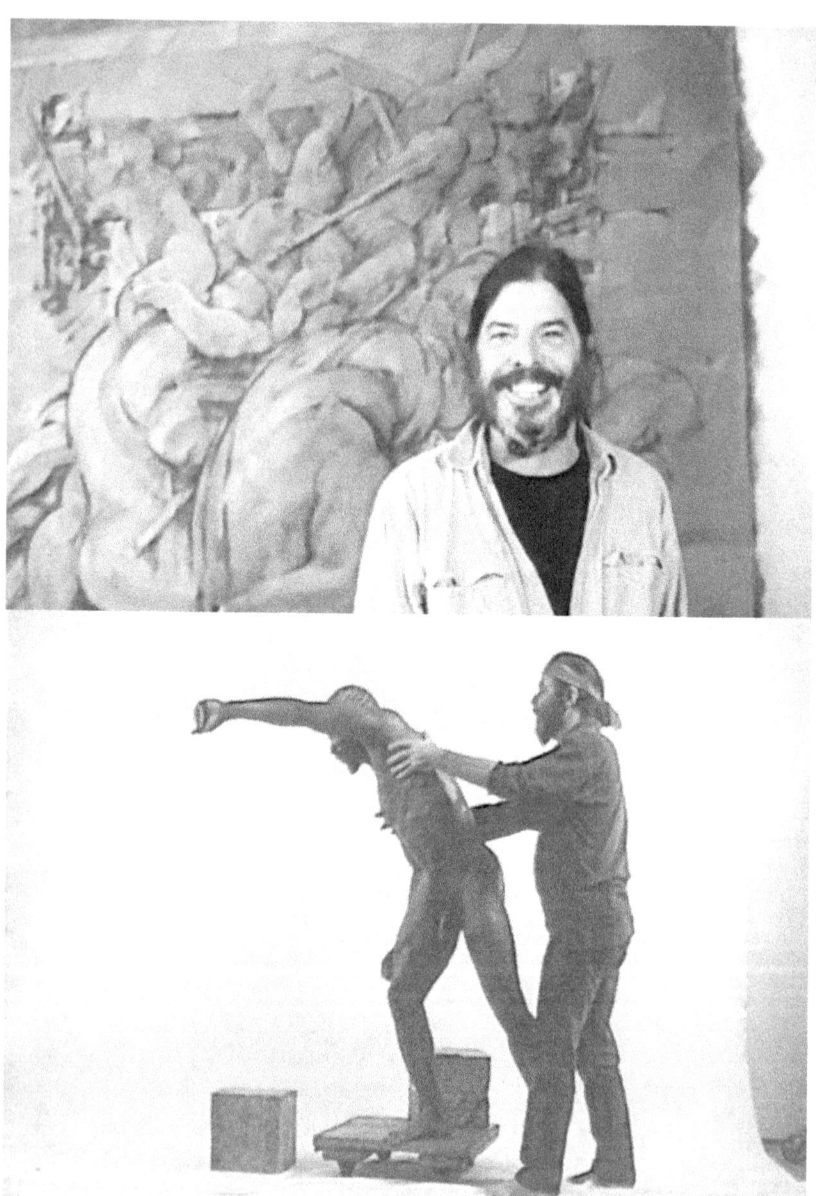

(Top) George Dureau installing his epic twenty-foot-tall canvas *Mars Descending* at the Contemporary Arts Center of New Orleans for its *War Exhibition*. April 8, 1991. Video photo by © Jack Fritscher

(Bottom) George Dureau posing his recurring photography model Glen Thompson for the documentary *Dureau in Studio*, April 10, 1991. Video photo by © Jack Fritscher

Foreword

These lively historic transcripts of legendary New Orleans artist George Dureau in conversation with Jack Fritscher act as a lens through which we're able to peer into one of 20th-century art's great questions of influence and mentorship: George Dureau and Robert Mapplethorpe.

New Orleans master craftsman Dureau holds court on art history, his life, lifestyle, and career, and both Fritscher and Dureau speak candidly about their longtime relationships with the recently departed Mapplethorpe.

Fritscher who knew both men for years leads us Virgil-like through these sessions held long distance, and up close on Dureau's French Quarter balcony, from 1989 to 1991 showing us Dureau in his early 60s, demanding and generous, as he continues to pursue his art despite the odds surrounding homosexuality, race, and disability.

This is George fit and on top at the end of the century before Hurricane Katrina, gentrification, and Alzheimer's took their toll on this great creative and (generally) blithe spirit who lived twice as long as Mapplethorpe.

Authenticated by his friends and family, these conversations illustrate Dureau's life and his work as inseparable. Fritscher handles the artist with the same empathy and care George showed his subjects.

Fritscher's release of this archival material is a great gift and an act of love for Dureau and Mapplethorpe and the models. It's essential art history giving a sense of time, place, and context while illuminating two Titans—one remembered, one nearly forgotten—at the end of the 1980s.

—Jarret Lofstead, writer/filmmaker, *George Dureau: New Orleans Artist*

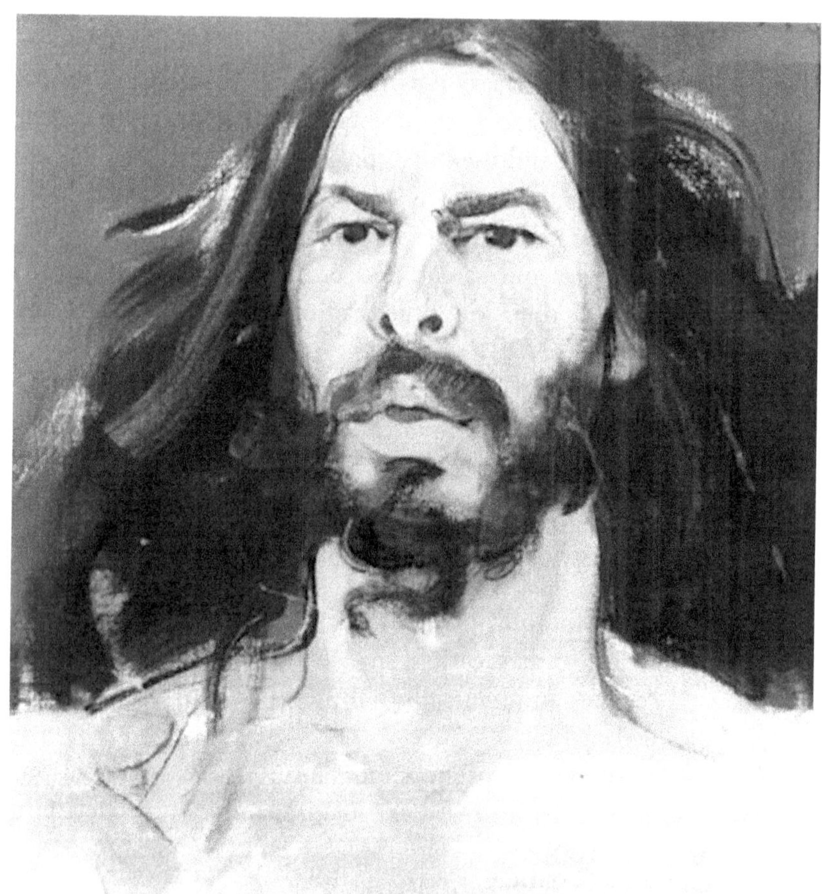

George Dureau, *Self-Portrait*, c. 1972. This assertive, baroque, and swashbuckling identity painting of the American man George Dureau, the homomasculine homosurrealist who was nobody's second fiddle, was first published on the cover of the exhibition catalogue *George Dureau: Selected Works 1960-1977, October 1-29, 1977*, with essays by W. Kenneth Holditch and Terrington Calas, New Orleans: Contemporary Arts Center, 1977, 32 pages. First Edition.

Preface

THE PASSIONATE FEW

Emancipating New Orleans Sun King, George Dureau, from the Mapplethorpe Eclipse

"And it is by the passionate few that the renown of genius is kept alive from one generation to another. These few are always at work. They are always rediscovering genius. Their curiosity and enthusiasm are exhaustless, so that there is little chance of genius being ignored. And, moreover, they are always working either for or against the verdicts of the majority. The majority can make a reputation, but it is too careless to maintain it. If, by accident, the passionate few agree with the majority in a particular instance, they will frequently remind the majority that such and such a reputation has been made, and the majority will idly concur."
—Arnold Bennet, "Literary Taste: How to Form It," 1909

Toward the 2030 Centennial
of the Birth of George Dureau

In the *Rashomon* of stories around George Dureau, I tip my hat to the Passionate Few who have had the pleasure of knowing George far better and longer than I who met him in April 1991 to shoot what he directed as his seminal video interview "for posterity" on his Dauphine Street balcony talking about his career and that of Robert Mapplethorpe whose double mentor he was in both photography and race relationships.

For too long the Mapplethorpe shadow has eclipsed George who, like Robert, was also a genius in a class and city of his own. In the way Stephen Sondheim spun a musical out of a painting to illuminate the other George, Georges Seurat, limning his *A Sunday*

Afternoon on the Island of La Grande Jatte, the time has come to spin new art, thinking, and scholarship out of the storyboard painting, photography, and sculpture of George Dureau.

This book is a mandate of sorts because both George and my 1970s lover Robert asked me to write about them. For over forty years, I've told their stories in essays and books and onscreen documentaries recalling the way they were before their lives became legends that became myth. George passed at 83, and I, now 84, sorting my archives, simply wish to add my recorded conversations with George and my eyewitness observations about him to the sodality and solidarity of relatives, friends, critics, scholars, filmmakers, and art lovers who have championed him for so long.

George made everyone he met feel like a longtime friend.

To know George was to have a heartfelt platonic affair with him that endures to this moment.

"I'm capable," George told me, "of carrying on affairs with everybody on earth at the same time. Not successfully, but energetically. My life and my work are identical. There's a lot of warmth and passion, and a lot of dinners and candles in my life."

In 1994, George contributed his lovely 1979 photograph of a healthy Robert Mapplethorpe for the cover of my Mapplethorpe memoir which has its own Dureau chapter.

I cherish the last time my husband Mark Hemry and I were together with George in this life. It was Paris, May 3, 1996. We were strolling the Grande Allée path of the Tuileries on a sunny afternoon in the park with George. With our video camera filming, and George, vivacious and laughing, we were on our way toward the Maison Européenne de la Photographie where that night in the gay Marais at 5-7 rue de Fourcy, George was to be honored and our two video documentaries, *Dureau Vérité: Life, Camera, Canvas* and *Dureau in Studio*, were to be received into the permanent collection.

A dozen of his photos and one of his paintings hang, like a shrine to a New Orleans saint, in our living room where his lively spirit abides.

While George voices his authentic opinions and speaks for himself in my video documentation and telephone transcripts, may I say, out of respect for the *Rashomon* of other voices, stories, and opinions, that my efforts at scholarship, and my assertions, which I hope are compatible with others, are my own as are any errors in my book written to honor George.

Working as an academic gay historian since 1965, I have the greatest respect for the diverse efforts of the Passionate Few in New Orleans so long dedicated to keeping George's life, work, and legend alive. My thanks underscores my appreciation of the eyewitnesses who have written and spoken about, filmed, and cared for George so that my effort here can quote and assemble their voices together to organize existing information to offer research support to a new generation creating Dureau essays, biographies, films, and scholarship in the run-up to his hundredth birthday in 2030.

My particular appreciation to Don Dureau, Arthur Roger, Jonathan Webb, Jarret Lofstead, Michael Alago, Jim Marks, Edward Lucie-Smith, and especially George himself for the hours of his oral history transcribed here as he requested "for posterity."

Jack Fritscher, PhD
San Francisco
May 2024

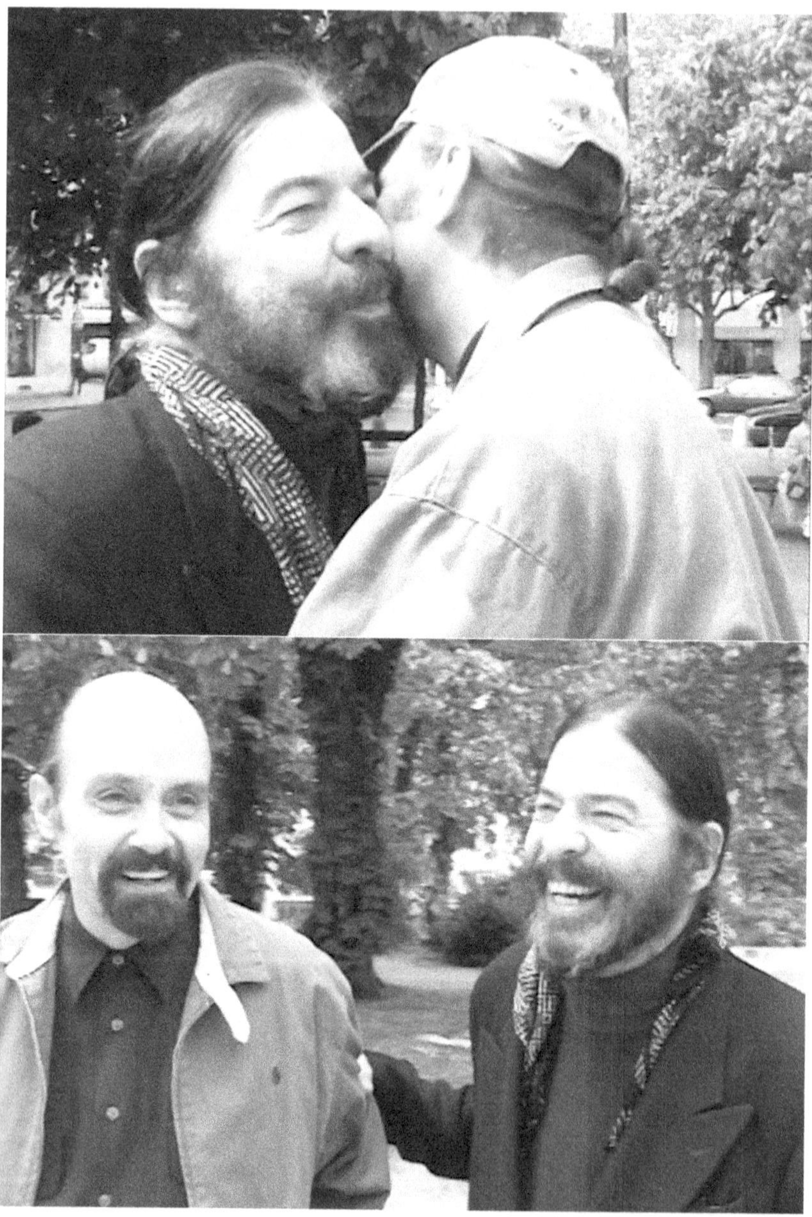

George Dureau and Jack Fritscher strolling the Grande Allée, the Tuileries, Paris, May 3, 1996, on the way to La Maison Europèenne de la Photographie at 5/7 Rue de Fourcy where that evening George was being fêted as the two Dureau documentaries by Fritscher and Mark Hemry were being inducted into its permanent collection. Video photo by © Mark Hemry from his unpublished footage of Dureau in Paris

Contents

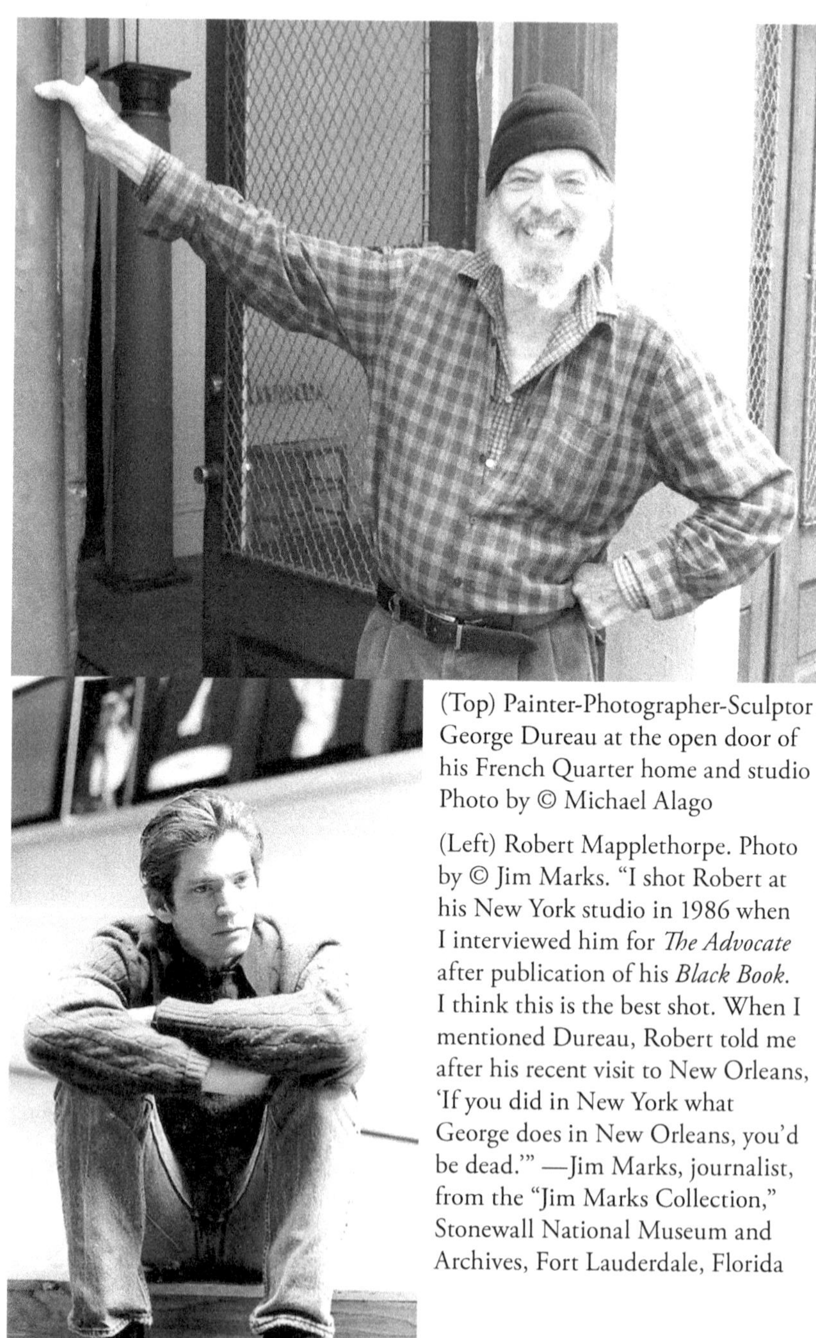

(Top) Painter-Photographer-Sculptor George Dureau at the open door of his French Quarter home and studio Photo by © Michael Alago

(Left) Robert Mapplethorpe. Photo by © Jim Marks. "I shot Robert at his New York studio in 1986 when I interviewed him for *The Advocate* after publication of his *Black Book*. I think this is the best shot. When I mentioned Dureau, Robert told me after his recent visit to New Orleans, 'If you did in New York what George does in New Orleans, you'd be dead.'" —Jim Marks, journalist, from the "Jim Marks Collection," Stonewall National Museum and Archives, Fort Lauderdale, Florida

TAKE 1

AN EYEWITNESS CAMERA

George Dureau and Robert Mapplethorpe
Through a Lens Darkly
But Then Face to Face

Mentoring Mapplethorpe on Photography and Race

"The camera is a mindless lunatic."
—George Dureau
28 December 1930 – 7 April 2014

On April 8, 1991, after three cordial long-distance phone conversations between California and Louisiana, I met George Dureau who shot Mapplethorpe who shot Dureau who sat for my eyewitness camera. Like Manet's canvas-slashing friendship with Degas, theirs was a gentlemen's rivalry fit for the iconic Dueling Oaks in New Orleans. "Daguerreotypes at dawn!"

When they met, George, forty-eight and laidback in horizontal New Orleans, was already "The Dureau." Robert, thirty-two and climbing in vertical New York, was not yet "The Mapplethorpe." Robert first learned of the charismatic Dureau when he set eyes on the Dureau pictures being collected by his millionaire lover Sam Wagstaff in the 1970s before the three were introduced in person by New Orleans art collector and radiologist, Russell Albright, MD, in 1979 beginning their intermittent and fractious nine-year friendship.

George, fit and quick-witted and speaking for himself with vivid memories reclaiming his history, told me, "Robert wrote to me and bought some of my photos in the late 70s before we met in person in 1979 when we shot each other.[1] My photograph *Wilbert Hines* [1977, leaning against a mantelpiece], was the first one he bought. He asked me how I did it and like a fool I told him."

He prized his photos of the fresh-faced Robert and he gave me one of those able-bodied portraits—to document Robert's healthy look when he and I were just men together—for the cover of my 1994 memoir *Mapplethorpe: Assault with a Deadly Camera.*

George said, "I'm sending you the cute ones of Robert I took up at his place in 1979. It's very much the style that comes from my drawing that I've been doing since the 60s, the way it's posed and put into the circle. I transposed my figurative drawing into my photography. It represents him very nicely in the period that you and I knew him best."

The reciprocal portraits by the two gay alpha males with extravagant personas pulsate with the kind of *frisson* expected by fans of Tennessee Williams, Louis Armstrong, Anne Rice, and the *Gris-Gris* of Dr. John eager to experience the magical realism of the prismatic French Quarter where something behind appearance may be the reality of the story behind the story. Each single frame they shot contains plot, character, and mystery similar to the kind Oscar Wilde found in a single frame picture of Dorian Gray and David Hemmings found in a single frame in Michelangelo Antonioni's 1966 film *Blow-Up.*

Dureau inflected Mapplethorpe who without the infusion of Dureau's extra-strength-added might have been less than "The Mapplethorpe." Punished for his good deed, Dureau was cursed with the label "Mapplethorpe's mentor." He who hated the suffocating caption and refused to play second fiddle to anyone will always be double-billed as a supporting actor in the Mapplethorpe drama in the way one can't say "Mapplethorpe" without saying "Patti Smith."

Theirs was not a solidarity relationship, but neither was a villain. Robert was not the first Northerner rummaging opportunity in the American South disfigured by war and disabled by defeat. John

---

1   All quotations of George Dureau, unless otherwise cited, are sourced from his interviews in this book.

Berendt in his nonfiction novel *Midnight in the Garden of Good and Evil* called the modern type "Gucci carpetbaggers."

"Robert was so famous," George told me, "his fame shit all over him, and not just over him, over me as well. Because people got such a load of Mapplethorpe, it's hard for them to understand my work. He doesn't have anything to do with me. His famous style laid a wet blanket on every other photographer."

In the early 1980s, the two frenemies, sharing the male bond of the hunt, cruised Mardi Gras together in search of models and sex. George said, "We both liked bowlegged boys." During the years George knew Robert, he skipped the new parades and only went to Old Line ones like Proteus and Comus until 1991 when Proteus and Comus refused to stop discriminating against race, disability, and gender orientation.

In the late 1980s, in *The New Yorker*, Pulitzer winner Hilton Als, the African-American author of *Black Male: Representations of Masculinity in Contemporary American Art* who saw his first Dureau photo in 1986, pronounced Dureau's 1985 gaunt portrait of Mapplethorpe as "creepy."[2] George more gently termed his eye-witness take on Robert as "a bit bedraggled." Shot at the height of the AIDS emergency, this important picture by the master photographer of disability is an iconic Dureau portrait revealing Robert's specific anorexic disability from drugs, tobacco, and HIV while giving face to the universal horror of AIDS disablement.

Accepting George's invitation, I flew with my husband, video producer Mark Hemry, from San Francisco to New Orleans to interview him at his antebellum home and studio which he rented at 1307 Dauphine Street, a 6,000-square-foot bohemian loft where he had lived for six years at $1500 a month mostly on the second floor in two huge main rooms each measuring fifty-five by thirty so he could stand back and look at his very big and bold paintings from fifty feet away like his enormous *Doing the Pollaiolo at the New Firenze, Three Maenads and a Centaur,* and *The Poseurs Illuminate the Eighth Deadly Sin.*

---

2   Hilton Als, "A New Orleans Photographer's Eye for Male Beauty and Imperfection," *The New Yorker*, July 30, 2016

"It's an ordinary 1840 house with guillotine windows, but a hundred years ago, it was gutted and made into a warehouse so," he joked, "it's got a Queen Anne front and a Mary Anne behind."

The larger space was his grand living room arranged around his paintings, easels, antiques, and four-poster bed. The other was his open kitchen, a man's galley, the welcoming heart of his home, just six indoor feet away from his in-home studio, and his side rooms in which unhoused models, some wearing prosthetics, sometimes slept, and his storage rooms filled with unfinished work because perfectionist George was never done with his drawings and paintings which galleries sometimes had to pry out of his hands to meet deadlines.

"It has," he said in a nod to Warhol, "the flexibility of a little factory."

When George finished his four years of courses for his Bachelor of Fine Arts from Louisiana State University in 1952 as well as courses in architecture at Tulane University, his family, who ran several successful local businesses, set the twenty-one-year-old up in a boutique lamp store, Letolier Lamps, in the 100 block of Royal Street where he also framed pictures for clients and hung his paintings that soon outsold the lamps. So he took up painting and when he was drafted in 1955, he closed the shop.[3]

Entering the U.S. Army for two years, 1955-1957, George had to negotiate his place in a straight world not welcoming to queer folks whose very existence was down by law with arrests and sentencing to jails and mental hospitals. Then as now, gay men, told they were broken "freaks of nature," had to buck fear, danger, and homophobia to get out of bed, go out the door, and live. The Army placed him for training in counter-intelligence in Maryland until military spies on the sniff for deviates detoured his tour of duty off to a stint in clerk school in New Jersey which allowed the twenty-four-year-old boy from New Orleans to experience New York for the first time when the odds were against lads like him in 1955.

---

3   Don Dureau, "Interview by Mark Cave," Oral Historian, Historic New Orleans Collection, May 26, 2015. https://s3.us-east-2.amazonaws.com/thno-caudio/mss629.19_web.mp3

In 1950, five years before George was drafted, U.S. Senator Joe McCarthy's hysterical House Un-American Activities Committee's witchhunt had ignited the ongoing Lavender Scare about subversive queers. In 1953, two years before George put on his uniform, President Eisenhower had issued executive order 10450 banning "sex perverts" from all federal and government jobs which destroyed lives for forty years until repealed in 1995.

In the worst ever decade to be gay in America, George, assessing his military career and calculating the homophobic odds against him, figured that his background checks—arguable and ambiguous even with the beards of his several women friends—caused him to be downgraded from counter-intelligence to an outpost in Indiana where he worked closeted off as a desk clerk and librarian until mustered out in 1957. Despite that, he said, "When I was in the Army, I seduced a mountain of people. I didn't go for sex first. I went for romance first. I worked at it because sex was a wonderful jewel in those days whereas today it's thrown on the counter like meat. I'm still romancing everybody who has ever appeared in my photographs. There's a lot of warmth and passion, a lot of dinners and candles in my life."

Having come home to New Orleans, the Army veteran and painter trying to kickstart his career in 1959 had his first art show at his LSU alma mater where ten years earlier in 1948, the "fabulous" Russian émigré dancer and choreographer Tatiana Semenova, founder of American Youth Ballet, much to George's flamboyant pleasure, had recruited the well-built sophomore with a dancer's body to lift and spin teenage ballerinas until George told her: "That's enough."

When he waltzed out Tatiana's door, he took the flowing movement, shape, and drive from dance into his brush, his first tool, and put it on canvas. When he took up the camera, his second tool, in 1970, he choreographed his models into personally expressive poses across the basic positions of dance. And Tatiana, "My Fabulous Tatiana," became one of the big-gestured stories he dined out on forever.

"I downright seduce the people I shoot," George said. "I put them through all kinds of directorial changes. I make up all kinds of stories to liven them up. 'Oh, let's do this one as if you're waiting for the bus to come and get you.' I'll babble at them and stroke them, and once in awhile we're having sex when I take the picture. I play with people a lot. I don't mind stroking them and kissing them and carrying on. Sometimes my pictures are foreplay or afterplay as the case may be. The foreplay experience of greasing my black models isn't a bad idea. I got that from my kickboxer friends [his models pro-athlete Al Mims Jr., Jeffrey Cook, and Byron Robinson] who grease themselves to look good under the lights. Robert got that from me.

"There are pictures in which I have directed things toward an ideal pose during a shoot, and others in which I have left the awkwardness in them. I just don't want to iron the person out of it. I try to keep some contact with their faces and personality. I'm kind of a slave to my models, in the camera, but not in painting. I serve them with my camera because I think it might be their only or last chance to say who they are, particularly if they have one arm and a scar on one cheek. It might be their one chance to speak to posterity.

"My camera gives them voice. So I frequently, always, let them do a couple of their own poses because they seem to crave something that they've been saving up for years. I give them space, step back, and kind of rearrange their ideas and hope for a compromise between my idea and their idea.

"I'm inclined to see my pictures in the eyes of the people I photograph, not the buyers. When Robert did a scary picture he was always thinking of the eyes of the beholders, the rich people who would buy it, look at it, and have to swallow it. His photos were like the painting of the reclining nude female hanging over the bar in a western cowboy saloon, quite passive, invitational, for horny men to speculate on and use in their heads as they will. But mine do the opposite. My pictures flip that dynamic. My pictures look back at the cowboys looking at the picture. My models make eye contact which can make viewers feel uncomfortable or guilty.

"Robert's models are meant to be looked at. His work is synthetic in the sense of his flattening his models against geometry. He pushed them all into a sort of come-hither calendar-boy pose that, even when they're looking menacingly at you, you're saying, 'Oh, that Robert's *Mr. December.*'"

"He knew," I said, "the sexual market value of his men."

"One thing I'll give him. He was very good at editing his pictures and figuring out what was the most bombastic and best. He also cropped his frames which I don't. He has many cropped images that might not be so impressive if they weren't cropped. So his work is very edited, and what's edited is edited. What's not edited by him now he's dead must be edited by someone else. So it's not the same original as him doing it."

In the way both Dali in 1939 and Warhol in the 1950s designed windows for Bonwit Teller on Fifth Avenue, George in 1959 began decorating windows for Kreeger's, the stylish women's emporium on Canal Street where he became art director. In the perfect frames of those plate-glass windows, the twenty-eight-year-old painter dedicated ten years of his life during the Swinging Sixties—except for nine months in New York in 1965—rehearsing disability by staging the postures of his mannequins' disjointed torsos, with boxes full of moveable and removable arms and legs and hands and feet, next to his props to engage window-shoppers the way his gay gaze would soon direct his models and his *mise en scene* within the frame of his photos to engage his viewers.

Film documentarian Jarret Lofstead, confirming the timeline in George's archive at the New Orleans Historic Collection, said that "while George was creating the windows for Kreeger's," he, who always loved the passing parade of the streets, was inspired to "reach out to the Orleans Gallery and the Downtown Galleries to provide art for the displays" to bring art to the people.[4] What an interesting 21st-century gallery show it would be exhibiting George's emerging eye if only he had taken up the camera in 1960 instead of 1970 and shot a treasure trove of documentary photographs of his ten years of staged and framed public window art.

---

4   Jarret Lofstead, email to Jack Fritscher, January 2, 2024

New Orleans Rhodes Scholar Keith Marshall—the brother of Don Marshall, current president of the Jazz & Heritage Foundation—was the director of the Contemporary Arts Center for Dureau's big 1977 show *George Dureau: Selected Works 1960-1977*. Keith wrote that their mother, Naomi Marshall, gave George his first show in her Downtown Gallery in 1961, and exhibited him five times up through 1965. He recalled the always stylish George Valentine Dureau in his 2014 "Valentine for George" in *ViaNolaVie* online. He had incidentally witnessed George channeling midcentury queer fashion gayly sourced in Oscar Wilde's secret code of the green carnation. "George wore a green woolen three-piece suit, even in summer. He dressed that way when Mother finagled him into being a judge for the Miss New Orleans Pageant held at Pontchartrain Beach that year."[5]

Don Dureau,[6] George's compatible half-brother and executor, a jovial Sagittarius centaur/archer born December 2, 1942, twenty-six days before George, a horned Capricorn goat/satyr, turned twelve on December 28, said, "George always dressed up especially when he was around women. In the early 60s, when he went out on his own, he wore black pants and a man's longsleeve white dress shirt tied up into a knot at his waist."[7]

George's home was a stage fit for a Tennessee Williams drama because he was very like the archetypal kind of male whose life-force Williams could not resist. In the way Williams' plays put beds center stage, George arranged his main public living room around the dramatic 19th-century Southern walnut four-poster canopy bed inherited from his grandmother by way of his beloved mother Clara who, having divorced his father in 1935, raised him with her three sisters, one of whom taught the boy to paint courtyards, moonlight, and magnolias.

---

5   Keith Marshall, "How's Bayou?: A Valentine for George Dureau," *ViaNo-laVie*, April 15, 2014

6   Unless otherwise noted all quotations from Don Dureau are from "Don Dureau: 'The Dureau Family Interview,' with Jack Fritscher," December 30, 2023.

7   Don Dureau, "Interview by Mark Cave," *op cit.*

Living inside art history, he so often posed stretched out like a reclining Matisse *Odalisque Couchée aux Magnolias* on that signature bedstead for photographers that those butch boudoir shots can be shuffled like a deck of virtual selfies lensed by cameramen he directed.

"Get this," George said to me. "I was talking to this woman [Rosemary James] who has this beautiful little house, something called 'Faulkner House Books' here in the Quarter, and she had also just been photographed for the *Classic New Orleans Homes* book. She said, 'Did they photograph your bed properly?'

"I said, 'It's a great angle. The bed's three quarters of the way into the picture.'

"She said, 'Oh, the bed from the front.'

"I said, 'Yes. It looks like a Federalist bed [1788-1800] that I draped sort of like Manet's *Olympia*. It has this Federalist appearance that really describes my nature. Like *Olympia* with her come-hither stare, I'm forthright, upright, but you could get to me if you tried.'

"She said, 'Did he get all that?'

"I said, 'I'm afraid it didn't come out as well as I thought he could have done.' But he must have liked it because he asked if they could shoot a few more photos for *Southern Accents* [a home, antiques, and luxury magazine]. *Southern Accents* here we come! All the magazines get a notion to do me, but some drop out because they decide there's just not enough 'precious stuff' in the house."

In truth, his domestic sanctuary was large enough to contain his huge paintings, his cameras, his photographs, his sketches, his collections of other artists, his antiques, his household treasures, his pots and pans, and his ebullient self.

Off-stage outside his guillotine windows, the base beat from car radios cruising past, the distant barking of dogs, the street voices calling out, the floating echo of a spasm band of young rhythm boys busking a mile away on Bourbon Street wailed like a blues soundtrack up to Dureau's wrought-iron balcony, where, having a go at spinning Tennessee Williams, he entertained guests over his famous crawfish étouffée dispensing to each and all the kindness strangers always depend on. Or yelling at walkers, as we saw one afternoon, to pick up their dog shit.

Immediately upon our arrival he greeted us like long-lost friends and, with his natural command presence polished by military training, got us down to business videotaping him rushing and brushing his final strokes on an epic twenty-foot-tall canvas, *Mars Descending*, due that day for delivery to the Contemporary Arts Center of New Orleans for its *War Exhibition*.

He was full of good ideas, fresh history, and deprecating humor. "Of course, I *had* to be a figure painter when it was so out of style in the 1960s. I've always worked against the grain. Back then I was a drunk and talking all the time before I quit all that, shut up, and got down to work." [*George Dureau: Self-portrait with a Wine Glass, within a Circle*, charcoal on canvas]

While Mapplethorpe shot self-portraits sometimes like a character actor in drag, George was a leading man who deemed it "odd to pose yourself pretty like a lady." As a star window dresser on Canal Street showcasing women's styles, he said, "I didn't dress like a girl when I was young. I'd maybe dress with ribbons around my dick, but I didn't dress in ladies dresses."

George drew and painted romantic self-portraits but did not shoot selfies. He knew his face without studying his identity on camera where Robert searched for his. George whose swashbuckling panache partying in a port city was as picturesque as the cover of a romance novel described himself to me: "I have a Minoan profile. I've got an exaggerated profile and I always think of it as my Minoan profile, you know, like the pottery that has satyrs and whatnot with very strong profiles. My hair is in a tight little braid down my back. I have a rather garish, deep profile."

While some journalists trying to heroize George report the wishful math that he served in the U.S. Army during the Second World War, he didn't. He, who was nine months younger than the starry composer Stephen Sondheim and six weeks older than star-crossed actor James Dean, was only a lad of fourteen when the war ended one year before Robert Mapplethorpe was born. As a veteran, he rarely spoke about his service, but he often wore his dog tags alongside other fetish necklaces resting on his bare chest in his open shirt, and, sometimes, he painted his dog tags as a kind of signature in his art.

He said, "I like to do things political, and I'm glad that today I'm just as happy to do that as I was in the 60s. I like to push people into a corner of social and political problems, but I always try to bring a broad universality to it. My gut politics guide my work. Does politics trivialize painting? Think of Picasso's *Guernica*, Delacroix's *Liberty Leading the People*, Jacques-Louis David's *Death of Marat*."

On the evening of July 29, 1964, just after the Civil Rights Act passed, George was arrested in his Speedo swimsuit during his own private party in his home-studio located at 611 Esplanade simply because he happened to be the bohemian artist living upstairs over the Quorum Club where he was a charter member. "I was having a soirée with Negroes on my porch," he said. The Quorum was the only integrated coffee house in Louisiana, where the audience had come to hear black male blues singer and guitarist Babe Stovall (1907-1974).

In a culture where militant segregation was the norm, George said, "In 1945 [when he was about to turn fifteen], I sat behind the 'Colored Only' sign on a bus and the bus driver was furious."

Listening for years to boys' adventure programs like *The Lone Ranger, Sargent Preston*, and *Sky King* with his outsider queer-kid ear pressed close to his family's big radio, the precociously aware twelve-year-old winner of a local art contest woke up in the home of his liberal mother. In 1942, a month after the shock of Pearl Harbor, the start of World War II, and the draft of boys six years older, he could not help absorbing radio news about January race riots two hundred miles away in Alexandria, Louisiana, and February race riots in Detroit, and the summertime arrest in Nashville of a black man (the gay Bayard Rustin) for his sit-in on a bus. In a then-white city, young George intuitively identified with blacks the way gays often do because race prejudice, although different, seems akin to anti-gay prejudice. Ten years after George's 1945 sit-in, Rosa Parks refused to give up her seat to a white passenger on a bus in Montgomery, Alabama.

The Quorum hosted poetry, dance, chess, conversation, and voter registration, but was raided because the coffee house was according to undercover police "a hotbed for communism, propaganda, homosexuality and racial integration." For all that jazz, the price of membership was a cup of coffee.

To prompt civil rights discussion, the coffee house discussed topics like white racists's favorite film, D. W. Griffith's *The Birth of a Nation*. On its advertising poster, the three-hour film originally titled *The Clansman* featured a white-robed and hooded Ku Klux Klansman standing next to a burning cross. Making heroes of the KKK and villains of stereotyped blacks played by whites in black face, it was a huge box-office hit and the first film ever screened in the White House.

In the *French Quarter Journal*, Mary Rickard reported: "Although one of Dureau's frightened party-goers managed to escape arrest by jumping out a window, vice squad officers still rounded up 73 unsuspecting Black, white and Creole people, citing them with disturbing the peace with 'tuneless strumming of guitars and pointless intellectual conversation.' But undoubtedly, every person arrested understood the real reason for the bust: integration."[8]

So complicated was segregation around race and gender that on July 31, Quorum manager Jim Sohr told the *Times-Picayune*: "When we got down to the police station, they really had to wrack their brains to figure out how to separate us. They had to put the black females in one cell. The black males in another cell. The white females in one cell and the white males in another cell."

One of the policemen, blind to the fact they'd mixed gays and lesbians with straights in all four cells, explained, 'We don't mix 'em here!'"

Soon after, they were all bailed out by civil-rights activist Ernest "Dutch" Morial who later became New Orleans first black mayor in 1978. Thanks to him and the ACLU, all charges were dropped

---

8   Quorum information and quotations, Mary Rickard, "Everything Under the Sun: The Quorum Club," *French Quarter Journal*, March 30, 2023

including against Dureau who had been collared for, among other crimes against humanity, "resisting arrest" after the cops threw the Army veteran down the stairs three times and he could not get up from the floor.

George was thrown down the stairs of segregation yet again seven years later in 1971 when—like a foreshadowing of the censorship of Mapplethorpe's photos being put on trial in Cincinnati in 1990—he had to deal with nerve-wracking city rumors that cops were threatening to close his exhibit of paintings and drawings at the Orleans Gallery because black and white male nudes were paired within the same canvasses. Adding insult to injury, "Alberta Collier, art critic for the *Times-Picayune*, didn't like the exhibit…. Dureau…felt it was an assault on his character. He was quick to point out that there was no sexual activity in those works. As a matter of fact, unlike Mapplethorpe and others, there are no sex acts in any of Dureau's art…(thirty years later he can still recite her offensive words almost verbatim). The public rejection provoked in him a period of self-reflection, even depression. He declined to exhibit again for six years…. It was in this period of artistic hibernation that he discovered photography."[9]

When George was a dashing young buck acting up in the 60s, he flaunted segregation laws and continued to party and dance with black and white and brown Marines on shore leave at the sailor dive bar, La Casa de los Marinos, which, although illegal because it mixed all races, was ignored by the police and the Shore Patrol who turned blind eyes to the necessity of the venue. "The French Quarter," George said, "was full of sailors and soldiers from World War II and Korea and the Army. You could fall in love!"

Richard Balthazar recalled an hallucinatory mural on the walls over the crowd that perhaps impelled George to paint his own baroque allegories of classical myth on the walls of New Orleans restaurants and bars.

"The third room," Balthazar recalled, "had its own even more powerful juke box and a hallucinatory mural on the walls over the

---

9   Doug MacCash, "Opening the Shutter," *The Times-Picayune*, October 22, 1999

crowd. Around the room in a dreamlike swirl ran a dark flood of writhing nudes, racing motorcycles, a matador with sword, and a charging bull. As above [on the walls], so below [on the dance floor]. It was here in the dense throngs of the third room that the ecstasy happened, the Dionysian transports of *merengues* and *cumbias*. The clock was forever stopped at ten of three, though that was usually an early hour in an evening's revelry. We'd dance till dawn, even after."[10]

After Don Dureau turned the legal drinking age of eighteen in New Orleans, he often ran across his thirty-year-old brother at La Casa where they skirted a respectful distance around each other, not so much because of family estrangement or age difference, but because George was out and Don was not.

Don Dureau's eyewitness testimony, at once so parallel and parallax to George, provides a foundational voice documenting in sharp relief how Dureau Family Life, a struggle of patriarchy and matriarchy around divorce and homosexuality, impacted the patri-archal George who created as counterpoint his own chosen family shooting what he called his "family pictures" of nonnormative men exiled by society.

"I used to go to La Casa," Don told me, "with my high-school fraternity brothers and dance with girls. I'd see George and we'd wave at each other, and I'd go and tell him hello, and he'd hug me, and that was about it for our relationship. He'd then go off and be sitting at the bar with his legs crossed, looking around and scoping out the guys. I knew what was going on even though he always had lots of women in his life. One time, I was going into Al Hirt's Jazz Club on Bourbon Street with a girl and some other couples and someone said, 'There's your brother.' And there was George on a date with the girl my parents thought he'd marry."

George told me in 1991, "Three months ago, I turned sixty. I've been laying men, devotedly laying people, some women, since the 1940s. I've changed some with age, but back then I would go danc-ing and have a riotous good time in the Spanish or Greek bars. If

---

10   Richard Balthazar, "La Casa de los Marinos," January 18, 2015. https://richardbalthazar.com/2015/01/18/la-casa-de-los-marinos/

you fell in love with somebody, wasn't that wonderful? And if three months later they screwed you over, well, that was just a different period. You could fall in love with a sailor and wait for him to come back from some endless war."

Robert Mapplethorpe who was not a dancer and was never arrested wasn't particularly political or patriotic. As a teen cadet in the Pershing Rifles at Pratt Institute (1963-1969) during the Vietnam War, he gladly submitted like Anthony Blanche in *Brideshead Revisited* to the thrills of the meaty boys hazing him. Turned on by the inches of rifle they shoved up his bum, Pratt's "Imp of the Perverse"—who did things simply because he could—would soon have his nipple pierced and a whip up his ass. Picture the boy Bob becoming the man Robert conjuring himself in his dorm room, mirror-fucking himself through a glass darkly in his full-length mirror, creating the perfect moment of a live selfie in the fever dream of his framed reflection.

Recalling three years of intimacies with Robert in his early thirties, I can retrofit an impressionistic flashback of the teenage enigma picturing himself like Cocteau's "Orpheus" approaching the mirror, loaded on his first LSD, standing in front of the mirror, wearing his ROTC military uniform as a sex fetish, admiring his dick hanging out like a penis in a polyester suit. Imagine him invoking the gay gods Eros and Priapus and jerking off to the magical thinking of masturbation, conjuring his new self-image while smoking his first cigarettes. Think of him who could get no satisfaction wanking to the beat of his leather-clad idol Mick Jagger singing "Sympathy for the Devil" and hailing Satan and erecting his future. Every picture Robert ever took was autobiography of his forty years of longing.

In the closets of the 1950s, gay men often paired with women as self-defense against anti-gay prejudice. This pre-Stonewall vestige continued socially in the 60s and 70s in trendy pansexual venues like Warhol's Factory and Studio 54—and with men like George, and Robert who met his beat-punk muse in fellow Pratt student Patti Smith in 1967. In 1968, he dodged Vietnam by showing up for his induction physical stoned on acid. What "Americana" he shot was declarative fundamentalist American iconography of handguns, assault rifles, knives, a Navy aircraft carrier, and a tattered American flag or two.

Robert's weapons pictures, often featuring himself brandishing his fetish guns and knives, went unnoticed by gun-culture conservatives, but his leathersex pictures put a target on his back during the Satanic Panic of the Reagan 1980s when religious fundamentalists lost their minds fantasizing about AIDS as divine judgment, gay satanic rituals, and the prolonged McMartin Pre-School child molestation case (1983-1990) that all exploded into an Ohio witch trial around Robert's pictures.

George's only gun pictures date from 1996 when in response to the murder rate in New Orleans, he photographed his amputee models holding guns decommissioned by the police for the group show *Guns in the Hands of Artists* at Jonathan Ferrara's Magazine Street gallery, Positive Space.

George and I met at a pivotal moment in the American culture wars. Six months before, on October 5, 1990, jurors ended the Mapplethorpe censorship trial in Cincinnati with a not-guilty verdict. Six weeks before, Republican President George H. W. Bush's Gulf War (August 2, 1990 – February 28, 1991) had ended in ignominy and was sharing the endless headline news about the Mapplethorpe verdict and the television polemics of the Republican defunding of the National Endowment of the Arts.

"We Americans find it very easy to turn success into moral right," George said. "Because we were 'successful' in this Gulf War, we tell ourselves 'You see, we are morally correct.' And unfortunately, I think we're going to do a lot of that thing soon with cops and fascism. I'm afraid that we're on a tear now that we've discovered where we've failed economically, and where we've failed politically and morally. We [think we] can clean up all that [our national moral failure] by using our guns and make "ourselves" *like* "ourselves." We really look like we're on that path."

Robert had been dead only twenty-four months. He had fame in the inside baseball of the art world and notoriety in the gay world, but he had no idea how world famous he would become a hundred days after he died when Jesse Helms, the Republican Senator from

North Carolina—not realizing the irony that his loud censorship was a million bucks of publicity even Robert could not buy—denounced him by name on the floor of the U.S. Senate and made him a pop-culture icon, a cultural lightning rod, and a legend.

"Robert's been gone that long?" George said. "I can never remember birthdays and anniversaries."

In the living room of his beautiful residence and studio that had, he said, "the biggest and best balcony in the city," George, who was born to play to the balcony, stood vibrant and barefoot on his enormous unstretched canvas that cascaded from the ceiling down the wall and fell in folds around his feet. At the top, he'd painted a military tank charging in 3-D perspective out of the painting. At

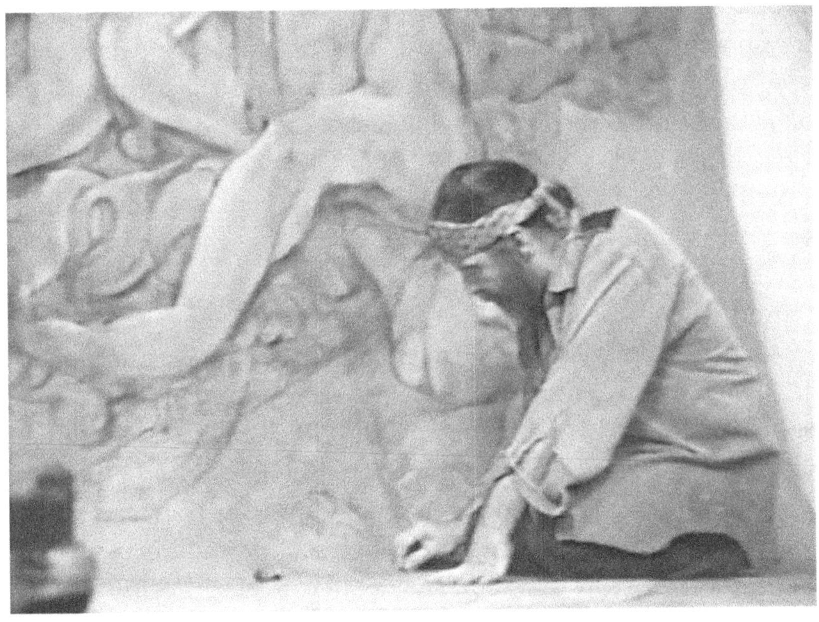

the bottom where the canvas dropped and spread like a rug across the floor, I filmed George crawling on his knees across his canvas while painting his final swirling Persian carpet patterns where he knelt.

Doug MacCash, astute in his continuing coverage of George, wrote in his *Times-Picayune* obituary for George: "He painted like a dancer."[11] George had so internalized the aesthetics of ballet and modern dance at LSU that in 2015, Dureau, the effulgent painter, the visionary photographer, would have been a perfect convivial mentor to the Scottish Ballet's ecstatic production of *A Streetcar Named Desire*. His figurative paintings of dancing satyrs and diaphanous women, like his strutting male quartet in *George and His Closest Friends*, his four-figure balletic *Classical Tableau*, his theatrical *Scandal at the Forge of Vulcan Café*, his 8x22-foot widescreen triptych *The Parade Paused* in Gallier Hall, and his untitled three-panel mural at Cafe Sbisa, are masterful storyboard sources of theatrical character, costume, and choreography.

An hour later, Mark and I and painter-photographer Jonathan Webb, George's personal assistant from 1982 to 1998, helped him transport his still-wet painting to the Contemporary Arts Center two miles away at 900 Camp Street where we three helped him hang and unfurl the falling folds of his unframed canvas for our video camera.

"This *War Show* is not anti-war," George said. "It's simply about war. Although my painting certainly dramatizes the current war."

"Another war to protest," I said, "while we're busy protesting censorship."

Perhaps because George Valentine Dureau, Junior, the hyphenate painter-photographer-sculptor, was the son of a resilient mother, Clara Rosella Legett Dureau (1909-1994), and an alpha father, George Valentine Dureau, Senior (1905-1994), who was a wedding and party supplier, he became a natural-born bon vivant and raconteur. He was the man New Orleans high society, and rich Texans in town to turn oil into art, wanted to sit next to at supper.

His resonant voice and genuine laughter made the new people he met feel like longtime friends. There was no falseness or hypocrisy in the man. He had that charming quality of storytelling peculiar to Southerners like William Faulkner, Eudora Welty, and Tennessee Williams who, himself a Sunday painter like Welty, once lived around the corner from George in an attic apartment

---

11 Doug MacCash, "George Dureau, New Orleans master painter and photographer, has died," *Times-Picayune*, Nola.com, April 8, 2014

at "722 Toulouse Street" where he began drafting *Vieux Carré*, his play about a painter and a photographer set at "722 Toulouse." Had George who told me he was "wildly dyslexic" read Thomas Wolfe's *Look Homeward, Angel*, an immersive Southern novel of disability narrated by the kind of triumphant alienated body "freak" beloved by Dureau, he would have cum over Wolfe's own orgasmic paean to "the romantic charm of mutilation."

Dureau addressed the gravitational pull of Southern time and place and artists in a panel discussion on "Pre-Pop Modernists," Arthur Roger Gallery, September 12, 1989. George, who grew up learning to paint during the popular regionalism movement in the art of the 1930s and 1940s, said about his staying put deeply immersed in the French Quarter: "...my purpose is to create a universal kind of statement in my pictures, but coming from certain particulars which back them up. Because of that, my own life has to be, I think, like the Southern writers who stay in one spot following the same people over and over and over, until, finally, out of these particular environments, I pull some universal sort of statement."[12]

Looking out at the French Quarter from his veranda, he told my camera, "I think New Orleans is about the size Paris was when Paris was great. I mean for creating art, for knowing your subject matter, for knowing the people you're dealing with, for reusing them and them being there when you need them for reconsidering things, for redrawing a picture and throwing it away and doing it another way. The people are there the way you know the grocer you've known for thirty years."

It's relative to the Dureau synergy and gestalt that in 2015, the Ogden Museum of Southern Art in New Orleans, George's home museum which had honored him with its Opus Award in 2011, hosted *Tennessee Williams: The Playwright and the Painter* exhibiting nineteen of Williams' paintings including his mixed-media *Sulla Terrazza della Signora Stone* based on his novel *The Roman Spring of Mrs. Stone.*

---

12   George Dureau, Arthur Roger Gallery, Video, "Panel Discussion: Pre-Pop Modernists," September 12, 1989. https://arthurrogergallery.com/1989/09/arthur-roger-gallery-1989-panel-discussion-pre-pop-modernists

Williams' *Vieux Carré* scratches Tennessee's own itch for rough trade and erotic street cruising into his archetypal tale of art and sex and a dying painter who recruits models off the street, and an orgiastic young gay photographer whom Williams describes as "New Orleans's most prominent society photographer" who shoots "artfully lighted photos of debutantes and society matrons" and recruits his other saltier models off the street.

Williams began writing *Vieux Carré* in 1938 and finished it in 1977. Over those forty years, his observant queer eye accumulating the local color of his play's street narrative had to have spied the vibe of the Quarter's flamboyant star character who was everywhere.

Meant for each other, the two artists were kindred spirits covering the waterfront in their fetish-like fixations on broken bodies. George, who said he grew up fascinated by Long John Silver's peg leg and crutch, created pictures of men he found maimed in New Orleans where disabled vets hobbled home from wars and drunks, passed out at night on streetcar tracks, woke up as amputees.

Tennessee who was partially paralyzed as a child featured a crippled girl in *The Glass Menagerie* (1944) and invented short stories and a canon of plays dramatizing processes of disablement through dismemberment and cannibalism and castration and medical lobotomy like "Desire and the Black Masseur" (1948), "One Arm" (1948), *Suddenly Last Summer* (1957), and *Sweet Bird of Youth* (1959).

By the late 1960s, Quarterites were becoming aware of Dureau as the very model of a modern major painter roaming the streets picking up talent for his canvas and camera. In 1991, George, who emphasized that his avatar "Tennessee lived right around the corner from me," identified himself to me as Williams' "Big Daddy" from *Cat on a Hot Tin Roof.*

"I had to put together my art and my insistence on telling stories my way," George said.

Claude Summers noted in *An Encyclopedia of Gay, Lesbian, Bisexual, Transgender, and Queer Culture* that many of Dureau's paintings include provocative narratives: *Nude Beach* (1965), *Reception with a Waiter* (1962), *Black Tie to Petronius* (1970), and *Poseurs Illuminate the Eighth Deadly Sin* (1997).

In both his white and black narratives, George's models with their backstories were his protagonists, but he was careful how much street drama named disaster was safe to recruit. Don Dureau said, "It was not really popular for a white man to be taking nude pictures of black men in the South and George really walked tiptoe around that all the time. While he didn't have any real problems with the models, he did get comments from some in the art world who said, 'We don't want that stuff in our show.'"

Regarding the street as a casting couch, George said about the models their cameras depended on, "Robert's models are too available whereas mine look like something just dragged in off the street which they were. His were dragged off the street too, but he presented them in a way that every good faggot will know what it means. With mine, every good faggot doesn't know what it means."

In daily practice, because street trade is often rough trade, George kept danger at bay by managing his models with care, vetting them, knowing who they were, and who their families were, to avoid the inevitable risk involved when a gay man violates the first commandment of gay safety and invites strangers into his lovely home.

"I have discretion," he said. "I have to be a bit choicy, but not too much. I still get enamored by someone's appearance and bring him home. So many older queers think they're something and hold themselves royally apart for no good reason. I think being older gives me more advantages to offer more to the cute things I'd much rather pickup. I'm a recognizable nice man who is an artist who will lay you if you want it.

"Robert would see a black man he'd say was 'scary.' I was careful not to disillusion him and say, 'Oh, yes. He used to be my delivery boy.'"

Even so in 1986, Mapplethorpe judging George's New Orleans "recruiting" style to Jim Marks, the first executive director of the Lambda Literary Foundation, deadpanned like the pot calling the kettle black, "If you lived like that in New York, you'd be dead."[13]

His New Orleans neighbor, the closeted painter and photographer John Burton Harter who was a secret multi-millionaire was

---

13   Jim Marks, Facebook message to Jack Fritscher, January 28, 2024

killed, age 62, in 2002 at his Faubourg Marigny home-studio in the kind of unsolved murder which is an all-too-familiar trope—no aspersions on victim Harter himself—about gay men hiring strangers as nude models off the street. In a kind of polite erasure to keep the usually rich, older, white, gay male victim from seeming like he "asked for it," a queer New York institution, denying reality, reported the soothing prevarication that "Harter died suddenly."

Assessing George's reaction around gay murder, Don Dureau recalled, "I once went with George and Richard Gere to the Vera Cruz restaurant where George went two or three times a week before it closed [around the time of Hurricane Katrina] because the owner took in street boys and was murdered, and George would not talk about it."

Like all gay men living under a constant state of siege when homosexuality itself was defined as a psychiatric disability, George lived inside the unspeakable stress of gay cautionary tales in New Orleans art circles. When he was seventy-four in 2005, the year of Hurricane Katrina, he was shocked when his sixty-two-year-old friend Russell Albright, MD, was attacked on Bourbon Street. Albright was the board member of the New Orleans Museum of Art who had introduced George to Robert who frequently stayed in the old slave quarters at Albright's mansion where he and his partner Michael P. Myers fussed over The Mapplethorpe in ways Dureau wouldn't. The radiologist who had retired in 1992 was pushed to the sidewalk outside Galatoire's allegedly by a presumably straight twenty-eight-year-old tourist from Texas, Anthony Creme, who followed the retired Navy veteran out of the restaurant because he reportedly took offense that Albright had tossed a mint onto the his table where he was dining with friends—not knowing that mint tossing, which George enjoyed, was a light-hearted social custom in the restaurant.

Perhaps thinking Albright was flirting with him—and so what if he was?—the Texan allegedly followed him out of the restaurant and attacked him who fell and fractured his skull causing permanent brain damage that required the doctor be hospitalized for two months and under care for the last twelve years of his long life

(1934-2017). When a settlement was reached in 2006 after Albright requested the court drop second-degree battery charges against Tony Creme who had filed for bankruptcy protection, the Dallas, Texas, *D Magazine*, saluting the forgiving Albright as "a mensch," could not resist the pun headlining the fiasco, which was no laughing matter in New Orleans, as the "Creme de Mint Affair."[14] George, suffering the onset of Alzheimer's, was not amused.

"I had my humanistic needs," George told me. "I just had all these needs to talk about people, tell their stories, and help them solve their problems, and it all ultimately led to a real patriarchal kind of lifestyle where I'm the Big Daddy who knows how to paint pictures about you. Sometimes looking for interesting models, I'd place my photos on the back seat of my Jeep so hitchhikers would ask if I could shoot pictures like that of them. They pose for me because they want to record their youth and good looks. I may, or may not, have sex with the models, but when I finish a shoot, I collapse."

George nicknamed his Jeep "Clara" after his mother who was, according to Don Dureau, "the love of his life. He constantly talked about her to everyone."

George grinned. "I do this wonderful thing where I just go out to the streets and ride and ride around the city on my bicycle," always in black, sometimes wearing a gay leatherman's peaked Muir Biker Cap, "until I can't ride anymore and then I come home and I just lie on the floor and beat my meat or let the air blow over me and just lie there until a new creative thought comes into my head."

"Dureau's paintings and drawings are, for me," the British critic Edward "Ted" Lucie-Smith wrote for the Arthur Roger Gallery in 1983, "prolix, turbulent and simultaneously indulgent and self-indulgent. One would use the same word to try and give the flavour of William Faulkner and Tennessee Williams. And this is not perhaps so surprising when one considers that Dureau comes from a similar cultural background. What makes Dureau's art work is a kind of

---

14 Adam McGill, "Crème de Mint Affair No More?," *D Magazine*, online, December 19, 2006

over spilling abundance, a gift for rhetoric. The cultural flotsam is carried along by a torrent of visual energy. The same thing happens in Tennessee Williams' long speeches, where the words coalesce in baroque clusters, till the subject becomes language itself. Dureau the painter, like Williams the playwright, is a celebrator of the medium which is being used."[15]

In 2013, the last full year of George's life, the Arthur Roger Gallery, Dureau's gallery since 1988, celebrated George's Southern DNA in its show, *Southern Gothic: An Insider's View with Paintings and Drawings by Willie Birch* [African-American born New Orleans 1942], *and Paintings, Drawings, and Photographs by George Dureau.*

When Arthur Roger, whose father was a transit conductor on the ancient streetcar line named *Desire,* opened his 2018 postmortem exhibit, *Mapplethorpe and Dureau: Photographs,* the first-ever exhibition of the two artists co-starring together, Dureau's friend John D'Addario, arts professor at the University of New Orleans, noted that while there was the 2016 HBO documentary *Mapplethorpe: Look at the Pictures,* "Dureau's death [from Alzheimer's] in 2014 did not even merit an obituary in *The New York Times*…the full story of Mapplethorpe and Dureau is still one that needs to be told."[16]

Like Robert, George Dureau was a solo act. "I'm not," George told me about group exhibits, "going to play second fiddle to anyone. Especially when I think of all the images that [Joel-Peter] Witkin and Mapplethorpe lifted from me. I don't like people sipping wine at a group exhibit coming up and asking me, "Now who are you, dear?' I'm not going to take that. I don't need an exhibit where I'm just another photographer who happened to have done certain images before Mapplethorpe. That doesn't say anything about me. When the *New York Times* did Gene Thornton's major piece about me ["Critics' Choice," March 1, 1981], I look back now and see Wagstaff and Mapplethorpe pulling strings."

---

15   Edward Lucie-Smith, "George Dureau: Classical Variations," *New Orleans Art Review*, May 1, 1983. https://arthurrogergallery.com/1983/05/george-dureau-classical-variations-n-o-a-r/

16   John D'Addario, "Side by Side: Dureau and Mapplethorpe Shared Friendship and Art, but Not Fame," *The Advocate*, New Orleans, January 16, 2018

Like a proverb around George and Robert, Flannery O'Connor, the Catholic Southern Gothic novelist of disability, wrote in 1965 what could be the tagline of the Dureau-Mapplethorpe relationship and movie. "Everything that rises must converge."

In a split-screen montage of queer convergence, both George and Robert had brothers who were many years younger and caught up in family drama. George was turning twelve when Don Dureau, his only sibling, was born in 1942. Robert was fourteen when his brother Edward Maxey Mapplethorpe, one of his three brothers and two sisters, was born in 1960.

When Don was a boy, his mother tried to keep him away from George because George was gay. Because of this, the teenage Don did not really see much of George even before George was recruited into the U.S. Army in 1955 until Don came out as gay in 1986. Edward said when he was a little boy of three, and Robert age sixteen began commuting to Pratt, he felt his cool and remote brother was "magical."[17]

With his own successful career in business computing, Don, closeted and married nineteen years with wife and two sons, became close to George after Don came out and took courses in photography as did Edward who studied photography at SUNY and graduated in 1981. As Edward built his own career as a photographer, Robert forbade him to use the Mapplethorpe name. So, for the next twenty years, the kid brother became "Edward Maxey" before he became Edward Mapplethorpe with his own successful photography career.

While Robert disconnected from Edward by denying him his identifying surname, George with disabled memory lost the identity of his half-brother. When Don would call on the phone around the time of Hurricane Katrina, George would say, "I don't have a brother," and would hang up. In the care home, George would introduce himself to his visiting brother saying, "Hello, I'm George Dureau." Both Don and Edward expressed how their gay older brothers' open

---

17   Edward Mapplethorpe, "My Life as Robert Mapplethorpe's Assistant, Adversary, Baby Brother," as told to Justine Harman, *ELLE* Magazine, April 4, 2016

lifestyles and freedom helped keep them as younger brothers from being "ordinary" in New Orleans and Queens.

Did it mean anything that both the Dureau and Mapplethorpe fathers were athletic tennis players? George was not fond of his father for divorcing his mother. Robert was estranged from his Republican father who was too "ordinary" for words. Desperately seeking signs of heterosexuality in their artistic sons before Stonewall in 1969, George's family believed he was always about to be engaged to a woman he dated and Robert's parents presumed and feared he and Patti were married.

In the kind of thrust-and-parry Freudian rivalry George had with his father, Robert told his father who was an engineer and amateur photographer who had his own basement darkroom that he was going to become "New York's greatest photographer."[18] He rarely returned from Manhattan to the family home only twenty miles away where his father who never accepted him told him he couldn't care less about Patti Smith. Robert cut him and his mother out of his will and left his estate to his Foundation which has donated millions to AIDS research and the Robert Mapplethorpe Residential Treatment Facility in Manhattan. George died without wallet or will and his longtime business lawyer worked pro bono to sort out the disposition of his drawings, paintings, and photographs. Both artists died disabled after long illnesses with incurable diseases.

While George cared for his elderly parents who both lived until 1994, the Mapplethorpe family from 1986 to 1989, lost two sons, and a mother. Joan Maxey Mapplethorpe died May 25, 1989, two months after Robert passed on March 9. George's father, according to Jonathan Webb, was an Archie-Bunker loudmouth who, Don Dureau said, was "very artistic and made pottery and plaster figures of David and Goliath and biblical and Greek figures in his backyard workshop that he sold all over town while running his Dureau Rental Service catering party supplies and tableware.

"Whenever George would talk about our father," Don said, "he'd say, 'YOUR father did this today.' He was not that fond of

---

18   Kim Masters, "Harry Mapplethorpe, A Father's Tale," *The Washington Post*, May 3, 1990

our father because he thought he didn't do right by his mother. He thought our dad was rather harsh and rigid in his thinking and always right. But my father was never harsh like that to me. My parents were party people, and New Orleans is a party town, and I was the only child at home. So they were not very strict with me. My parents had rules for me, but I had a lot of leeway. In grade school, I was a little bitty thing and began riding my bicycle to the park, where my grandfather had donated a lot of land, because I knew places in the bushes to have sex. No doubt George knew them too.

"The worst thing our father ever did was always know more than anyone else. Even before the internet, he knew everything. He read a lot: the paper, always looking up stuff, the dictionary seven to nineteen times a day. My father had a love of reading. George didn't care that much for him, but was always there for him maybe because George with his big opinions was so like him. He also helped take care of my mother in her nursing home."

Don later recalled their own Big Daddy's sissyphobia and amateur gay conversion therapies that kept Don in the closet and drove George out. "Back in those days [the 1930s, 40s, and 50s of the brothers' boyhoods], if you had a limp wrist and walked with a limp wrist, well, I thought that was a game, but anytime I did that my dad would slap my hand. I remember the two of them locking horns. George wouldn't do anything he said."

Perhaps homophobic slaps like these from George, Senior, caused George, Junior, who may have been slapped into presenting as masculine, to resent their father whose second wife seconded his homophobia by warning their "straight" son away from his gay half-brother. Perhaps this abuse was one of the reasons George's mother divorced his father to save her beloved son who early on estranged himself intermittently from his father, even while caring for him on into his old age. Is there a satisfying ironic slap-back at his father that London's Barbican featured George's work in its 2020 landmark exhibit *Masculinities: Liberation through Photography*?

"So after I came out," Don said, "George told me he wanted to shoot a picture of our father slapping my hand, and we did. The three of us grownups. And it came out really good because you can tell what's happening. I don't know what happened to that picture."

George, shooting a verbal selfie, pulled no punches when he told me, "There's a lot of rather flamboyant, womanish behavior in me sometimes. I get a little like a woman when I get really mean."

George's typical kindnesses as Big Daddy-big brother extended to warm family scenes with Don who on a 1983 visit to San Francisco became startled and scared when a trick alerted the thirty-nine-year-old Texan to the reality of the AIDS epidemic. When Don turned on the local TV news and saw people dying on stretchers in hospital hallways, he immediately flew home to Dallas and asked a fundamentalist preacher to cure him. Three years later when Don finally told his wife he was gay, he said, "She held my hand and said, 'So, that's what's been bothering you? There's nothing wrong with you being gay. Stop that church. You know better than that. You know you can't do anything about being gay. There's nothing wrong about being gay. I'm not happy about this, but I understand.' She understood, but she was still blown away. She always understood about George. The day after I came out, my now ex-wife said I had to call George. 'Go visit him.' I told him and he said, "Well, it's about time. I've known since you were a little boy, all those curls you had!'

"I stayed a week with him and he was wonderful. He told me I could stay as long as I wanted unless he was getting ready for a show. I brought my boyfriends to meet him, and they came back and one bought a painting. In the 1970s George had a longtime friend. They never lived together, but they were always together. I asked him why he didn't have a lover, and he said, 'Donald, you must know if you want to hang on to someone, you have to let them go.' He had close longtime friends and he had lots of sexual relationships. Most were good. But at the end, his model [white muse and lover since 1982] Troy stole paintings during George's last months in the studio."

George took nostalgic pleasure telling my camera about his sex life. "In 1971, I started photographing blacks. I picked up my camera as a kind of 'proof of life' about my amputee models because people thought I was doing special effects with trick photography. So I was in my very black period, but I've always had white lovers, maybe eight or nine great loves over the years, especially when spring is in the air. I should be dead now from all the sex. [He was HIV-negative.] Oh, those lovers were such difficult numbers. They were all white, and I didn't photograph them much."

When the 1960s counterculture revived Tod Browning's 1932 movie *Freaks*—beloved by the Surrealists and the Quorum club—with eye-opening midnight campus screenings, students fashioning their own alternative hippie anti-war lifestyle as "freaks" wanted to discuss the powerful film that de-stigmatized disability and was cut to confetti by censors because its first audiences fled to the exits triggered by the mindfuck of seeing its cast of atypical-looking actors portrayed as humans whose nonconformity challenged their body images of normality.

"Some people," the nondisabled George told me, "respond foolishly to the handicapped. Sam Wagstaff was one of them. Some people don't know how to respond to the beauty of deformity and missing parts. I think gay men respond well."

"Because of gay body dysmorphia, gay body fascism, and our boyhoods when people informed us flawed beauties we were broken freaks?"

"Yes," he said. "But sometimes they're embarrassed about their hidden attraction and affection for deformed people. I'm not particularly interested in sorting their psychology."

"Does grooving on a guy because he's handicapped or black or straight reduce him to a fetish? Like Tennessee Williams' hunger for blonds?"

"I often tell people that because some people who are beautiful and sexy have a stump on one side doesn't mar their sexiness or their beauty. I often tell people who don't get it that you don't say, 'Let's just throw out this little Roman sculpture because it's part broken.' It's still there. We're still here."

Perhaps some people responding to Dureau's pictures of disability are triggered ambivalently with lust and guilt around his eye-opening work. Not feeling whole themselves, they are pleased but shocked to find erotic attraction and psychic awakening in fantasies around amputation, castration, paralysis, blindness, and prostheses. Like Stoics imagining the worst to overcome their fears, they graduate from Dureau's literal pictures of "born freaks" to Mapplethorpe's metaphorical pictures of "made freaks." The endlessly perversatile find sexual pleasure, rebel power, and counterphobic healing in Robert's designer pictures of men made physically challenged by sadomasochistic fetish-sex rituals: immobile in bondage, blind in blindfolds, disfigured by scarification, helpless by infantilism, penetrated by prosthetic sex toys of artificial body parts, penises and fists, made from silicone, rubber, and plastic.

In the origin story of Dureau half-eclipsed by Mapplethorpe, Dureau DNA can be traced in Tod Browning, the 1930s movie director who at sixteen had run away with a traveling circus freak show. Dureau as a child was a fan of Browning's daring vision. As an artist shooting the challenged men with whom he identified emotionally, George actually lived the equality of the movie's punch line of inclusion in which a whole-bodied person surrounded by other-bodied persons is told by the freaks: "Now you are one of us." Taking on his models' burdens and support, something Mapplethorpe rarely did one-on-one, George became "one of them." Browning's empathy tutored Dureau's empathy for the diversity of differently abled humans.

"When I was eight," George said, "my parents took me to a side-show, a freak show—that was acceptable then—across Canal Street where I saw an armless artist, a very nice looking man, who held a pencil in his toes to draw pictures. I desperately wanted him to draw me. He stared at me twice. He must have thought I was worth drawing, but my parents moved us on to see a movie at the Saenger Theater where I loved watching Busby Berkeley, Lana Turner, and Judy Garland."[19]

Mapplethorpe was also entranced by freak shows. As a child, Robert visited Coney Island freak shows as did Arthur Tress and

---

19 *New Orleans Artists John Burton Harter and George Dureau*, Film Tribute, Jarret Lofstead, editor/producer, The Bend Media + Production for Saints+Sinners LBGTQ Literary Festival, March 2021, with support of the John Burton Harter Foundation

Joel-Peter Witkin who as a boy took his camera into a Coney freak show. As a curious teen hanging out in seedy Times Square in the 1960s, Robert was fascinated by Hubert's Freak Show and Museum of "born freaks" and "made freaks" where Diane Arbus was taking pictures while he was studying the faces cruising in the 24/7 Mardi Gras parade of motley freaks walking bawdy 42nd Street.

"Later," George said, "a girl in my school asked me to go home with her to study, and in her living room her uncle was sitting on a chair. It was the armless artist and he drew me. I'm an artist who grew up thinking about what an artist is supposed to be—living a warm involved humanist sort of life with lots of people around me. If I contribute something strong to photography, it's probably my ability to picture the model's sexuality in their brain or their life as told through their human face."[20]

Digging through George's archives, Jarret Loftstead addressed the raconteur's *Rashomon* repertoire. George was not unreliable in his twice-told tales because, he, "insistent on telling stories my way," was fabulous like a standup improv actor tailoring his performances to his audience. "George," Lofstead said, "reports two stories about the armless painter, both fairly apocryphal. In both, George sees *Zeigfeld Girl* with his aunt and her friend, and then they go to the circus. In one version, weeks later, George walks home with a friend, and the painter is the friend's uncle. In the other, following the film, George's aunt takes him to her friend's apartment. The painter is brother to the friend, and George is left with the painter while George's aunt and friend go out to get a bottle. The painter asks George to help him in the bathroom."[21]

"For the show *Drawing Monuments II*," George told me, "I drew a tall drawing of a statuesque guy, with the head of a dwarf snuggled up under him, with the dwarf's hand wrapped around the perfect leg and the dwarf's arm pointing up directing this big beautiful Indian-looking creature. It's this dwarf directing this big gorgeous monster to look at the stars."

---

20 *Ibid.*

21 Jarret Lofstead, email, *op. cit.*

George, who studied Velázquez, and loathed deformity as entertainment, genuflected to the sassy power of Diego's bold portrait of dwarf Court Jester Sebastián de Morra painted with defiant eye contact and an attitude of body self-rule: *The Dwarf, Sebastián de Morra, at the Court of Felipe IV* (1644).

"I'm pretty much aware of art history with my camera, but I wasn't interested in the history of photography. I mean I knew of nice pictures by Avedon and Irving Penn. But when I make an adjustment or insert a comment during a shoot, I jump the bridge into art history. I say, 'This boy is through-and-through Velázquez.' And, jumping the bridge, I'll make the light even stronger, or sometimes I make a comment to myself that will cross in from another medium. My model Troy, for instance, a beautiful blond with long curly hair is from North Carolina, but when I draw him, he's a total Michelangelo. That's all he can be. His proportions are about the same proportions as Michelangelo's dream boys: a thick square body and big square shoulders and a head just a little too small. My Troy pictures were all Michelangelo because he had what Michelangelo's boys had. But I never think about other photographers.

"Everyone knows Robert's photography is distilled from other photographers's work. It's hysterical how many of Robert's poses and attitudes and mock poetic postures are not real 'Mapplethorpe' photos because they are really 'George Platt Lynes' photos. For all his creativity, Robert seemed to have lifted everything. It's very strange. He wasn't comfortable with just the object or the person in front of his camera. He had to frame it in terms of a style of someone else. I guess I might think that because I'm so styleless."

When I asked George if photography is as good as painting, he said, "As a painter I have to tell you, 'No. It ain't.' Photography is an editorial art. It's not a creative art in the sense that painting and drawing are in which you start with nothing. You're given a lot. The camera will give you too much so all you have to do is shut it up by editing it. The camera is just a mindless lunatic. You have to edit down what it's going to take in. You don't have to tell it, like you do a paint brush, how to make something look like a finger."

"The camera is a mindless lunatic. I'm going to quote you."

"That's why I'm talking. For posterity. I must tell you that blacks are the first people I shot. Before the blacks, I never shot a white person. Before Robert saw my work he had never shot a black person. I was one of the peculiar people who get to the age of forty without knowing anything about cameras. I would hold up a camera and say, 'What button do I push?' I started out with a used $65 Vermeer Lens and an eleven-year-old 2-1/4 square camera [a Mamiyaflex before his Hasselblad].' I photographed for three years with natural light and two fill lights before I bought a light meter. Essentially, Robert—who bought some of my earliest pictures dating back to 1972—and I used the same camera, film, paper, and format which gives us a similar velvety quality.

"Robert was not drawn as I was to people who are handicapped, particularly to people who are triumphant while handicapped. I've always loved tough dwarfs. I've always been attracted to little people who act strong and big—like the triumphs of superheroes.

"Often times, his photographs, like his picture of a mean-looking tough little Spanish guy, maybe a kickboxer, making a fist, look like a mockery of my style."

George juggled themes of ability and disability. Don Dureau recalled "George liked wrestlers and boxers for their form. He had piles of books with pictures of classical athletes from Greece and elegantly dressed Roman women. He'd have a book laid open when he was painting. When he'd get stuck, he'd go to those books and his videos to find images to inspire him. It was wonderful to watch him work.

"One time I was sleeping in a corner of his big room where he had put a circle of easels up around my bed to give me some privacy and some of them were paintings he was working on. One morning I felt my bed shaking and it was this little guy Peanut who used to clean George's place hitting my bed with a push broom. The easels had moved. I said, 'What happened to that one painting?'

"Peanut said, 'George was up early two hours painting while you were still asleep and you didn't hear him.'

"I said, 'Well what happened to that painting? It's changed. The subject was facing me. Now he's not.'

"George had moved the shoulder around.

"When I asked George, he showed me his process, how he does it. He said, 'That's why I do oils because you can change it. You just pick up the oils and move them around.' George was not structured around time. He worked late into the night and worked a lot in the mornings when the light was good. Sometimes he didn't work for months, and then he'd paint a lot.

"He loved people, even the ones on the artist tours of the Quarter. He'd have food out for them. Cooking was his ritual. If someone was visiting, he was always cooking with loud music, usually opera and the blues. He loved the blues. He loved Nina Simone. His favorite was her 'I Want a Little Sugar in My Bowl.'"

George said about his always-open house, "It's so interesting when tourists come in to see my drawings and photographs. A process. A man, very often with the wife, will ponder which one they're going to buy. Frequently it's a drawing that's going over their bed. Whatever that all means, I don't know. Very often they are very intellectual straight people who worry and ponder such things like they are psychiatrists. Very often with the photographs they will line up three amputees, and they'll talk about them, go home and ponder, and come back again. So it's kind of delicious to sell things out of my home instead of a gallery. It's kind of a bother to have people come into my home, but it's kind of delicious because we have time to talk, no pressure, and it's interesting to hear their worrying and reasoning and help them choose the right one."

Both Mapplethorpe and Dureau grew up to be masculine-identified gay men shooting heteromasculine men and homomasculine men. While Robert shot some women, George shot mostly men. His gay gaze boldly exchanged the straight male gaze in New Orleans by switching the gender of sitters shot by his famous New Orleans predecessor, E. J. Bellocq (1873-1949). After seeing Bellocq's hidden work about women exhibited for the first time in 1971, George took up the camera to shoot figure studies for his male paintings. He said he had no interest in becoming a famous photographer.

Bellocq, the subject of Louis Malle's controversial 1978 film *Pretty Baby*, pictured women of the streets in Storyville in the 1910s the way George after Stonewall pictured men of the streets from the 1970s onward. (George turned down a cameo in the movie.) While Bellocq's pictures seem shot for his own private spank bank, Robert and George, two able-bodied white artists, wanted to reveal to the world the hidden beauty inherent in the race and abilities of their sitters.

In pursuit of the platonic ideal of the human body, Robert sought perfect models like *Ken Moody*, 1984, and ballet dancer *Peter Reed*, 1980, for ice-cold perfect moments. George also sought perfect men like *Byron Robinson*, 1985, but he favored the perfect moments of "imperfect' men like *B.J. Robinson*, 1983, a goodlooking "human torso" born without legs and sitting on hips, to whom he could draw warm attention in his unflinching pictures.

Twenty-five years after Robert's death and ten years after George's, those who don't know or remember the last midcentury might fancy a little sidebar of parallel history to compare and contrast how George pollinated Robert.

While George in his thirties, nearly twice as old as Robert, was thriving as his own man with brush and canvas in 1960s New Orleans, he was unaware he'd become the French Quarter connection to one of the matched pair of New York performative characters in their early twenties trying to invent themselves in the Manhattan pop-culture of Warhol's *The Chelsea Girls* (1966).

It was a Hollywood story as old as Broadway tap-dancing down 42nd Street. The girl from New Jersey who had not yet sung had given up her newborn for adoption. The boy from Floral Park who had not yet touched a camera had given up his soul for success. So in 1969, the two "young, young, young" Tennessee Williams characters, the fugitive kind, in search of a lifestyle took lodging from 1969 to 1972 in the tiny inner sanctum of 1017, a room of their own, in the arts-immigrant sanctuary hotel that was the Chelsea where they sought and found their first access to influence and money.

That maze of backstairs art fusions was, in the unities of time, place, and action, its own Vieux Carré. "From the outside," *Vanity*

Fair observed, "the Chelsea Hotel looks as if it were the only building in New York that was flown in from New Orleans."[22]

In a quick movie montage of what happened almost sixty years ago, the ambitious androgynies guised themselves as just kids slouching from Yeats to Didion to be born as artists.

They made themselves available busking the hallways and taking door-to-door master classes in *La Vie Bohème*. On fire escapes and stairwells where Isadora Duncan danced, they rehearsed and performed their breathless starving-artist act with waif gravitas for gonzo photographers slumming through the twelve stories of the legendary dump of tenants and transients that I entered as an academic pilgrim writer on the road in search of Jack Kerouac over the weekend of October 20, 1968, made memorable as the shocking day Jackie Kennedy married Onassis. A bit too much of a good thing, the Chelsea was an unsafe vertical skid row, a boho freak show of robberies, room fires, celebrity sex, and murder.

Playing at being androgynous Chelsea girls, the pals made themselves camera-ready, playing themselves the way Warhol actors played themselves in New York and George played himself in the French Quarter. They posed for Gerard Malanga from Warhol's Silver Factory and German filmmaker Albert Scopin in 1970 at the same time Stanley Amos gave *pauvre* Robert his first collage exhibit at Amos's "gallery" inside Amos's tiny room at the Chelsea, and Sandy Daley gave Robert his first camera, a Polaroid, just as George was buying his first camera, a used 1962 Mamiya C3 twin lens reflex. In 1971, the year Diane Arbus died, Daley shot Robert in her all-white room in her thirty-three-minute Warholian film of Robert's personal masochism, *Robert Having His Nipple Pierced*.

By 1970, the Chelsea couple changed partners. The liberated girl took the straight and married playwright Sam Shepard as her lover. The beautiful boy took fashion model David Croland who would soon introduce him to Sam Wagstaff as his.

"I lived in New York once for about nine months in 1965," George said. After his first solo exhibit that year at New Orleans's

---

22 Alex Beggs, "The Chelsea Hotel: We Knew It Well," *Vanity Fair*, October 8, 2013

Delgado Museum of Art (now the New Orleans Museum of Art), he flew to Manhattan making the rounds of galleries peddling his portfolio of drawings and paintings like *Reception with a Waiter* (1962) and *Nude Beach* (1965). "I liked it while I was there."

"Why did you leave? While Robert stayed?"

"To remain human. As soon as I got home, I thought, "Oh, thank God, I'm home. I'm not aggressive. I don't like to knock on doors and have to go tell someone that they're supposed to love my art like Robert did. I'm not aggressive the way he was. I'm not a traveling salesman.""

After the Swinging Sixties when assassination, civil rights, the French New Wave, Warhol, the peace movement, The Beatles, the moon landing, feminism, and the glitter bomb of the 1969 Stonewall Rebellion broke the *status quo*, Robert and George both took up the camera for their post-Stonewall work. At the same time, the entrepreneur businessman Sam Wagstaff was strategically planning to market and sell photography by declaring it a fine art.

Sam in his visionary evangelism to position photography as an institutionally legitimate art invoked F. Holland Day, Alfred Stieglitz, Ansel Adams, and painter-photographer Edward Steichen who all declared photography a fine art. He also took a pop-culture-changing strategy from silent-film director D. W. Griffith who adapted books into moving pictures more controversial and racial than Mapplethorpe's images. Griffith assailing the strict norms of art was the first American to insist as Warhol did that movie photography be regarded as art. And then he made films about sex, race, and gender to prove his point the way Robert, with Sam as his marketing director, shot ambitious silent pictures of sex, race, and gender to prove himself an artist who was a photographer which—a surprise to wannabe Mapplethorpes—is quite different from photographers who are not artists.

Holly Solomon who exhibited Robert in her Manhattan gallery in 1977 told me what she and George witnessed around Sam Wagstaff, Robert's Pygmalion, whom George called a fascist. "Sam," Holly said, "was the great curatorial person who helped photography achieve its identity as art. Other photographers, of course, had presented their work as art, but Robert was determined to legiti-mize the camera through a kind of aesthetic assault on the art es-tablishment. I was trying to introduce Robert as an artist, not just a photographer."[23]

Robert collected and pursued George because George was an artist who was a photographer capturing the French Quarter the way Robert wanted to conquer Manhattan. Dureau, who said "My drawing is handwriting," was also with canvas and camera "writing" the narrative of the Quarter that Tennessee Williams was penning on paper. Williams who was a teenager when Dureau was born in New Orleans in 1930 said about himself that he learned so much in New Orleans he should have paid tuition. Just so, Robert, the un-dercover student with a spy camera flying reconnaissance into New Orleans, learned so much at George's knee, the tormentor should have paid his mentor.

Williams and Dureau and Mapplethorpe created the homosur-real mythology of their statuesque satyrs and horse-hung centaurs out of their own variously beautiful and offbeat gentleman call-ers. George said of one of those gentlemen, "Along with my mod-els Wilbert and Oscar, Robert liked my little friend Jeffrey [*Jeffrey Cook*, 1984] which is really funny because Jeffrey who is my protégé is a gorgeous little mulatto boy and karate person with washboard abs. Robert loved Jeffrey so much that he bought four pictures of him to give to people over the years."

Dureau fostered a French Quarter repertory company around his most frequent core models, the whole-bodied athletes, the de-formed, and the amputees whom people often think must be Photoshopped: Troy Brown, B.J. Robinson, Glen Thompson, Terrell Hopkins, and Earl Levell. Men like Troy Brown (*Troy Brown*, 1979) or Christopher Fisher (*Christopher Fisher*, 1985) or Glen Thompson (*Glen Thompson*, 1983) could be cast as the platonic ideal of any number of Williams' males from Stanley Kowalski, Brick Pollitt, and Chance Wayne to the hearty Black Masseur—while Robert's flowers could illustrate Sebastian's French Quarter garden in

---

23 Jack Fritscher, "Holly Solomon Interview 1990," *Mapplethorpe: Assault with a Deadly Camera*, Hastings House, New York, 1994, page 137

Suddenly Last Summer or the *flores para los muertos* in *A Streetcar Named Desire.*

Williams wrote in his poem, "Carrousel Tune," that "the freaks of the cosmic circus are men." He was outing the disabling fact that some gay men in pursuit of the platonic ideal of beauty in themselves and others, feeling they are not in the right or best queer body, suffer greater body dissatisfaction than do straight men.[24]

Both the maimed men of Dureau and the fetish freaks of Mapplethorpe's leather period in which his pictures of bondage and scarification are metaphors of literal movement-and-body impairment also illustrate Williams' comic and cosmic circus of broken male specimens in his books of Southern-Gothic short stories, *One Arm* and *Hard Candy.*

Tennessee who tried to write screenplays at MGM in 1943 was swimming laps in local N'awlins color in 1947 when he was finishing *A Streetcar Named Desire* at "632 St. Peter Street" dramatizing Stanley shouting his barbaric yawp for "Stella-a-a-a!" outside their tenement at "632 Elysian Fields." That "632 St. Peter Street" address was only five minutes from the future *atelier* on Dauphine of the then seventeen-year-old Dureau.

As a queer rite of passage, every gay man alive during Williams' long life (1911-1983) has his own "Meeting Tennessee Story." In the way Wagstaff picked up the twenty-six-year-old Robert by walking up to him at a cocktail party saying a line worthy of Williams, "I'm looking for someone to spoil," it's credible in the six degrees of cruising culture what photo-journalist Jason Storm reported in *The Rolling Storm*, October 18, 2014, that George told him about "being picked up by Tennessee Williams as a young man."[25]

After trying to reach Jason Storm to no avail, I asked Jarret Lofstead about this ambitious gay urban rumor. He said, "Getting picked up by Tennessee Williams for sex sounds specious. According to Kenneth Holditch, George never met Tennessee, even though

---

24   Tennessee Williams, "Carrousel Tune," *In the Winter of Cities*, New Directions, 1956, page 95

25   Jason Storm, "George Dureau," *The Rolling Storm*, October 18. 2014. https://therollingstorm.com/ramble/george-dureau/

he had the opportunity to do so at a party at Marti's Restaurant. But George was too drunk and nervous to meet the writer whom Holditch himself had only met twice." While neither Dureau nor Mapplethorpe shot a formal portrait of Williams, Don Dureau told me he remembers a candid photo George had snapped like a paparazzo of Tennessee socializing at a party at Marti's or at some gallery or museum. Don gave that photo to the wife of the attorney who handled George's estate.

Had Dureau, an avowed top, met Tennessee, an avowed top, in the six degrees of cruising for gay sex, what a "meet-cute" moment in gay history. "Icons collide in 20th-century art." If it didn't happen, it should have, and indeed, may have—never to be mentioned if the sex spark between the two authorial men (who would submit to no one) misfired. Two tops fighting for the top in a world of eager bottoms. What a Samuel Beckett sex comedy. Much can be learned from apocryphal juxtapositions like the urban legend that Albert Einstein met Marilyn Monroe. Having shot two Dureau documentaries, if I were scripting a Hollywood film about him, I'd remember he told me, "Any movie about me needs to be big and baroque and operatic exactly like my life, an extension of my life."

So, indulging an expressionist "aside" like Romeo's first thoughts on first seeing Juliet, I might at George's insistence for the "baroque and operatic," tease open the wide-screen Technicolor biopic of events—changed for dramatic purposes to suggest the Dureau-Williams gestalt—in 1947 when George, who won his first art prize as a pre-teen, was a hot *beignet* of sixteen and Tennessee, who was writing *Streetcar* upstairs, was a hot daddy of thirty-six. The one-minute establishing shot would be golden footage of quiet beauty portraying Tennessee *being* Tennessee soaking up streetlife, standing, smoking a cigarette in the doorway at "632 St. Peter Street," watching a man like Stanley and then a woman like Blanche pass by, when the handsome young George *becoming* Dureau—sporting his first pencil moustache like Hollywood stars Zachary Scott and Clark Gable—comes riding slowly by on his bicycle cruising past once, then twice, then stopping a third time to shake out a cigarette saying to the original Big Daddy, "Got a light?"

Then there'd be a quick cut away from that ambiguity (Was that actor supposed to be Tennessee? Did they or didn't they?) to an expository montage purpose-built to introduce the audience to George's versatile public career from his cast-bronze nudes on the gates outside the New Orleans Museum of Art to his enormous 1999 bust of Artemis on the pediment gable frieze of Harrah's Casino, now Caesars New Orleans, at 8 Canal Street; his mural inside Cafe Sbisa; his painting of a Mardi Gras Parade in Callier Hall, as well as his paintings, drawings, photographs, and posters for art, jazz, and symphony events. In addition to Artemis on his monumental baroque pediment frieze, George depicted New Orleans arts figures of dancers, actors, musicians, singers, and two fauns, one playing a flute.

In November 2023, Caesars replaced the sculpture in the pediment triangle with its shiny corporate logo of Caesar's golden head wreathed with laurel. George's original is "said to be in the possession of Barry Kern, son of Mardi Gras float fabricator Blaine Kern."[26] While this removal is nothing compared to the censorship of Mapplethorpe art, the "corporate erasure" of art smacks of insult to George and to the cultural heritage of the city of New Orleans.

Doug MacCash observed in his April 8, 2014, *Times-Picayune* obituary that "At Cafe Sbisa on Decatur Street, his mural of glamorous French Quarterites has shined for decades in the spotlights above the bar. When fire broke out in an adjacent building this winter, art lovers called to express concern for the beloved painting."[27]

To script the vibe around Mapplethorpe meeting Dureau, I'd make the point that Robert—who wrote to me in a letter dated May 21, 1978, that "I want to see the Devil in us all"—would marvel at George's cocked-eyebrow satyr "look" documented in his self-portrait paintings that his close friends described as "Mephistophelean."

Robert and George were both raised Catholic and Catholics as an article of faith must believe in the Devil or go to Hell. Altar boy Robert pictured like an angel, age six, in his First Communion picture in Floral Park was a believer. Mardi-Gras boy George in

---

26 Jarret Lofstead, email, *op. cit.*

27 MacCash, *op. cit.*

America's most Catholic city was not. In David Zalkind's 2007 video, Zalkind chats casually with George chipper and charming, straddling his bicycle on the sunny corner sidewalk in front of the Faubourg Marigny Arts & Bookstore at 600 Frenchmen Street.[28]

A Zalkin question leads to a Dureau stand-up comedy routine. George regales the camera saying when he was a boy of eleven as America entered World War II, the idea of receiving his postponed First Holy Communion made him vomit. His father, divorcing, had left the Catholic Church for Protestantism; and George himself was not into receiving into his mouth—what Catholics must believe—the Body and Blood of Christ under the appearances of bread and wine. "I'd run outside the church and vomit. I did that three or four times. I used to do that when Jesus said to stay in that church. I have never vomited since. I escaped the nuns because my family moved to twelve different houses in Mid-City when I was young. Jesus can come and get me when he wants. I keep my bathroom clean."

George may not have believed in Catholic doctrines of Communion and Resurrection of the body, but he told me, "I believe in the renaissance of all things."

For Mardi Gras in 2008, George's friend John D'Addario snapped him, as did others, costumed as the Devil with dime-store plastic horns and a fun pitchfork for the photo: *George at the St. Ann Ball*.[29] That casually comic image matches Robert's intentionally impish *Self Portrait (with Devil Horns)*, 1985, which twins with his photo of the bust of a classical horned marble statue *Italian Devil*, 1988.

For George playing Falstaff, the Devil was camp.

For Robert playing Faust, the Devil was real.

While George who loved Mardi Gras put blue-collar men at ease with his rumpled blue-chambray work shirts, Robert who loved Halloween conjured identity and authority in his daily

---

28   David Zalkind, "George Dureau: The Sidewalk Interview," Faubourg Marigny Arts & Bookstore. 600 Frenchmen Street, Youtube.com, 2007

29   John D'Addario, "Remembering George Dureau," Hyperallergic.com, April 10, 2014

black-leather costume. Like Patricia Highsmith's *Ripley*, the talented Mr. Mapplethorpe appropriated whatever he needed to climb the straight social ladder all the way up to Princess Margaret. To build his gay brand all the way up to Tom of Finland, he sucked up homosurreal foundation images of leathermen, piss, whips, Christ, skulls, guns, and devils from gay Satanic Magus Kenneth Anger's brilliantly blasphemous and censored film *Scorpio Rising* (1963).

Robert struck poses on both sides of the camera like Edgar Allen Poe's "Imp of the Perverse" just to lark about. The conjure power of the camera and the wizardry of the cameraman empowered him, the sex magus who wore the occult voodoo jewelry he designed. His black-magic photo, *Snakeman*, 1981, a virtual selfie, matching Richard Avedon's *Nastassja Kinski with Serpent*, 1981, iconized a seductive white devil in a black-leather horned mask curling a huge python around his body like a serpent selling apples in Eden. He took delight knowing that ever since the dawn of photography people suspected photographers were magicians, snake charmers, freaks stealing souls with their cameras. He certainly hoped that was so.

Mapplethorpe illustrated the 1986 limited edition of Rimbaud's *A Season in Hell*. Dureau created covers for *Leon Galatoire's Cookbook* (1994) and for the deluxe edition of Anne Rice's *Memnoch the Devil* (1995), the fifth book in *The Vampire Chronicles*. George's photos could also light up Williams' "French Quarter Canon" from his *Streetcar* and *Suddenly Last Summer* to his exquisite stories of amputation, "One Arm," and of inter-racial love, "Desire and the Black Masseur," and his one-act play of female mastectomy *The Mutilated* set in the French Quarter on Christmas eve. As if writing specifically about one of the broken human figures Dureau lensed, Williams compares the maimed sailor in "One Arm" to classic Greek marbles that also appealed to Mapplethorpe who studied sculpture at Pratt and turned hot models into cold statuary.

Like Dureau romancing disability, Williams wrote that his maimed hustler Oliver Winemiller had been the boxing champ of the Pacific fleet before he lost an arm. "Now he looked like a broken statue of Apollo…[with] the coolness and impassivity of a stone figure."[30] Ted Lucie-Smith, whose own photo book, *Flesh and Stone* (2000), juxtaposed contemporary gay flesh with ancient marble statues, was one of the people who introduced me to Dureau in June 1989.

In 1985, Ted, working toward a *catalogue raisonné* for George, had written the "Introduction" to the first volume of Dureau's work to be published, *New Orleans: 50 Photographs*, Editions Aubrey Walter, London. In his essay, Ted made literary comparisons of Dureau's images of athletes and amputees to Baudelaire the way Robert and Patti connected their lives, songs, and photos to literature from Rimbaud and Verlaine to Baudelaire and William Burroughs.

George who drew "Dureaugrams" of storyboarding, a sequence of sketches, which he called "visual notetaking" for both his paintings and his photos said, "Robert's photographs were like slices out of an intimate movie—the one of him with the whip, the leather boys." He added, "Who knows? I might take up shooting video. I'm the *fin de siecle* artist. *Fin de siecle*, here I am!"

On April 9 in his studio, Mark Hemry and I handed George his first video camera and filmed him shooting his first video portraiture as he added the dimension of motion to his still pictures.

Robert left more than 120,000 negatives, 500 Polaroids, and 200 artworks of drawing, collage, sculpture, and jewelry through his Mapplethorpe Foundation to the Getty Museum.

George summing up his career told me, "I've done thousands and thousands of drawings. My drawings are my favorite things. I've always drawn and painted. When I picked up the camera and started making pictures, they looked like my paintings and drawings. So the precedents for whatever Robert got from me come from my paintings and drawings of men. I have hundreds of thousands of negatives. If someone is worth shooting, I will do ten rolls of twelve. So there's a 100 to a 150 sometimes very similar exposures of anybody I find worth photographing."

---

30   Tennessee Williams, "One Arm," *One Arm and Other Stories*, A New Directions Book, 1948, page 7

Don Dureau revealed that the painter was not keen that his photographs eclipsed his paintings. "George quit taking photos in the late 1980s."

George and Robert shot photos from 1970-1988.

"He realized how good he was and never took another one and went back to drawing and painting. He said, 'I have more photographs than I need. I'm not going to drag that camera out anymore.' When he was done with something, he was done. He didn't realize that's what people are going to remember him for more than his painting."

In 2014, Don Dureau and Arthur Roger gathered up George's work in the repository of the Arthur Roger Gallery. Don told me, "At the gallery, we have at least a thousand photographs which we've sorted and cataloged." Arthur Roger noted that Don was intent on preserving the archival integrity of his brother's work. Don said, "At George's last apartment, we found boxes with stuff lying around on the floor, but he had a file cabinet with hundreds of pictures in different sizes. About ninety percent were signed." And then came a nurturing care scene. "When he was in the nursing home, Katie [Machod] sometimes took four or five photographs to prompt him to recall them and talk about them. So sometimes he'd remember who he was and want to sign them. All of his originals, signed or not, now have certificates of authenticity."

In Don Dureau's interview with the Historic New Orleans Collection, he said that George's *Mars Descending*—the painting we had bonded over the day we met and filmed him hanging at the Contemporary Arts Center, 900 Camp Street—was donated as an "unmounted painting" to the Ogden Museum, 925 Camp Street, which had requested it as important.

In 2014 and 2016, Philip Gefter crossed Robert's white calla lilies with George's black tulip magnolias in his two books *Wagstaff: Before and After Mapplethorpe* and *George Dureau, The Photographs* which spans forty years with ninety-eight images funded by friends and produced by the Aperture Foundation founded in 1952 by Dorothea Lange, Minor White, and Ansel Adams. That was as close as George ever got to 23rd Street, the ground zero of canonical gravity for photography galleries, studios, and publishing in New York where Aperture had moved to 20 East 23rd in 1985, two minutes from the five-story building where the dying Prince of Darkrooms—who moved the same time as Aperture—held court in his new top-floor condo at 35 West 23rd Street.

In 1988, Anna Wintour, then editor of *House & Garden*, pictured Robert's carefully curated apartment as the best showplace in the best block. It was there the BBC interviewed him, and he hosted his last gala birthday party for the chauffeur-driven gowns and wallets of the limousine carriage trade he had created by double-daring them with his sales pitch: "If you don't like this photo, you may not be as avant-garde as you think." George, cracking wise about the ambitious Mapplethorpe doing "retail" and selling Dureau knock-offs told me, "Robert ran himself like a department store."

These fusions and confusions in mixed-media pop culture tighten the degrees of separation around Williams, Dureau, and Mapplethorpe. In 1977, Tennessee Williams scholar Kenneth Holditch (1933-2022) who was George's longtime champion wrote the "Introduction" to a retrospective of Dureau's work at the Contemporary Arts Center. In 1987, Holditch, a professor of English at the University of New Orleans and a high-school classmate of Elvis "King Creole" Presley, commissioned Dureau to draw the inaugural poster for the first (and second) *Tennessee Williams' New Orleans Literary Festival* started by Holditch at La Petit Théâtre du Vieux Carré. In 2021, Holditch made one of his last public appearances in the fifty-minute video produced by Jarret Loftead, *New Orleans Artists: John Burton Harter and George Dureau*, paying tribute to both painters in an oral-history documentary produced during Covid in 2021 for the Virtual Saints+Sinners and LGBTQ+Literary Festival.

Offscreen, in the rooms where the women come and go speaking of George Dureau who was no hesitant J. Alfred Prufrock, they remember his kindnesses to models and other artists like his mentoring his young neighbor, African-American artist Vernon Thornberry, teaching him about painting, allegory, and nudes. Thornberry's painting *Decline of the Sun* is very Dureavian. Because Thornberry had no heat or lights in his tin-shack studio on Esplanade, George ran electrical extension cords to him from his own home next door.[31] Don Dureau remembered George's constant neighborhood generosity casually taking him along to visit an "old lady he took care of" and to bring food to his models' families.

In the 1970s, New York exhibits and photography books, including the startling new gay photography books, were favoring Diane Arbus, Peter Hujar, and Arthur Tress with no Dureau and only minor nods to the tempestuous Mapplethorpe who was once so publicly jealous and personally censorious that he demanded that the tempestuous Hujar be removed from an upcoming group exhibit, or he'd withdraw. Neither he nor George liked group shows. When Robert got his way with Hujar, he realized by force of personality he could raise his profile through aggression. Seeking publicity beyond the closed camp of New Yorkers shunning him, he flew out of JFK to introduce himself to the power of the national gay press. He did what Evita Peron did and Dureau didn't: he went on a Rainbow Tour.

As a result of Robert's aggressive 1977 marketing campaign traveling to meet editors to promote what would become his *X Portfolio*, he had a banner year of free publicity in 1978 print media. He came to me at *Drummer* in San Francisco because I was actively promoting erotica as art which was also his goal and ultimately his signature contribution to modern art as proven by the verdict in the Cincinnati trial. He had not yet met Dureau when I commissioned him to shoot a photo of my friend leather-biker Elliot Siegal for the cover of *Drummer* and published nine of his *X* pictures in my special arts issue *Son of Drummer*. In New York, editor Michael Emory included six of his *X* pictures shuffled in almost anonymously among thirty-four other young photographers in *The Gay Picturebook*. In Paris, *Creatis* magazine devoted its entire issue seven to his work.

---

31   Megan Wahn, "The Renaissance Man of Athens: Vernon Thornsberry," *The Red&Black*, August 3, 2020. https://www.redandblack.com/culture/the-renaissance-man-of-athens-vernon-thornsberry-captures-local-culture-in-new-exhibition/article_a0650f1c-855f-11e8-9996-47b6d45f00ca.html

The morning after the riotous first-class party cruising the Titanic 1970s hit the iceberg of HIV, the gay press in an AIDS frenzy of reactionary censorship tried to silence Mapplethorpe, the unrepentant champion of 1970s sex, by blacklisting his images and leathersex from its 1980s magazine and newspaper pages. At this time, while Dureau was mentoring, socializing, and dueling with Robert, George received his first coverage in the national gay press when *The Advocate* headlined him on the cover of issue 333, December 1981. Three months later in March, 1982, the same magazine took a swipe at gay leathermen like Robert with its cover story "Is the Urban Gay Lifestyle Hazardous to Your Health?" Gay censorship cost Robert fame and fortune until straight censorship added to his fame and fortune.

Dissing Robert in the *San Francisco Sentinel*, April 28, 1983, erstwhile *Drummer* contributor Steven Saylor typifying gay resistance to Robert coincidentally wrote dialogue that would have made George laugh.

"Robert Who? I've been dropping his name a lot lately, since getting hold of his first [*sic*] book of photographs, *Lady Lisa Lyon*. No one seems to recognize Mapplethorpe's name....He's a court photographer to the fashionable SoHo set, where New York literati and nameless punks in leather rub elbows with socialites in Halston drag....Yet you've probably seen his most famous work—an arresting, disturbing series of bodies trapped in latex and leather—in the artier gay magazines [*Drummer*] and in chichi card shops."[32]

Dureau was cursed with the label "Mapplethorpe's mentor." He who hated the suffocating label and refused playing second fiddle to anyone will forever be double-billed as a supporting actor in the Mapplethorpe drama in the way one can't say "Mapplethorpe" without saying "Patti Smith."

Village Voice writer and essential New Yorker Gary Indiana who knew Robert spun a clever riposte of "intellectual disability" giving the finger to politically-correct fundamentalists when he confirmed that "Robert took a lot of shit from the gay community....

---

32   Steven Saylor, *San Francisco Sentinel*, April 28, 1983

Mapplethorpe's work…challenged the 'sexually crippled and re-pressed' who see pornography as 'ipso facto evil.'"[33]

In 1991, George was shocked when I told him that in the November after Robert died in March 1989, I had such an uneasy premonition about politically-correct prejudice against the rich, white, male, leather photographer that I called *The Advocate* and sug-gested Robert for their "Person of the Year" cover. I was informed that the lesbian attorney and AIDS activist Urvashi Vaid was their chosen "Person." Over the next week, I suggested that this year of Robert's death was the last and only year Robert, then the most fa-mous gay man in the world, was eligible to be their "Person." No of-fense to social justice warrior Vaid who could be celebrated the next year. After much friendly persuasion, the editor pictured Vaid and Mapplethorpe gendered side by side in two headshots billed on the December 19, 1990, cover of issue 566 as "Woman of the Year" and "Man of the Year." After that, *The Advocate* switched to "People of the Year."

On April 9, 2014, two days after George died, *The Advocate* post-ed a 186-word online notice headlined by a copy editor: "Dureau was a longtime contributor to *Drummer* magazine." By actual count over three years, George contributed only ten photos (1986) and two photos (1989) in two issues out of 214 issues from 1975-1999. Because The *Advocate* had no obituary prepared for George, arts re-porter Christopher Harrity rose to the moment and made the most of the column inches allotted, and then concluded the news brief with a Youtube link to the 1991 video interview with George on his veranda.

Six months later on October 17, 2014, *The Advocate* pub-lished Nathan Smith's 1082-word Op-ed profile "After 25 years, Mapplethorpe's Photos Still Crack the Bullwhip." In a politically-correct culture disrupting norms around race, maybe George was lucky he was shunned and ignored. On May 17, 2017, *The Advocate* published an essay by Charles Stephens, the African-American founder (born 1980) of the Counter Narrative Project, titled "The

---

33   Joe Nalley, "S/M Activists Debate Meaning of Censorship," *OutWeek*, October 8, 1989, page 17

Sexual Objectification of Black Men from Mapplethorpe to Calvin Klein." Stephens made no mention of Dureau's cautionary mentorship of Robert around race when Stephens called Robert a racist: "The perfection sought by Mapplethorpe was inherently a sadistic enterprise...having sex with black men does not exclude a white man from racism, and in the case of Mapplethorpe, black men were not only a fetish but racism itself."[34]

George with his first pioneering exhibition at Naomi Damonte Marshall's Downtown Gallery in New Orleans in the spring of 1962 was a frontrunner for Mapplethorpe who couldn't get arrested. That's why Robert—who started his career making collages (*Leatherman #1*, 1970) from "found" photos in gay porno magazines he bought in adult bookstores on 42nd Street—flew hat in hand to San Francisco to pitch his pictures at *Drummer* to cash in on its monthly print run of 42,000 copies sent out internationally to subscribers he saw as potential models and clients.

When Robert unzipped his portfolio at my desk a few days before the Gay High Holiday of Halloween in 1977, his visions so outdistanced received gay photography that I immediately invited him into our *Drummer* salon. Would that Dureau had done the same because he could also have been swept to stardom on the immense international popularity of *Drummer* that helped create the gay culture of arts, ideas, and sex we reported on.

George said, "For a number of years, *Drummer* kept asking me for something but I said, 'I can't because, well, there's one serious problem. The men I shoot, most of my models, even though I sometimes lay them, are straight. They live a straight life. I'm attracted to people who are not flamboyant or don't have a gay lifestyle.' It seemed unfair to compromise them in a gay magazine."

Not until a dozen years later did *Drummer* finally persuade Dureau to publish ten of his conformity-disrupting photos in the April 1986 "Maimed Beauty" issue of *Drummer* 93 headlined by San Francisco photographer Mark I. Chester who wrote the cover feature. Three years later in issue 129, June 1989, *Drummer*—a first

---

34   Charles Stephens, "The Sexual Objectification of Black Men from Mapplethorpe to Calvin Klein," *The Advocate* online, May 17, 2017

draft of leather history and the leather magazine of record—published two more of George's photos to illustrate "Chester," a story making a sex fetish of erotic disability written by disabled-rights advocate Michael Agreve.

On the make in the 1970s, Robert, although often in group shows, managed to book very few solo shows. By 1985, his hard work, charm, and grit had scored more than forty small solo shows around the world. By his death four years later, he had logged more than two hundred solo exhibitions. Between 1965 and 1977, George had no solo shows, mostly because he retreated into himself after the "bad" 1971 review from Alberta Collier in the *Times-Picayune.*

George had his first one-man New York show at Robert Samuel Gallery in 1981 when Robert—the duelist no one knew was a secret active partner influencing the business of the gallery[35] —invited his mentor to exhibit in Manhattan. The minute Sam saw George's porfolio, he and Robert began an uptight Wagstaffian curation, picking and choosing Dureau pictures to George's chagrin. George, feeling set-up, told me sarcastically, "Sam and Robert 'cleaned up' my pictures."

Slapped repeatedly in the face, George recalled that Robert and Sam in 1981 had allegedly meddled with the *New York Times* over a feature article written by critic Gene Thornton who told him of editorial issues. "You may remember," George said, "the anecdote I told you about the *New York Times.* That peculiar incident when Gene Thornton wrote a major piece on me and it was pulled. At the time, I didn't get particularly hysterical. I thought, 'Oh, isn't that a shame.' But now that I look back at the hegemony of Wagstaff and Mapplethorpe, now I understand that there may have been something else than the *Times* saying, 'Oh, we don't want to do a piece on photographs about men, and Dureau wouldn't be the person who we would do it on if we were going to do it.' That was just the opposite of what Gene Thornton had told me. He said, 'Before I saw your work, I never even *wanted* to do a piece about men photographing men.'"

---

35   Frances Terpak and Michelle Brunnick, *Robert Mapplethorpe: The Archive,* Getty Publications, Getty Research Institute, 2016, page 140

The New York show drove Dureau to drink and his drinking at that time, like Mapplethorpe's drugs, presented difficulties. To survive the passive-aggressive power couple sorting his pictures and short-sheeting him on Robert Samuel Gallery walls and in the *Times*, George sought refuge sitting in front of Baudelaire's friend Manet absorbing his rebel style and life-size tableaux at the MOMA.

George told me, "When you enter a vicious mainstream like New York, you have to give up things. New York thinks it's the mainstream and I'm an eddy. In New Orleans, I'm the mainstream and they're the eddy. I don't sell my work at top New York prices. I sell at top New Orleans prices. I used to get drunk and frustrated back in the 60s by all this, but I don't do that anymore. I'm very controlled about eating and drinking."

In 2012, Higher Pictures Gallery in Manhattan opened George's touring solo exhibit, *Black 1973-1986*, which the *New York Times*, suffering from the art world's "Mapplethorpe Tourette Syndrome," gave short shrift in its 274-word review that, scrying George through the Mapplethorpe lens, could not resist mentioning "Mapplethorpe" three times, and that Dureau, named four times, was "black" which he was not. The *Times* printed a correction the next day.[36]

Is it possible that through the years, George's career was marginalized because he was thought to be black? Or because his photographs pictured blacks and disability? Or because he was regional and Southern? Or because he was gay? Or because he was presumed to have AIDS which he didn't?

In 2018, *The New York Times Style Magazine* published George's portrait of his white friend New Orleans painter Robert Gordy in a photo-spread of artists killed by AIDS.

In 2015 at the Armory Show, Higher Pictures opened its second solo Dureau exhibit, *The French Quarter, 1970s-1980s*, featuring his male nudes and street scenes. At the same moment, just a year after George, a cultural griot and gay elder, died famous and beloved as New Orleans's most significant artist of the late 20th and early 21st centuries, the text artist Kenneth Goldsmith

---

36 Roberta Smith, "George Dureau: 'Black 1973-1986,'" *New York Times*, June 21, 2012

canonized Mapplethorpe as his protagonist in his thousand-page homage to New York City, *Capital: New York, Capital of the 20th Century*.[37] In his introduction to his thirty-six-page anchor-chapter, "Mapplethorpe," Goldsmith wrote, "Mapplethorpe, the Ultimate New Yorker, embodied New York in the 1970s in the way Baudelaire did mid-19th-century Paris."

Arthur Roger said the same about Dureau who also contained the essence of a city now changed by time: "George, the quintessential New Orleanian, had this quality that you would only see in New Orleans in that particular time."

Art critic D. Eric Bookhardt reviewing a Dureau exhibit at Arthur Roger Gallery for *Gambit* in July 2013 wrote: "It was Dureau's singular genius to be able to meld Charles Baudelaire's poetic otherworldliness with Walt Whitman's utopian American egalitarianism in singularly striking images that reflect something of the soul of his city."[38]

"Because of the circles Robert operated in," George, whose Dureau ancestors three or four generations back immigrated from Paris, said in our interview, "particularly in Europe where people knew my work, I heard from people come back from some university in Belgium or from Paris who'd say, 'Well, everyone over there knows you were Mapplethorpe's master. Everyone knows he had this master in New Orleans whom he would visit like a pilgrim.'"

Robert rushing past his mentor who was content to let the world come to Dauphine Street was well on his savvy way to global conquest creating his charitable Mapplethorpe Foundation in 1988 the same year as his triumphant first major solo museum exhibit at the Whitney *Retrospective* where Jonathan Becker photographed my once-spermatic dear friend gone gaunt and bravely receiving guests at his own wake, confined to a wheelchair, smiling, and grasping his Death's Head Cane to illustrate Dominick Dunne's article, "Robert

---

37 Kenneth Goldsmith, "Mapplethorpe" by Bruce Chatwin, Jack Fritscher, Patricia Morrisroe, and Edmund White, *Capital: New York, Capital of the 20th Century*, Verso, London, 2015, pages 501-537

38 D. Eric Bookhardt, "Paintings, Drawings, and Photographs by George Dureau," Arthur Roger Gallery, *Gambit*, June 17, 2013

Mapplethorpe's Proud Finale," for *Vanity Fair*, February 1989. If selling one's soul to the Devil actually worked, Robert would be alive today.

Suffering the passing of Robert, George felt sadness with no *Schadenfreude* even though his own success was trumped by Robert's *succès de scandale*.

When Robert Michael Mapplethorpe disabled by AIDS died at age 42, March 9, 1989, at Deaconess Hospital in Boston, Christie's appraised the Mapplethorpe estate at $228 million. When George Valentine Dureau disabled by Alzheimer's died twice as old as Robert at age 83, April 7, 2014, at Waldon Health Care Center in Kenner, Louisiana, he died poor, but money can't buy love of the kind Dureau elicited because he was the *mensch* Mapplethorpe could have been in America where the ultimate goal of the rich and famous is to become beloved.

During George's last impoverished days living with increasing dementia in a care home, his friend of seven years, Katie Nachod, the reference librarian at Tulane University and the Louisiana Supreme Court Law Library for whom he often prepared breakfast at his final post-Katrina home on Bienville Street, and other "Friends of George" held a fund-raising auction on July 13, 2013—*The Living Estate of George Valentine Dureau*—offering George's artistic tools and personal items like his famous four-poster bed, his kitchen table, and his photo props.

Professional appraiser Ruthie Winston said, "I know we won't have any trouble getting bids because George is such a part of our city's culture and he has left such an indelible mark; everything from the creation of his 'Professor Longhair' Jazz Fest poster or his exquisite black-and-white photos."[39] "Professor Longhair" was the black blues innovator, Henry "Roy" Byrd (1918-1980).

In the disco decade after the Stonewall riot in 1969 even as Marxist theories of class struggle were beginning to hijack popular gay liberation into the separatist fundamentalism of gay politics, Robert's business plan of resistance was to get his politically

---

39 Advertiser's Message, "Estate Auction to Benefit Artist George Dureau," *Uptown Messenger,* July 9, 2013

incorrect S&M pictures published in magazines as a trial balloon to pitch a book deal for his upcoming 1978 *X Portfolio*. When mainstream photo-book publishers also rejected his proposals, Robert, funded by Sam, turned to self-publishing thirty-nine of his photos in his *X, Y,* and *Z Portfolio* books from 1978 to 1981—even as he was studying, digesting, and cribbing Dureau.

In 1980, he and Sam engaged Galerie Jurka in Amsterdam to publish his *Black Males*. That book of fifty-eight pages, with Robert's *Bob Love*, 1979, on the cover was a vamp on Dureau's romantic blacks, specifically, George said with some pique, "My model Oscar. He kept my photo of Oscar hanging in the hall next to the bedroom when he was dying." To propel *Black Males*, Robert procured a key endorsement to catch the reflected glory he wanted from gay Manhattan mandarin and socialite Edmund White—whose middle name was *Valentine* like Dureau's—to write the brief introduction.

In the early 1980s, Robert's second influencer, not quite mentor, for his 1986 *Black Book*, was the pioneer gay white photographer Miles Everett (1912-1994) who, unknown to Dureau, had been photographing nude black men since 1931. Everett told me he had heard of Mapplethorpe through two photographers—Northern white peers of Dureau—who also influenced Robert.

One was Jim Jager (1933-1981) who, having shot his first blacks in 1958, photographed them in the 1970s for his Third World Studio which he ran in Chicago from 1976 to his murder in 1981. Word of Robert also came to Miles from Craig Anderson (1941-2014) who had been lensing blacks for his Sierra Domino studio in San Francisco since 1970. Studying Jager and Anderson in the doubly segregated world of white gay photographers and nude black men, Robert in 1981 visited the elderly Everett who was living closeted in Los Angeles with his unexhibited pictures because of his long career working for Hughes Aircraft and NASA. Robert's hunting trips with Everett describe how Robert acted on his hunting trips with Dureau.

"I didn't understand Robert then," Miles said during our interview on September 9, 1990. "I don't understand him now. He seemed extremely nervous. He smoked continuously all the time he was here. But he took his time looking through my work, and, boy, he pulled out my best stuff. Maybe twelve or fifteen pictures. He went on to shoot my model Marty Gibson several times [*Marty Gibson, on the Beach*, 1982]. I think he was influenced, maybe in his late pictures, by my style. I feel this because some of his late pictures use a black background. Now, he didn't ever before use a black background like I did. He'd tried whites and grays and all that kind of thing. But he saw in my work a certain beauty that he probably liked, and he went back and he duplicated it."[40] And then published the recreations in his *Black Book*.

By 1986, the year Robert's AIDS was diagnosed, work by Dureau and Mapplethorpe was trending everywhere in pop culture. The similarities of existing work caused confusion, contrast, and comparison between the two artists because, as Jonathan Webb said, "I had to hide George's work when Robert visited because if Robert saw a photo in New Orleans, six weeks later he'd be exhibiting his version in New York."

Floral Park came to New Orleans like Birnam Wood to Dunsinane.

"It was the kiss of death when Robert would buy something of mine," George said. "It was like he was paying a token price for what he was going to do with that picture. Put it in the Big Time! It was funny, because he would drain the soul out of it, that big slice of soul I created out of my personal experience, and not exactly for public consumption. I mean, so many of my pictures he'd copy in his brain. He'd see something in my drawings, paintings, and photographs that he'd carry back to New York where he started cropping his pictures to re-create 'profound Dureau compositions.'"

Speaking of the design of his photos bought by Robert, George said, "Robert lifted my 'Sitting Pose,' and sentenced it to death. There were two photos I showed in New York. One was Dave Kopay [*Dave Kopay*, 1982], the [gay] football player sitting sidesaddle with his arms around his knees and his dick and balls hanging out. The other one was a nude black boy [*Leonard Fazer (with Clarinet)* sitting

---

40   Jack Fritscher, "White Art, Black Men," *Mapplethorpe Assault with a Deadly Camera, op. cit.*, page 205

with dick and balls hanging out. And those sort of went together to make Robert's pictures of models sitting exposed on pedestals."

He added, "We didn't become enemies exactly. Over time, he became distant. He didn't know how to draw pictures of himself. He tried to draw me. His artwork was not very good."

The models Dureau humanized, Robert fetishized. What D. H. Lawrence, beloved by Tennessee Williams, wrote about Walt Whitman in his *Studies in Classic American Literature* may also be said about George. "Whitman came along, and saw the slave, and said to himself: 'That negro slave is a man like myself. We share the same identity.'"

Dureau called his pictures a "Family Album." As inclusive auteur, George titled his photos with the model's name and often had the model sign the photo prints next to his own signature. Robert as exclusive auteur titled his pictures with the model's first name and location as he pitched his work, signed by him only, to radical-chic white liberals.

"Robert cleaned up my pictures to make them respectable for respectable queers, especially queers with money. He wanted to give them something to talk about, bragging rights, like comparing the broken pottery of a boy to his perfect calla lilies. He was playing a game of 'Chicken' with his gay Mafia following. 'Look! I'm showing a dick with a mouth on it! Did you blink yet?' Baloney."

Robert's "Mondo Mapplethorpe" pictures of faces and fetishes were inspired by the million glossy gay sex photos he bought from bins in adult bookstores on 42nd Street. Those photos by text and subtext could have been virtual stills from the shocking international film hit *Mondo Cane* (1962). That movie which premiered at Cannes dared to turn its camera toward taboo by shooting never-before-seen cultural practices around the world. Its docu-fiction collage of bizarre visions was liberation for taboo-breaking *Mondo*-inflected photographers like Diane Arbus, Robert Mapplethorpe, George Dureau, Joel-Peter Witkin, and Arthur Tress, as well as for underground filmmakers like Andy Warhol, and Kenneth Anger with *Scorpio Rising* (1964), and John Waters with *Mondo Trasho* (1969) starring drag queen Divine of *Pink Flamingos* (1972).

In its 2017 exhibit, *Pride of Place: The Making of Contemporary Art in New Orleans*, the New Orleans Museum of Art displayed Mapplethorpe, Dureau, and Waters alone together and censored equally in an adult "private space" separated from the main show.

The Mapplethorpe-Dureau relationship had a perforated line.

"Robert would look at my photographs," Dureau told me as if Robert were the sex-starved Sebastian Venable cruising tasty teens of color in *Suddenly Last Summer*. George said, "Robert would look at my pictures of black men *devouring* them, discussing ways of making my rather romantic approach *nasty*, searching for the *shock* value." Williams wrote of Sebastian what he could have written about Robert out cruising the Quarter with George, the jolly chef, who said, "Robert devoured my art."

But drugs made the Irish-American boy, born with the Famine in his bones, anorexic. He, whose 24 Bond Street kitchen was never a place to cook, didn't like George's suppers, New Orleans cuisine, or eating.

"Robert should have eaten the food he photographed," I said. "He'd be alive today."

"His 'precious' grapes? I don't think so," George said. "All Robert wanted was an egg done his certain way and a Coca-Cola."

Grapes, 1985, was part of Robert's food photography like *Watermelon with Knife*, 1985, that suggests a summer picnic, but codes just a tad racist.

Tennessee Williams, who had his own regularly reserved window table at Galatoire's where he could eat and watch the hot dishes cruising outside on Bourbon Street, said about his insatiable sex-tourist Sebastian cannibalized by lads of color in a spasm band: "That's how he talked about people…as if they were items on the menu…delicious…appetizing…*he was really nearly half starved from living on pills and salad*."[41] (Italics added)

In the social intersections around Dureau and Mapplethorpe, when Jim McBride, the New York director of the 1986 neo-noir film, *The Big Easy*, wanted to capture authentic New Orleans locations

---

41   Tennessee Williams, *Suddenly Last Summer, Tennessee Williams: Plays 1957-1980*, Library of America, 2000, page 118

and picturesque *bona fide* characters, he persuaded George, who had painted *Reception with a Waiter* (1962), to punctuate the picture with a cameo star turn as the "Maitre D'" acting opposite Ellen Barkin on location at Antoine's Restaurant, 713 St. Louis Street.

In the second draft of *The Big Easy* script, authors Jack Baran and Jim McBride added to the original screenplay by Daniel Petrie, Jr.

Just then the 'Maitre D' appears with the telephone.
Maitre D': Miss Osborne? Call for you.

McBride's connection to Dureau came from his earlier 1976 connection to Mapplethorpe who shot one of his most controversial pictures of the director's five-year-old son, *Jesse McBride*, described as "Blond male nude child perched on top of chair with refrigerator in background," which was one of the seven photographs put on trial in Cincinnati.

In the popular culture of 1987, while George was a photographer beloved in Southern media and books like *New Orleans Elegance and Decadence*, Mapplethorpe, an elegant leather S&M graduate of Pratt and the decadent "Mineshaft School for Lower Education," increasingly disabled with two years to live, was at the apogee of his international career.

Robert had long been shooting gay cult icons like pornstar photographer Peter Berlin (b. 1942) who is Baron Armin Hagen Freiherr von Hoyningen-Huene, and collecting photographs of black men shot in the 1930s by Peter Berlin's cousin, the Jazz Age fashion photographer George Hoyningen-Huene (1900-1968) whose crisp silent-film lighting and in-frame composition directly influenced Robert's exquisite style. As he was growing his own celebrity plowing the pertinent on each continent, he did, in fact, clean up his act, graduating from the leather photography of his "High S&M *Drummer* Period 1975-1980" to his Dureauvian portraits of his "High Black Period 1979-1988."

Unlike Mapplethorpe, George grew up woke in the black culture of the New Orleans *entrepôt* that was 70-percent white when he was born in 1930 and 70-percent black by Hurricane Katrina in 2005. Robert grew up in the 98-percent-white calla lily that was Floral Park, New York.

While Robert was studying George's natural-born knack for racial presentation of his friendly neighbors, he set out to build his own racial street cred by waking himself to the black culture of skeptical black strangers inside black gay bars like "Blues" in Times Square. His tentative first black pictures were fetish portraits, not of black men he'd yet to approach, but of a pack of Kool Filter King menthol cigarettes, *Untitled (Kool Cigarettes)*, 1975, because while white men made a cowboy fetish of Marlboros, black men smoked Kools, and so did he because they did, and he could open a conversation with the offer of a smoke.

After Wally Wallace (1938-1999), the founding manager of the iconic Mineshaft sex club (1976-1988), told me in a video interview on March 28, 1990, how Robert cruised with him in black bars in New York in the 1970s, George confirmed in 1991 that Robert cruised much the same way in New Orleans in the 1980s.

Wally said, "I knew Bob as a person. I liked Bob. He shot a portrait of Mr. Mineshaft. [*Mr. Mineshaft, David O'Brien*, 1979] We weren't close friends, but we'd talk and compare notes. I remember one time [hesitates], well, he liked black men. He had heard of a place in Times Square called 'Blues,' which was a black gay bar. One of the few places that was openly promoted as a black gay bar. And Bob was afraid to go there. I don't why, but he was.

"So I went up there with him one time. He was like a kid so eager to go, but so afraid to go alone that you might have thought it was in the depths of Harlem. The night we were there, there weren't many hot men, but only a couple of black drag queens with their white boyfriends. It was not what he imagined. I know he went back there a few times. I know he went to Keller's a lot. That has now become a black bar. It was one of the original New York leather bars. It's still there; one of the longest-running gay bars."[42]

---

42 Jack Fritscher, "Wally Wallace: The Mineshaft Interview," *Profiles in Gay Courage: Leatherfolk, Arts, and Ideas*, Palm Drive Publishing, San Francisco, 2022, page 75

Dureau, mentoring Mapplethorpe's photography of blacks, more importantly tried to mentor Robert's behavior around race relations.

"I must tell you about my best time with Robert," he told me. "We had an absolutely splendid time cruising through the cold of Mardi Gras. Canal Street, the main drag, was mobbed. We were wingmen playing a cruising game like we were gunners in a war bomber.

"I'd say, 'Look at three o'clock: tall, skinny, tan.'

"He'd say, 'Look at nine o'clock: mean, black, dangerous, sexy.'

"That's what we shared the most mutual joy in, the hunt. He'd talk me into going into a black gay bar, and they'd recognize me and be all over me to shoot them. Robert would find someone he thought fabulous looking, and I'd drop him home with them, but often as not, afterward, he'd say, 'Oh, they weren't any good. They didn't do the right thing.'

"I thought him petulant. He liked what he saw, but often their performance never came up to New York standards. In the bars, his leather-wear made him look like a groupie with a boy band. Robert would stand in the corner and scowl at people, then say something. He acted the same punk way in a New Orleans bar as he would in a New York bar, looking petulant. I don't do that. I ask them about their wife and kids."

"Did Robert ask them what kind of drugs they liked?"

"I suppose he offered them drugs, because he didn't have enough confidence in his own charm. Drugs are the cheap and easy way."

"What is your take on Robert's wearing a button that said, 'N-word'?"

"That was a real problem with him, that N-word thing. I'd set him up with someone I knew and the next morning, I'd ask, 'How was he?'

"'Not too good,' Robert said.

"'Not too good?' Why not?

"'Well, he didn't want to do anything.'

"'I can't believe 'he didn't want to do anything.'

"'He wouldn't say,' Robert said, "'I'm your N-word.'"

"I'd go, 'Huuuh?' I've been accused of being a colonialist, accused of keeping slaves, despite my cordial behavior with my darlings. And I'd say to Robert, 'He wouldn't say, "I'm your N-word"? Isn't there an alternate, like, "Oh my darling, I love you'?

"Robert would say, 'No! Why couldn't he say, "I'm your N-word"? I say to them, "I'm your cocksucker."

"Well, do I have to explain why it's hard to say that? The problem was on his side. He wanted a scenario that was very set, inflexible. I mean that some person had to open his mouth and say, 'I'm your N-word.' Robert could have just thought that part as a fantasy in his head. What was he thinking? I think fetish scenarios for all of us come out of our deepest past."

"There's that picture of his, the one with the big black dick hanging out of the polyester suit. I own that polyester picture."

For all its threats and promises of racial potency, Robert's pars-pro-toto *Man in Polyester Suit*—coincidentally printed and released in 1981, the same year as John Waters's satirical *Polyester*—is also, to the gay gaze, an ironic picture of the erectile dysfunction size queens from the 70s recognize from men showing and growing at the clubs and baths: the endowed have a harder time getting hard and staying hard. In the gay press of the 1980s, it could also have served as a camp advertisement for a "Before Viagra" shot even without an "After Viagra" shot of the same man and pose with penis rampant.

George owned eight Mapplethorpes. Don Dureau retained one for the Dureau family and sold seven back to the Mapplethorpe Foundation to support George in the nursing home.

"Robert," George recalled, "told me he had major plans for that polyester model [Milton Moore]. He thought that was going to be some big lifelong affair.

"One time, he said, 'I wish I could find a smart one.'

"I said, 'What do you mean, a smart one?'

"He said, 'You know, I'd like to find one as good-looking as Bryant Gumbel.' [The handsome Bryant Gumbel was the popular anchor of NBC's *Today* show from 1982 to 1997.]

"I said, 'Why?'

"He said, 'I want one that has a brain of his own.'

"'Why? So he doesn't hang on to you?'

"'Yes.'

"'But, Robert,' I said, 'if there was a black man that was brilliant and beautiful and had a successful business, why would he want to go into a corner and say, "I'm your N-word" to someone like you?'"

Rimshot.

George was a swordsman who had perfected dueling to first blood in the fencing academies of gay bars.

In 1980, with less than nine years to live, Robert took to race-play sex and to shooting pictures of black men while embracing black lovers like his model and final partner Jack Walls—also photographed by Dureau—who standing by his man till he died, called Patricia Morrisroe's biography of Robert, "Shit."[43]

As an aging senior examining his career, George who had always been the life of the party was realizing he was becoming an endangered species in the gentrifying French Quarter where for years he had volunteered with city planners and served on boards of art commissions to protect the Quarter from Disneyfication.

Writing on a sheet of drawing paper, he took stock of self-disciplines of the kind Mapplethorpe never knew because Robert never had the advantage of growing old. He wrote about himself in the third person the way he often talked about himself in the third person—the way Catherine Holly in *Suddenly Last Summer* kept her journal in the third-person—before he began to suffer from dementia after Hurricane Katrina rattled him in 2005.

Having sheltered in place during Hurricane Betsy in 1965, George in 2005 rode out Katrina shuttered in his Dauphine home with four or five friends. Don Dureau said, "Around the time of Katrina, he got strange. When busses arrived to evacuate people, he got on a bus of refugees headed to Baton Rouge where he was given a ticket to Houston, but then got set up in a carriage house in Baton Rouge for a couple of months. What happened was that immediately after the storm, he crossed the street to a Catholic nursing

---

43   Tim Murphy, "Artist Jack Walls Survived His Boyfriend, Robert Mapplethorpe—and All the Haters, Too," *The Caftan Chronicles*, September 6, 2023. https://thecaftanchronicles.substack.com/p/artist-jack-walls-survived-his-boyfriend

home where a priest getting on one of the evacuation busses said, 'George, you need to come along with us to Houston.' But George got off in Baton Rouge after the Red Cross asked if he was on the bus and gave him a letter from friends who were good patrons saying he was welcome to stay in their Baton Rouge guest house while they were in Europe.

"When he got there, they had set up easels and paint and food. So he stayed there quite awhile. I told him he could come stay with me, but he wouldn't say yes or no. Then without telling me, he returned to Dauphine and was shocked that he had to vacate the premises because the landlord had lost his own family home.

"I went to his new home five times and he never answered the door. I called him many many times on the phone and he never answered, until one time he did, and said that line that haunts me, "I don't have a brother," and hung up on me. I thought maybe it was one of his jokes so I didn't worry too much or make a wellness check because friends said he was doing okay. He was already suffering from Alzheimer's. Our grandfather Dureau died in 1942 of extreme dementia."

In flowing script, the dyslexic George standing outside himself, feisty with deprecating irony or fighting semantic memory loss in his long goodbye, drew the words, as perfect as a soliloquy by Tennessee Williams, picturing his elder self estranged from his younger self in the third person.

"George quit smoking, quit what did not encourage his art and talent, quit drinking, quit living with another person (marriage [*sic*]), quit unhealthy goodies, quit drawing or painting in the style of others, quit laying women in 1960, scratch that, 1965, quit laying men in 2000, scratch that, 2002, quit driving, quit drinking red wine, quit flying to other places, quit keeping secrets, quit wearing popular clothes, quit dining around, quit promoting exhibitions, quit matching the popular times in art. He draws, paints, cooks, and bicycles conservatively around the Vieux Carré, but does not often visit elsewhere."[44]

---

44 *New Orleans Artists: John Burton Harter and George Dureau, op. cit.*

I told George when Robert asked me to write about him in 1977, he "wanted to be a story told in beds at night around the world."

George said, "Who doesn't?"

A month before Robert died in 1989, he told his first lover and model David Croland, "Tell them everything. Keep me alive."

All his life, George regaling reporters and talking to video cameras was courting the same eternity as Robert for his art. "I'm doing this interview for posterity," George told me. He wanted us writers to keep him alive. "I think my work will go on because it's loaded with humanity and stories of people's lives."

On Friday, May 3, 1996, five years after the perfect moment of our golden week together in New Orleans, George rendezvoused with Mark and me in Paris where Mark videotaped us three laughing and strolling the gravel paths of the Tuileries before we headed off for an early bite at a *brasserie* and then a quick walk to La Maison Europèenne de la Photographie at 5/7 Rue de Fourcy where that evening George was being fêted and our two Dureau documentaries were being inducted into its permanent collection. Joy remains in memories of that final Friday that was our "Sunday in the Park with George."

For the next few years we kept in contact by telephone until he no longer picked up his receiver. So that splendid springtime together cruising around Paris was the last time we saw each other in this life; but George's photographs hanging in our living room next to his handsome 4x3-foot painting *Legless Male Torso Rising Armless Off Greek Column* (1991) which he gave to my husband as a birthday gift, keep us forever mindful of him.

When beloved Big Daddy George disappeared from the French Quarter and died offstage out of town, he was sorely missed.

Katie Machod recalled, "An old man who sat for portraits by Dureau in the 1960s, teary-eyed and pleading, asked: 'Mr. George die?'"[45]

---

45   Steve Garbarino, "Artist George Dureau left his mark on the French Quarter like few others," *The Advocate*, April 15, 2014

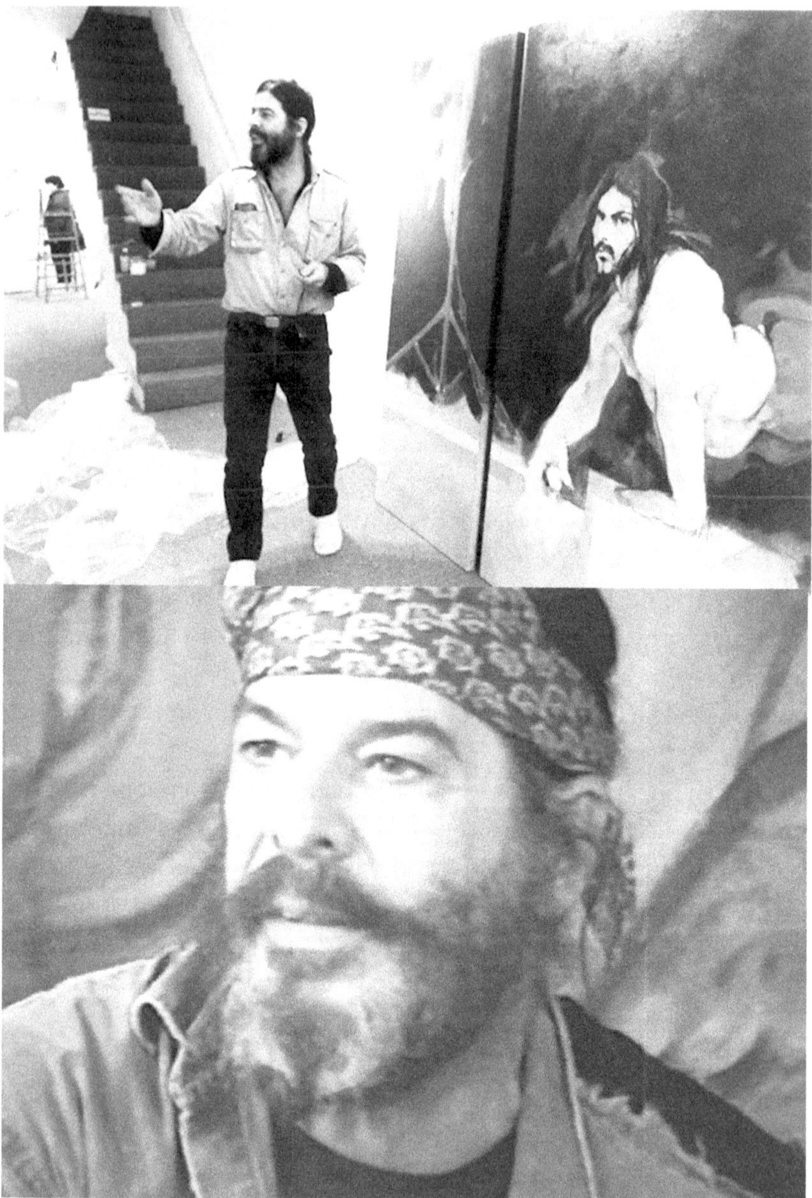

(Top) George Dureau installing his torso painting of his legless friend and recurring photography model B. J. Robinson, Martin Gallery, 2427 18th St. NW, Washington, D. C., 1986. Photo by © Jim Marks, journalist, *The Washington Bladee*

(Bottom) George Dureau in his French Quarter studio, April 8, 1991. Video photo by © Jack Fritscher

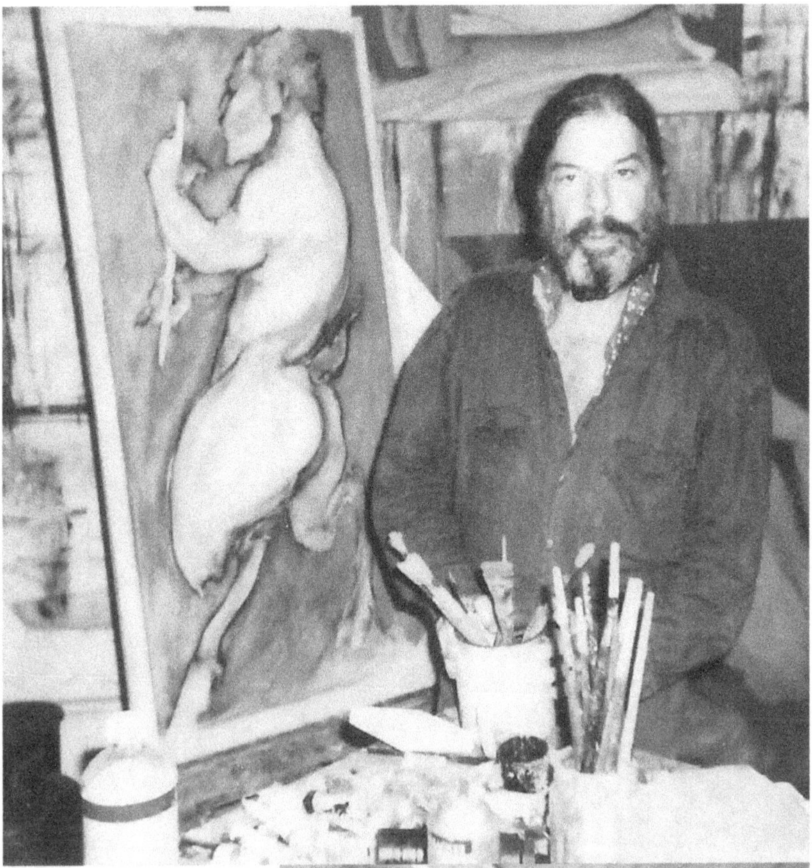

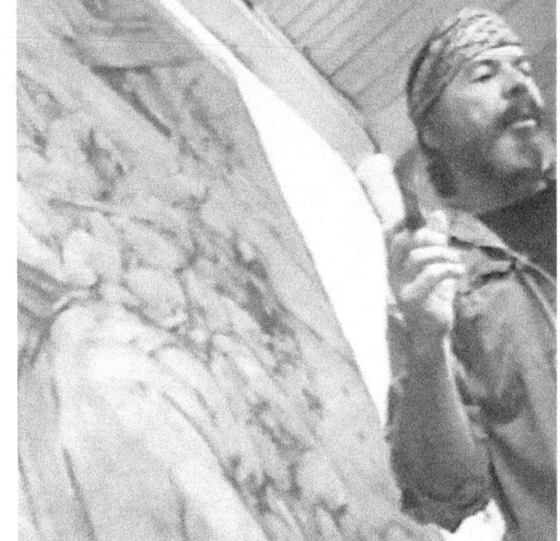

(Top) George Dureau with *Satyr* Painting. Polaroid photo by © Michael Alago

(Right) George Dureau to scale against his large painting *Mars Descending*, Contemporary Arts Center of New Orleans's *War Exhibition*. April 8, 1991. Video photo by © Jack Fritscher

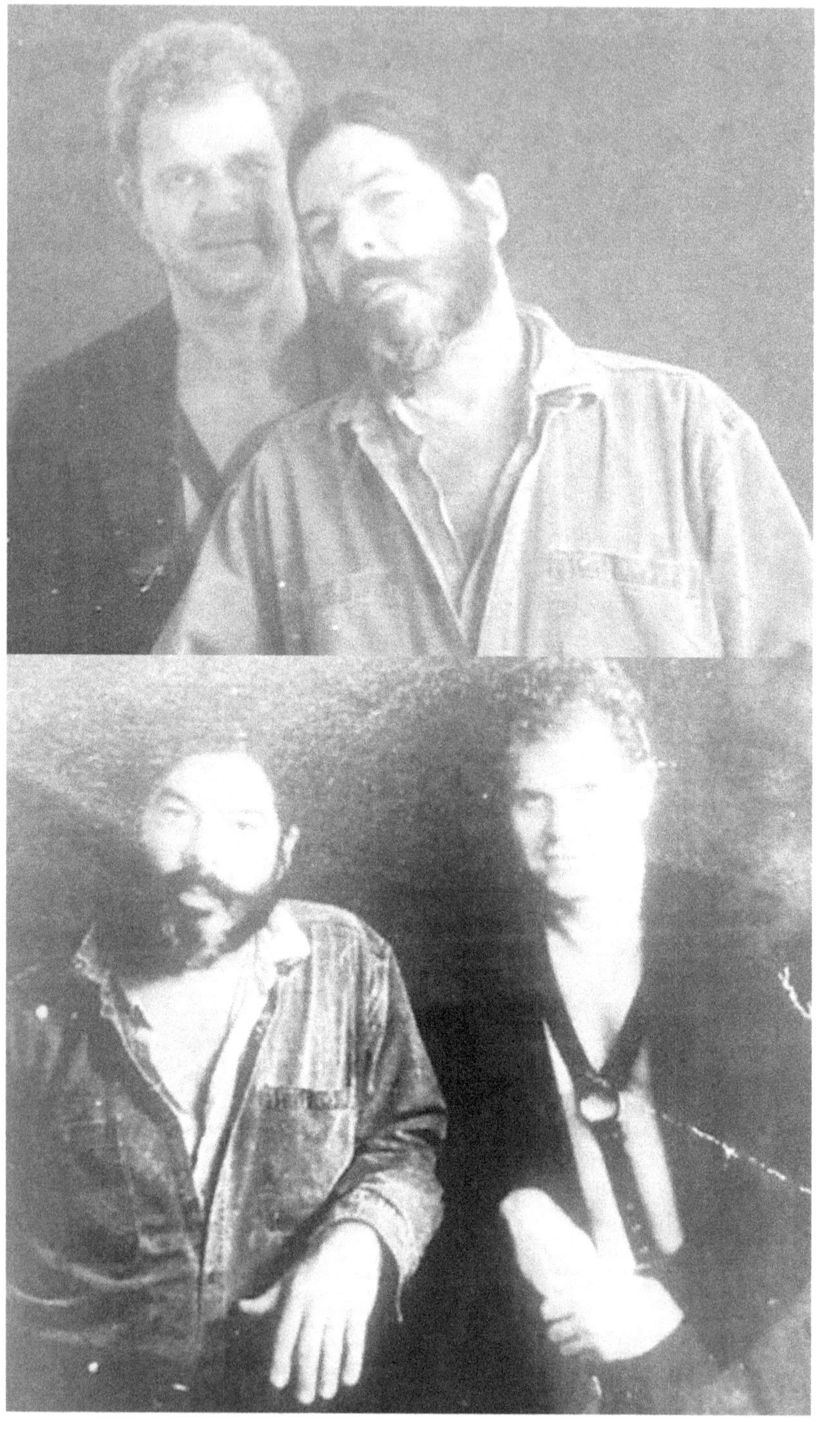

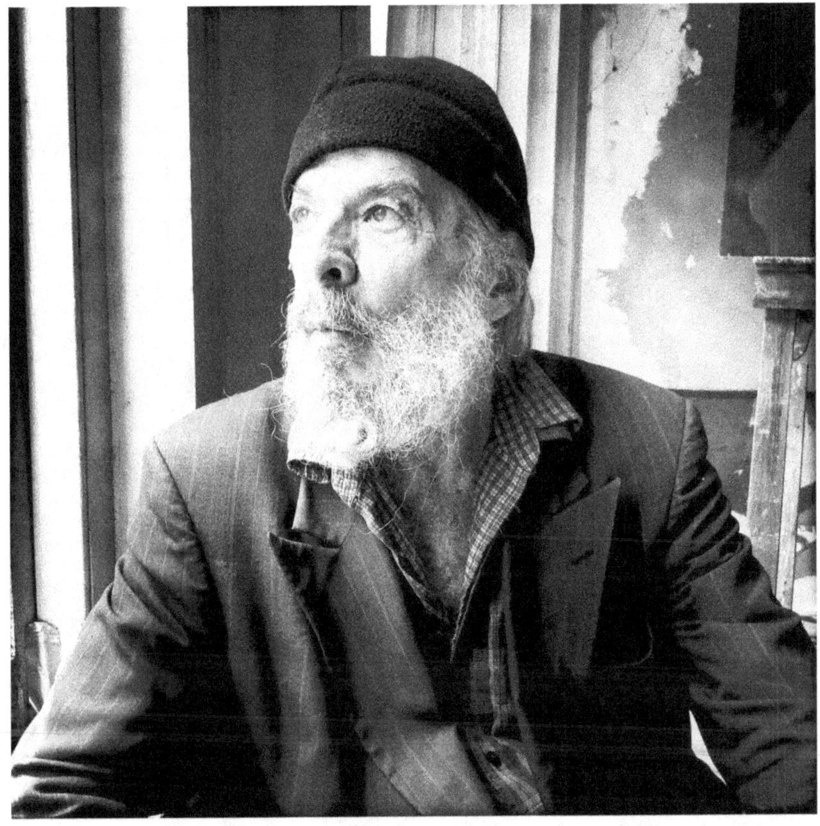

George Dureau at 81, French Quarter home and studio, 1307 Dauphine Street, New Orleans, 2012. Polaroid by © Michael Alago

(Opposite page) George Dureau and Don Dureau, New Orleans. 1986. Photos by © George Dureau. Courtesy of Don Dureau

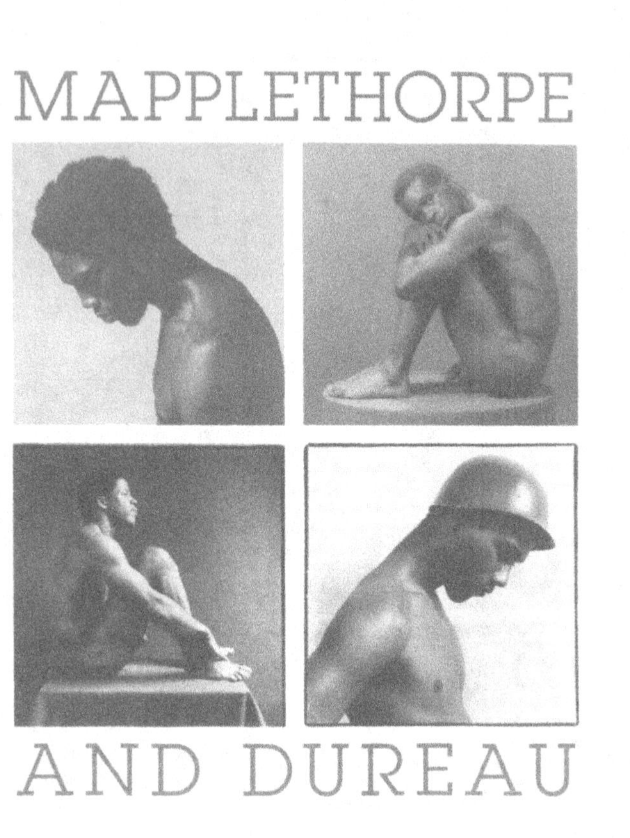

Who shot what? *Mapplethorpe and Dureau: Photographs*, January 6 – February 17, 2018, Arthur Roger Galley; Opening Reception: Saturday, January 6, 6–8 pm; 434 Julia Street, New Orleans, LA 70130; in collaboration with the Robert Mapplethorpe Foundation. Courtesy of Arthur Roger Gallery and Michael Alago

TAKE 2

INTRODUCTORY PHONE CALL TO GEORGE DUREAU

August 26, 1990

Primary Source Material
Dureau Speaks

Jack Fritscher: Hello. This is Jack Fritscher. Is George Dureau there?

George Dureau: This is George Dureau.

Jack Fritscher: George! How nice to talk to you. I'm a writer and a friend of Robert Mapplethorpe and have learned of your work from Keith Ardent who, when I was talking to him the other day, said, "There's this New Orleans passage in Robert's life that someone should pay attention to and the man there is George Dureau." I was wondering if you might consider my making a telephone appointment to ask a few questions.

George Dureau: Yes. Are you writing a book or what?

Jack Fritscher: I am. May I record this? To make notes? I won't take much of your time.

George Dureau: Of course. Ask away.

Jack Fritscher: I've been working on my Mapplethorpe book off and on since 1978. A couple of chapters are based on my feature articles about Robert. I'm not so much interested in the controversy about him as I am in presenting him as a person. And in your case, as your student. People have heard he had a mentor, but they think it was Sam Wagstaff.

George Dureau: So you see him as he was?

Jack Fritscher: As I saw him for three years when we were together. Robert has been lost as a person in all this controversy over censorship. What I'm trying to do in my book is present him as a person who, as with all young photographers, had teachers, mentors, friends. You helped him along and taught him things about photography. Robert was not born to the camera. The camera found him.

George Dureau: I knew even less about photography than he. We may have started photographing about the same time, but because I've always drawn and painted, when I picked up the camera and started making pictures, they looked like my paintings and drawings. So the precedents for whatever he got from me come from my paintings and drawings of men. Robert was much more a student of photography than I. He and Sam had gathered up a collection of historic pictures by all kinds of photographers and Robert studied them and distilled them into what he wanted his work to look like.

I must say, I never thought about what my own work would look like. It just looked like my painting. Robert certainly never came to me to learn anything. He saw some of my photographs at Robert Miller Gallery. He and Sam were reviewing my work, and fell in love with a couple of them. He wrote me a letter and asked could he buy one. So he bought that first one [*Wilbert Hines*, 1977], and he continued thereafter to buy them, and I must say that they influenced him a lot.

I'm very much a humanist and I'm very involved with the people I photograph. My pictures are family pictures. Very sentimental, shall we say. They're very humanist. And that was highly inappropriate for the New York market he was aiming at. Sam, not even for one moment, would never have tolerated Robert photographing people with as much compassion as I did. Quite true.

Robert, looking through a large stack of my photographs, just kept staring at me as if to say, "You must be crazy to like these people." My pictures quite clearly say that I like everybody that I photograph. So anyway, Robert cleaned them up. That is, he used some of the aesthetics of my kind of old-fashioned good posing that I had developed over twenty or thirty years of work, but he made it into a much more stylized, art-for-art's-sake kind of art which suited him and the much more chic audience he had in mind.

The New York people to whom he appealed, none of them, were as compassionate as the people in New Orleans who were amused by my pictures. There was a coldness about his work, either because he was like that or his audience was. He always used to sort of smile and give a "Ooh, how could you do it?" look about my pictures being so tender and involved. He came around here a good bit, you know.

Jack Fritscher: So you knew him rather well. Personally. And through your lens.

George Dureau: Yes. I have a good many photographs of him, and some he took of me down here. There's two or three really lovely ones of him. One that I took when we first met face to face, 1979, I guess, and then I also took some later when he was not as well, looking a bit bedraggled. I don't know when that was, maybe 1985.

He came down here and stayed in the French Quarter. In those days I had a big house right outside the French Quarter on Esplanade [Avenue]. Now I live in the French Quarter. We went out together. Ran around together. He had that sweet baby-sister behavior. A come-hither kind of behavior.

We shared quite a bit of the same taste about men we liked, but I don't think there was any similarity about our sexuality. I'm an old fashioned Greco-Roman patriarch queer, not a flip-flop queer. I mean, I'm the dominant male about the house. I have a lot of gorgeous boys who work for me and do things for me. My house is a kind of colony of the underclass, but I'm Big Daddy always. I'm not anything similar to his sexuality which, I believe, was much more modern gay.

Jack Fritscher: It was. It's a perfect hook to talk about because I had many of the same observations about him myself during our affair.

George Dureau: Well, let's consider the people. It's wild the tenderness I afford to my models. They're my children. They're usually people that I'm doing for, like they're adopted. I keep them around so when I hire them to model, it's quite different from Robert's one-shot thing. Bring them in, shoot them, pay them, throw them out.

Robert asked, "How can you get them so cheap?"

I said, "You can get them cheap if you don't mind having them for life."

Where he would pay $400-$500 to get them to drop their pants in front of the camera, I would seduce people because I loved them and then I would have them to dinner or for life, to paint from or to draw from or to fuck or to photograph. If I paid them $100 to pose for me they would be back the next day anyway to get money to pay their momma's rent or the water bill or something. I could have paid them $1,000 and they'd still be back.

It's so different when you live in a congenial little town like New Orleans. You can't shoot them and leave them. At any given time, I have two or three at the door, even though I've found out they're not people I want to spend the rest of my life with. I have discretion. I have to be a bit choicey, but not too much. I still get enamored by someone's appearance and bring him home.

Jack Fritscher: When you and Robert went out, how did you find him to be? Was he predatory? Did you find him under the influence of drugs?

George Dureau: When we were out, Robert would always have to go home to make a pit stop for his powders. I didn't have to. I did smoke in the 60s and a little into the 70s. I used to be quite an alcoholic and drank quite a bit, but I've never been addicted to drugs. So we had a different mentality. The drugs matched very well with his hard vision of what people could do for him as opposed to my sort of Big Daddy way of what I'm going to do for them. It's a very funny thing. I see people as somebody I might adopt, do for them for awhile, while Robert would see them as "What's this one going to do for me tonight?" His was a very modern-day gay behavior, but not something I could do. I think it ties in much more with drugs and immediate satisfaction. I'm the king of low-key living.

Jack Fritscher: I tend to be more like you.

George Dureau: Where do you live?

Jack Fritscher: In the countryside north of the Golden Gate Bridge. Just so you know, because you mention Big Daddy, I wrote my dissertation on Tennessee Williams. So I get it when you call yourself Big Daddy.

George Dureau: Tennessee lived right around the corner from me.

Jack Fritscher: Ah, the Vieux Carré.

George Dureau: In some ways, I'm the older Big Daddy and someways I'm the younger Brick [two characters in *Cat on a Hot Tin Roof*]. I looked at myself when I was thirty-five….

Jack Fritscher: The average age of a leading man in Hollywood…

George Dureau: …back when we all had long hair in the early 60s, and I would go into hippie bars with hip people. And then I looked in the mirror one day and it dawned on me that I had attained the age of my own fantasies.

"Oh, my God," I thought, "now you're a daddy!"

I suddenly became the daddy instead of the pursued person and I must say it's the best thing that ever happened to me. So many older queers think they're "something" and hold themselves royally apart for no good reason. I just think being older gives me more advantages to offer more to the cute things I would much rather pick up.

Jack Fritscher: Robert was that way in a sense. He was very good looking, but he was that type. Aloof. Objectifying. Everything he did around leather guys he met was an audition for his photography.

George Dureau: Yes, it was. I however still do blind "fall-in-loves." I have this immediate passion for almost all human beings which is incredibly stupid sounding, but I give everybody one hundred per-cent. Then I let them chip away at that. Essentially I just love people unreservedly, whereas he!

Let me tell you a story. He was here one Mardi Gras and we had an absolutely splendid time out in the cold cruising the Mardi Gras parade and crowd. Now this was swell to him like he was paging through a book of beauties or something. I was his wingman.

I'd say, "Look at 3:00 tall and skinny, tan, eyebrows."

And he'd say, "Look at 9:00."

We'd do this sort of behavior, walking through the crowd, the endless, massive crowd, especially when you went down to Canal Street, the main drag. Do you know New Orleans?

Jack Fritscher: From music, movies, and books. When my husband Mark Hemry was younger, he often went to Mardi Gras and has stories to tell.

George Dureau: Canal Street is the main drag, but it's also the meanest street because that's where most of the black people hang out, on the main drag, and so we could go cruise through them. Actually, that may have been my best time with Robert because the fun of seeing them and cruising them was what we enjoyed the most. What happened with them after he saw them, or I did, was so dissimilar, it was strange.

We'd go into a black gay bar. There's many, but they're not the kind of places I can go into because the city is so small. The guys would be all over me because they want me to photograph them or hire them for a little job around the studio. They know me too well.

But I did take him around for a little education.

We'd go into a black bar and find someone he thought was fabu-lous looking. Then I'd drop him home with them, but often as not he'd say later, "Oh they weren't any good," or, "They wouldn't do the right thing."

I would think: that's odd. He liked them when he saw them, but when they didn't do what he wanted, or come up to the New York standards, he complained.

As a matter of fact, when I moved to New York in the 60s, it took me no time at all to find I was not going to perform up to the predictable New York pattern. I was far too romantic, yes, and came on sort of "southern literary" or something, southern country behavior, country compared to New York. There was a gentility to my life before I went there. I thought, "My God, if I stay here, I'm going to have to give up everything I hold dear." I stayed about nine months.

Jack Fritscher: Do you think Robert's urbanity tripped up his humanity?

George Dureau: I don't know. I just saw how he acted in New Orleans. He could pick up anybody he wanted to, but you don't have to behave that sharp way in laid-back New Orleans to pick up people. They're all over the place. I find my satisfaction in having a more humanist relation with people.

I'm fifty-nine. I'll be sixty in December. I've been laying men, devotedly laying people, since the 1940s. I've changed some with age, but back then I would go dancing and have a riotous good time in the Spanish or Greek bars. If you fell in love with somebody, wasn't that wonderful? And if three months later they screwed you over, well, that was just a different period. You could fall in love with a sailor and wait for him to come back from some endless war.

Jack Fritscher: Like Tennessee Williams' maimed young Navy sailor in his French Quarter story, "One Arm" [1948].

George Dureau: Yes. The Quarter was full of sailors and soldiers from World War II and Korea and the Army. I was in the Army myself. I seduced a mountain of people. I didn't go for sex first. I went for romance first. I worked at it because sex was a wonderful jewel in those days whereas today it's thrown out on the counter like meat.

Jack Fritscher: What was Robert like when he went into a black bar with you?

George Dureau: Oh, just the usual petulant leather boy standing in a corner of the bar and scowling at people, then sort of sidling over to them and whispering something. He acted the same way in New Orleans as he would in a New York bar, looking petulant and kind of drawing them close into him whispering sex and drugs. I don't do that. I don't know how to do that. I ask them about their wives and children.

Jack Fritscher: Robert liked figuring out what drugs might make people available. He liked MDA.

George Dureau: He didn't have enough confidence in his own charm. So he always offered them drugs. That's the cheap and easy way to do it. He knew that I didn't object terribly to his taking drugs. I didn't participate. A joint once in awhile. I've never used coke.

Jack Fritscher: Wally Wallace [Manager of the Mineshaft bar in New York who allowed Robert to shoot *Mr. Mineshaft, David O'Brien*, 1979, on location] introduced him to black bars in New York and told me for the record on video that when he took Robert into his first black bar, he was terrified, and yet he went around wearing that lapel button that said "N-word." So...

George Dureau: Well, that was a real problem with him, that N-word thing he had.

Jack Fritscher: Like a fetish-trigger buzzword that made him hard, something he could say to a partner to propel a scene.

George Dureau: I can remember one time he brought a rather cute black man back from a bar to my home. In this small town, I recognized him. So you can see one of the problems in New Orleans is sexual history. I'll see a guy who is twenty-eight-years old, handsome, and good looking, and I remember him when he was my paperboy because I go so far back, because I've been a recognizable nice man who is an artist who will lay you if you want it. I go way back. I've laid their big brothers. So Robert would see somebody cute who turned him on because he seemed real scarey. So I'd have to be careful not to disillusion him and say, "Oh, yes. He used to be my delivery boy."

Jack Fritscher: He needed that mix of beauty and terror.

George Dureau: Exactly. So one time when Robert was staying with my friends, he took home somebody who was quite handsome. I had an idea who he was, and the next morning Robert came over to have breakfast with me.

He was often the houseguest of my friends Russell Albright and Michael Meyers. Russell is a radiologist and Michael is a decorator. They have a big gorgeous house here, and they bought a lot of paintings from Robert Miller and they're sort of art climbers. So they would make a "Big Score" saying, "Oh, Robert's staying at our house." Okay, fine.

It would not be fun for Robert to stay at my house because I work all over my house all the time in my big live-in studio. But it was fine for him to stay at Russell's because there's a slave quarters building across the patio, and more guest rooms in the big mansion. So I knew they would find a nice place for him and give him all the liberty in the world because they don't make guests have to eat with them or drink with them or anything else even though they're quite social.

So anyway he would stay over there and come over the next morning to my place, and I would say, "How was Danny boy?" Or whoever.

"Oh, not too good."

"Why not?"

"Well, he didn't want to do anything."

"I can't believe he didn't want to do anything."

"He wouldn't say, 'I'm your N-word.'"

I'd go, "Huuuh?" I've been accused of being a colonialist, accused of keeping slaves, and all sort of things, but I have this cordial, sweet saintly behavior with my darlings. And I'd say, "He wouldn't say, 'I'm your N-word?' Isn't there an alternate? Like, 'Oh my darling I love you?'"

Robert would say, "No. Why couldn't he say, 'I'm your N-word?'"

Well, do I have to explain why it's hard to say that?

I'd say to him, "Look, if you said, 'I'm your cocksucker,' it might be a trade off for him to say, 'I'm your N-word.' Even so, why do you want him to say it? The problem is on your side, not on his."

We all have horrible fascist politically incorrect scenarios that go through our heads, but no one need say everything that comes into their head. You maybe create a private fantasy around a look in a certain picture, or around a guy, and then you hold your dick a certain way that turns you on, and then you lean up against something and fantasize two people falling in love with you, or something, and Whammo! It all adds up and you shoot your wad. It's often some kind of fetish scenario that comes out of your deepest past. It's okay, but I think it's so odd if you can't do it any other way. I mean that somebody had to open his mouth and say, "I'm your N-word." I mean in your head you could pretend that by his actions he was saying, "I'm your N-word."

Jack Fritscher: Floral Park where he grew up is very white. [Less than two percent black in 2020] He never said anything racist around me.

George Dureau: For all that, he would sometimes act like I was living a sweeter, warmer life than he. A couple times he wanted to come down and spend a couple of months here, but it never worked. He'd stay a week or two. He'd love it, but he couldn't stay off the phone, keep from doing business. He was just so ambitious to be well known.

Jack Fritscher: It's the American Dream.

George Dureau: Once he came down and said, "What have you been doing?"

I showed him some drawings and paintings.

He said, "No, Who have you been photographing? Got anybody new?"

I said, "I have new ones all the time. How about these?"

He'd look at the pictures and say, "Oh, look at him!"

I'd say, "Well, he's nice. but he ain't gonna say he's your N-word."

He said, "I haven't photographed any N-word I want in six months."

"Really?" I said. "What are you shooting?"

"Oh, I photographed some horses and some ads for Cardin."

I said, "Haven't you done any easel art or something you enjoy?" No?

Well, I thought, what a price. First you're famous and then you have to hurt yourself more. I'd like to be that famous, but his fame is so gigantic that it shits all over me all the time because it's so hard for people to understand that I am me without any need for Robert. He doesn't have anything to do with me because he sort of laid a wet blanket on everyone with his style.

My pictures, because they have other stuff going on in them, look less pure than his because they're not as stylized, as abstract as his. I'm much more concerned with the person, the whole human item. Do you know my work at all?

Jack Fritscher: Yes. I've seen your British photobook [*George Dureau New Orleans. 50 Photographs*, Introduction by Edward Lucie-Smith, GMP, London, 1985]. I know Ted Lucie-Smith who often stays in our guest room. And I appreciate your vision.

George Dureau: My pictures are like a record of a romance which is a big difference from him.

Jack Fritscher: Yes.

George Dureau: I'm romancing everybody who has ever appeared in my photographs. I have hundreds of pictures of the same people because they come back year after year and I photograph them. Sometimes it's hard to choose what to do with them, but each shoot I try to photograph different aspects of their personality.

Jack Fritscher: Robert went after the abstraction of a person, the platonic ideal.

George Dureau: That abstraction sometimes happens in my paintings because I sometimes talk the person into an ideal pose although I still keep some contact with their faces and personality. When I decided to make some photographs of the people I was painting and drawing, I had to resist the particular obvious things the camera was dying to shoot. I didn't want to spend my life taking literal pictures of a pair of big brown eyes with lashes on them, or of handsome amputees.

I used my camera as another way to get inside each person. My photographs also allow the person to "talk" which my paintings can't very well do. In my photographs, I have the person speaking back at you by looking back at you which, unfortunately, can make viewers feel guilty.

Jack Fritscher: Well, it's a shock to racist history when a black man can make direct eye contact with a white viewer and survive.

George Dureau: That's why some of my photographs were odious to some collectors like Sam Wagstaff, but not Robert who bought them. He had about thirty. He'd study them, take hints out of them, take the humanity out of them. He liked that my pictures would frequently make viewers feel uncomfortable. He wanted that with his pictures. I go nose-to-nose, beard-to-beard with you as the viewer, and then kind of come back at you again, and sometimes make you downright embarrassed.

Jack Fritscher: Your pictures have a gentle social consciousness. Robert's were rather aggressive acts of art for art's sake and commerce's sake. His leather pictures were like stills from a play in the Theater of Cruelty that assault an audience. The subtitle of my Mapplethorpe book will be *Assault with a Deadly Camera.*

George Dureau: "Assault," yes. His pictures were political, but a different kind of politics from mine. Somebody wrote, and this is very interesting, that his pictures belong to a speculative concept of art.

Jack Fritscher: Which is the gateway drug to the joys of pornography.

George Dureau: Yes, because his photos were like the reclining nude female painting hanging over the bar in a western cowboy saloon. It's hanging up there quite passive, invitational, for horny men to speculate on and use in their heads as they will. But mine do the opposite twist. My pictures flip the dynamic. My pictures look back at the cowboys looking at the picture. You hear what I'm saying?

Jack Fritscher: Yes.

George Dureau: It was a funny point, but it's kind of true. Robert's politics suited the gay mafia he catered to. Wagstaff was a real fascist.

Jack Fritscher: How so?

George Dureau: Wagstaff despised minorities. Not that anybody has to love them. I am one, but they piss me off sometimes too. Wagstaff really hated the whole idea of anyone saying anything nice about the poor.

Jack Fritscher: Do you think that attitude applied to Robert's women as well? When I look at Robert's women, I wonder if his gay eye was reductive around women. There's a certain passive deadness about them [*Lucy Ferry*, 1986; and about men, like the deadpan, *Roy Cohn*, 1981]. As if they're masks. Maybe he thought deadpan photography was cool.

George Dureau: But he's done that deadpan with practically everybody. There are very few of his black men that will look at you, except in a kind of odd sexy way. He bought one picture of my model, *Oscar*, and basically re-shot his version [*Bob Love* 1979]. He got it straight out of me. It was not the first picture [*Wilbert Hines*, 1977] he bought from me, but it was the very first picture of mine that he took a 'departure" from.

My friend Oscar himself had a pockmarked face and big bulgy pretty eyes that made him the king of peering out at you from the corner of his eyes and Robert did his "departure" of that picture [*Bob Love* 1979], and put it on the cover of his [pre-AIDS] *Black Males* [Galerie Jurka, Amsterdam, 1980, preceding his AIDS-era *Black Book*, 96 erotic photos of black men, St. Martin's Press, New York, 1986]. It's the head leaning forward. He's looking off to the side. Robert had my photo of *Oscar* hanging in the hall right next to his bedroom when he was dying.

There were three or four more of my pictures that he also took as points of "departure," one being the guy leaning on a mantelpiece named Wilbert Hines. The lighting and everything just intrigued Robert. *Wilbert* was the first one he bought. I didn't know Robert then. He had seen my work and wrote me and asked could he buy it.

Another one he bought was of a model who has little deformed arms, and a fierce expression. I photographed him with the arms curled up under his chin and I made three big 16x20s that Robert bought from the show because the lighting intrigued him. There's a big diagonal in the background and he went cuckoo over that.

Then there were two more that I showed in New York. One was Dave Kopay, the [gay] football player, sitting sidesaddle with his arms around his knees and his dick and balls hanging out [*David Kopay*, 1982]. The other one was a nude black boy [*Leonard Frazer (with Clarinet)*] sitting with dick and balls hanging out. And those sort of went together to make Robert's picture of a black boy sitting on a pedestal [*Phillip Prioleau (on Pedestal Side Facing)*, 1979, *Z Portfolio*].

I photograph a lot. I don't make a big deal out of it. I get these spells to do it. I might feel I love this person. So I'll take eight or ten rolls in one afternoon and maybe later just select one frame from it all. I do have a lot of negatives. Sometimes I go back and I see something in a picture, and I'll say, "Oh, my God. Robert must have loved this one."

My assistant [Jonathan Webb] would shake his head. "I know you love Robert. You must have had a good time together."

Robert would never go out cruising with Jonathan and me. He always felt that Jonathan was too quiet and vegetarianish. And Jonathan always felt wrongly he was not sophisticated enough for Robert's company.

And Jonathan would say, "Can't we hide these pictures when he's here? Because you know they're going to turn into Mapplethorpe pictures if you leave them sitting out here on the table."

It was the kiss of death when Robert would buy something. It was like he was paying a token price for what he was going to do with that picture. Put it in the Big Time! It was funny because he would drain the soul out of it. That big slice of soul was not an acceptable commodity to him. That soul that I shared came from my personal experience. It wasn't public domain.

Jack Fritscher: I find soul in Robert's pictures of Patti because he loved her. In his book *Some Women*, the last four pages are of her, and she looks, now, like the grieving Mrs. Mapplethorpe. But the other women in there, even Yoko Ono, I don't know. There is something dead about his sleeping beauties. [The ghostly floating face of *Doris Saatchi*, 1983]

George Dureau: I don't know how he acted with his models. Did he photograph you?

Jack Fritscher: Yes. Many frames. Also, in a kind of double-selfies, he shot the two of us curled up around each other.

George Dureau: He photographed me with one of my black models in New Orleans. It was a really nice photograph. I'd been photographing an old house, and I sort of came up with idea. The house had huge columns, and we stood on either side of these huge, battered columns. [*George Dureau (with Crouched Black Male in "Black Cobra" Sweatshirt)*, 1982] While it was my idea to stand there, Robert took the picture.

He wasn't very manipulative. He didn't spend a lot of time moving us about. I imagine that he must have spent a great deal of time directing people who were important to him, especially when he was desperate to make a good picture on commission, but he didn't fuck with me much in front of the camera when he photographed me as I didn't with him. Maybe it was because we knew too much about the thing. We didn't want to expose ourselves.

On the other hand, I downright seduce the people I shoot. I put them through all kinds of directorial changes. I make up all kinds of stories to liven them up. "Oh, let's do this one as if you're waiting for the bus to come and get you." I'll babble at them and stroke them, and once in awhile we're having sex when I take the picture. I play with people a lot. I don't mind stroking them and kissing them and carrying on. Sometimes my pictures are foreplay or afterplay as the case may be.

Jack Fritscher: I do the same verbal directions minus the sex when I shoot my video models. I tell them to put the sex into the camera for the viewers. I'm a writer, but I do a lot of magazine photography as well.

George Dureau: What kind of camera do you use?

Jack Fritscher: Minolta Maxxum.

George Dureau: Robert and I accidently used the same camera and the same paper and the same film and all that makes the pictures look similar. He had much more expensive equipment than me. When I began photography [1971], I used the light coming in the windows, with a little bit of fill light and then I got two more lights, but I've never been very technical and never spent much money on equipment. Essentially because Robert and I used the same film, paper, camera, and format, there's a similarity in the velvety quality.

Robert never photographed a black until he met me.

That's why he bought my pictures.

He asked me how I did it and like a fool I told him.

He told me he hadn't shot any black men, but he may have experimented.

He said, "I can't believe how you can get them to look like that for you."

Jack Fritscher: It was your relating to your sitters.

George Dureau: I think that he wanted to get rid of them as soon as he shot them. I know he would sometimes have major plans for a person, but I don't do that. I don't decide that this model is going to be my husband for life. And I don't do the opposite and throw them out after I've shot them. I enjoy our relationship that's nice while it lingers. I don't predict what our relationship has to be.

There was one picture Robert had of a sailor, the one with the big dick hanging out of the polyester suit, Melvin? [Milton Moore with whom Robert had a tempestuous relationship: *Man in Polyester*

Suit, 1980]. I've lost his name now. Anyway, he thought that was going to be some big life-long affair.

One time he said, "I wish I could find a smart one."

I said, "What do you mean, a smart one?"

He said, "You know. I'd like to find a good-looking Bryant Gumbel or something."

I said, "Why?

Jack Fritscher: To see if he could find a *what?*

George Dureau: A good-looking Bryant Gumbel [handsome television host of the *Today Show*].

He said, "I want one who has a brain of his own."

"Why? So he doesn't hang on you?"

"Yes."

"But Robert, if there was a black man who was brilliant and had a successful business, why would he want to go into a corner and say, 'I'm your N-word'?

What a success.

Jack Fritscher: His camera was a power tool.

George Dureau: I get embarrassed about things he did that I don't do. Things that are hideous to me. I don't know about the scat issue with him. I know he was into it one way or another, but I don't know what was going where, do you?

Jack Fritscher: No. That was not part of our scene. When he shot *grande dame* Katharine Cebrian in San Francisco [*Katherine Cebrian*, 1980], he did have SHIT spelled out in big silver studs on the back of his leather jacket. It was his bad-boy charm offensive.

George Dureau: Oh.

Jack Fritscher: When I was involved with him romantically, I should say "intelligently," he said what he wanted was "intelligent sex." I told him that some of his New York scenes were not my California scene. We had words about hygiene that [in 1980 before AIDS] turned our sexual relationship to friendship. I think I may be one of the few people who ever said "No" to Robert Mapplethorpe.

George Dureau: Have you been published?

Jack Fritscher: Since a wee gay boy of seventeen.

George Dureau: What's your recent work?

Jack Fritscher: My new novel is *Some Dance to Remember* [*A Memoir-Novel of San Francisco 1970-1982*]. It was published on Valentine's Day [1990].

George Dureau: Oh, yes. Jonathan is reading it. When we started talking, I had a feeling I knew who you were. Jonathan loves your book. He tells me some things in it from time to time. I'm wildly dyslexic so I read very little. So don't feel insulted. I try to put out of my head what people tell me they've written because I know I'm never going to get to it, because I'm the worst reader in the world.

Jack Fritscher: It's a lot of reading for anyone, five hundred pages about the 70s in San Francisco.

George Dureau: Jonathan says it's quite wonderful. I go to cocktail parties where he was talking to people about it and I was embarrassed not to have read it.

Jack Fritscher: Don't be. You can say you talked with the author.

George Dureau: There's something in it about you and Robert.

Jack Fritscher: The novel is dedicated to him. He's not in it, but his presence is felt in the fictional narrative about a photographer. Real people walk through alongside fictitious characters. There's a scene at the Fey-Way Gallery that is based on Robert's showing there.

George Dureau: Didn't he use another gallery in San Francisco?

Jack Fritscher: He used Edward DeCelle's Lawson-DeCelle Gallery [80 Langton Street] for his leathersex pictures downtown near the leather bars South of Market Street, and the Simon Lowinsky Gallery uptown near Union Square for his polite pictures.

George Dureau: I've begun pursuing a few galleries. I'm having a show with Fahey-Klein Gallery in LA.

Jack Fritscher: How wonderful. I've talked to David Fahey a number of times.

George Dureau: Well, I haven't. I'm leaving everything to my gallery manager here. He loves to manage things and keep everybody apart. I probably should give Fahey a call.

Jack Fritscher: He's very sweet on the phone.

George Dureau: I should certainly call him because he would probably like to know something more about me than what he's been told. What happened was he had several of my pictures. Do you mind staying on the phone for so long?

Jack Fritscher: No. Absolutely not. I'm all yours.

George Dureau: At one of the Chicago exhibitions, my gallery [Arthur Roger Gallery, his dealer since 1988] and Fahey decided to bring some of Witkin's work [Joel-Peter Witkin, b. 1939] down to New Orleans. They wanted to do a small show here, and I got the benefit of a trade-off deal.

I was embarrassed at first because Arthur had just a few of my works at the gallery and at first there wasn't that much of a response, but then all of a sudden, Arthur sold eight of my large prints and took orders for twelve more. So all of a sudden, there was this live reaction. So I get to have a show in February. Which is fine with me. I'm going to create, which is a first for me, a suite of eight or ten photographs that are real allegorical kind of compositions.

Jack Fritscher: Based on your paintings?

George Dureau: Well, based on what is in my head. There are some useable things in my paintings. My paintings are big and allegorical, not very complicated, not in the sense of neo-classic allegory. They are big, bland, kind of as if Cezanne painted people. I'm somewhat influenced by Manet too. There's a lot of flesh in my pictures. They're big, over life-sized, and very sexy. I draw very well. The drawings are frequently kind of unfinished looking, but I draw very naturally. Anyway, I'm going to have a show there in February.

Jack Fritscher: Congratulations.

George Dureau: A man in Seattle [Dan Fear] runs the Silver Image gallery [1973-1993]. He included me in a group show [*The Nude: Classic & Erotic*, July 19 - September 1, 1990]. He wants me to have a solo show too, and there's another gallery up there. It looks like the West Coast has discovered me all of a sudden. I wonder if it's because of Christie's selling so many of my photos when they sold so many Mapplethorpe pictures right after he died. Do you know there's a gallery in New York called Robert Samuel Gallery?

Jack Fritscher: Yes. Robert's longtime gallery [795 Broadway, opened November 1978].

George Dureau: Sam Hardison [Robert Samuel Hardison II (1942-1991) whose name fronted the gallery he managed in which Mapplethorpe and Wagstaff were active silent partners] talked me into showing there. I don't know if he's still alive. I think he is. I guess he's in Provincetown now.

Jack Fritscher: Some of Robert's work has been reproduced as greeting cards by a group in Provincetown. In fact, I set up a shoot for Robert with my then lover Jim Enger [*Jim Enger*, 1980] who is a championship bodybuilder. It was supposed to be a private thing Robert was doing for me and Jim for fun, but Jim was so gorgeous Robert couldn't resist making him his "model." Jim didn't fancy the switch. You know what happens when stars collide. The star bodybuilder and the star photographer. Jim refused to sign a release until after he saw the pictures. Somehow one of those shots was published as a greeting card of Jim's torso from the back with no head in the frame. [Other published Mapplethorpe photos of Enger, unlike the private originals Robert gave me, do not show Jim's face.]

George Dureau: Really? Because that's really trashy if that's what Sam [Hardison] is doing because Sam has had trouble like that before. Where did he get the photographs?

Jack Fritscher: Probably from Robert.

George Dureau: Robert sued Hardison to get back works that Hardison had stolen from him. He stole an enormous amount of stuff from me and others. Witkin and others. I didn't care to spend three years of my life fighting over the prints. So I wrote Hardison a scorching letter, told him to go fuck himself. What happened was there are notoriously gay couples who own galleries and talk themselves into thinking that they're going to make a great big go of everything. They think their intentions are so good and so noble that it will all come out okay. Anyway, Hardison would give work of mine to these eager people who would back him, keep him afloat, and then they'd flop. So an awful lot of my pictures were never returned.

They would periodically pop up at Christie's or somewhere like the Ace Gallery in LA. Ace got in touch with my gallery here and sent a whole lot of Xeroxes and asked would we identify the pictures. They were 8x10s and 11x14s that were meant for publicity. Robert Samuel might have sold them all off. So my pictures are drifting around the country all over the place, all these things of mine that Hardison confiscated and sold.

Hardison did buy some of Robert's pictures from me. I still have a few of his prints. I'm thinking of selling them. I think now might be the best time to sell them.

Jack Fritscher: Dead Celebrity Syndrome.

George Dureau: I don't think the market can go up. I have the polyester picture [*Man in Polyester Suit*, 1980].

Jack Fritscher: That's a main signature photo, of course. It's been in the center of all this controversy, in the Congressional Record, So that should command quite a price.

George Dureau: I have that one and I have another one. It's on the cover of one of his books from about 1979, I think. It's a white boy wearing thermal underwear, but just the boy's head was on the cover [Likely, *Robert Mapplethorpe: Foto's/Photographs*, Galerie Jurka, 1979]. I have the whole original picture where his hand is like squeezing his nuts. It reminded me of what my drawings look like. Once when Robert wanted to give me one, I took that.

Then he printed another one for me as a birthday present. I may have the only print of it. I don't like it much. It's has a smear on the lens or something. It's in a circle which is a mockery of my stuff which is frequently in a circle in a few of my photographs, but more so in my drawings and paintings inside circles. His picture shows a mean looking, tough little Spanish guy, maybe a kickboxer, making a fist, but it looks like a mockery of my style. I don't know why he made that picture for me.

Jack Fritscher: Maybe to acknowledge you. Like a student turning in homework for extra credit.

George Dureau: It may have been more about the type of model he thought I'd like. I have one or two people who fancy they're a model and they're wonderful. I like the complete innocence of somebody who is at last being given his chance to speak to posterity through my camera.

I'm kind of slave to my models, in the camera, but not in painting. I serve them with my camera somehow because I think it might be their only or last chance to say who they are, particularly if they have one arm with a scar on one cheek.

It might be their one chance to speak to posterity. My camera gives them voice. So I frequently, always, let them do a couple of their own poses because they seem to crave something that they've been saving up for years. I give them space, step back, and kind of rearrange their ideas and hope for a compromise between my idea and their idea.

Jack Fritscher: You say you're a slave to your models in the aesthetic sense. Do you think Robert might have been on a leather-bar master trip to some of his models based on his urban Plantation Fantasy of wanting them to be his N-word slaves?

George Dureau: Yes, which is comical. The master photographer dominating them to express what he wanted. What did they want? When I shoot them, it's *noblesse oblige* on my part.

I said to Jonathan once, "Why is it, you think, that men who look perfectly big and tough and fierce on the street, why is it that they know that I'm the fucker?"

He said, "Honey, any man who wants to get fucked knows a fucker when he sees one."

I think it's my Minoan profile. I've got an exaggerated profile and I always think of it as my Minoan profile, you know, like the pottery. Pottery that has satyrs and whatnot with very strong profiles. My hair is in a tight little braid down my back. I have a rather garish, deep profile.

Jack Fritscher: Have you done any self-portraits with the camera?

George Dureau: No. Not with the camera. In drawings.

Jack Fritscher: What do you think of Robert's self-portraits?

George Dureau: I think they're great, but they're pretty. I've never done that—made myself pretty. I've thought about doing it, but it may be too late. It's an odd idea to pose yourself pretty, like a lady. I didn't dress like a girl when I was young. I'd dress with ribbons around my dick hanging out or something, but I didn't dress in ladies dresses.

Jack Fritscher: Off camera, Robert didn't either. Gender bending was popular back in the 70s. David Bowie. Men with beards in glitter drag like the Cockettes and the Cycle Sluts.

George Dureau: There's a lot of rather flamboyant, womanish behavior in me sometimes. I get a little like a woman when I get really mean.

Jack Fritscher: You know I'm going to quote you.

George Dureau: Let me read it back afterwards.

Jack Fritscher: I will if you like.

George Dureau: I prefer it.

Jack Fritscher: Yes. I will.

George Dureau: I don't mind saying wild things, but I want a chance to clean them up.

Jack Fritscher: It's perfectly fine to let yourself go and say what you want.

George Dureau: That reminds me. Do you know Edmund White? He's sick.

Jack Fritscher: The gay press reports he's positive, but healthy.

George Dureau: He described me as a surprisingly graceful "bear." I'm not heavy, but it's very funny because I have kind of short legs. I'm very graceful, but it's kind of funny to have short legs and be very graceful, like something out of the Seven Dwarfs.

Jack Fritscher: Eddy wrote the introduction to Robert's *Black Book* in 1980. Robert and I had been working on a book of his pictures and my text back in 1978 when I was editor of *Drummer*.

George Dureau: When were you editor of *Drummer*?

Jack Fritscher: Issues 19 to 30. March 1977 to January 1980. At that time, I'd done half the *Drummer* issues in existence.

George Dureau: Would *Drummer* have any of my pictures there in the files?

Jack Fritscher: Listen, that office has always been dysfunctional. Manuscripts and photos would arrive in the mail and get tossed into a closet. I had words with the publisher about his not returning manuscripts and art.

George Dureau: They asked me for things. They did a spread on me ["George Dureau: Maimed Beauty." *Drummer* 93 (1986), pages 8-11].

Jack Fritscher: By that time I was long gone as the editor. By then, I was only a continuing contributor.

George Dureau: For a number of years, *Drummer* kept asking me for something. But I said, "I can't because, well, there's one serious problem. The men I shoot, most of my models, even though I sometimes lay them, are straight. They live a straight life. I'm attracted to people who are not flamboyant or don't have a gay lifestyle." It seemed unfair to compromise them in a gay magazine.

Jack Fritscher: I agree. I'd feel creepy putting my straight models in gay magazines unless I ask them and they say it's okay.

George Dureau: Exactly. So I sorted out where my men could be published. I didn't do magazines, but I did allow Gay Men's Press [London] to publish a little monograph of my stuff, but I had to really restrict it. [*New Orleans: 50 Photographs by George Dureau,* 1985] I made them [Aubrey Walter and David Fernbach] change their name to do it [from Gay Men's Press to GMP]. I told them that if they wanted to do it, they couldn't talk about *gay* all through the book because the men in the book are married or virgins because nobody else has screwed them.

I'm not bragging. Those men are just my specialty. I like men for whom I will end up being either their first or only lover. So I end up with a body of work of people who have a right to be looked at for some other reason than that their clothes are off to turn-on gay men. I told Gay Men's Press that I'd only do the book if it was of sexy-looking but handicapped people.

I told them that the pictures had to look like they had merit beyond gay because I didn't want the book to be construed as being a book of gay men for gay men.

Jack Fritscher: Did they pay you?

George Dureau: I always expect a small amount of money. That may have been four years ago, and then two years ago, GMP asked me to create some more pictures to illustrate one of their authors who wrote up some trashy, romantic little piece about falling in love with a guy with two artificial legs or something, and the thrill of watching him walk across the room.

Well, that was really hard. I considered two different existing pictures that I sent them I had one model with two artificial legs, but I didn't want to use his face or anything that would identify him. And I had another model who had only one leg, and I didn't really want him to be recognized either. So I prepped both pictures in a way no one could tell who they were.

Jack Fritscher: That's very interesting, kind of a short circuit in the world of gay body dysmorphia that some call gay body fascism because the whole gay subculture and its art and photography are always presenting and making a sex fetish of not ordinary men but super, heroic bodies and dicks, and your take is the opposite, presenting ordinary people who also have bodies different from the average.

George Dureau: I've photographed a lot of just drop-dead gorgeous people. I have some black guys who are just marvelous looking. They're good buddies of mine. Some of those gorgeous guys are also deformed. What I do with that is different and it gets a reaction because that combination overwhelms some people. They don't know how to respond to the beauty of deformity and missing parts.

Jack Fritscher: Do homosexual men respond to these men well? With our boyhoods and people telling us we're broken freaks?

George Dureau: I think they respond well. Sometimes foolishly. Sometimes they're embarrassed about their hidden attraction and affection for deformed people. I'm not particularly interested in sorting their fetish psychology.

Jack Fritscher: Grooving on a guy *because* he's handicapped or black reduces him to a fetish.

George Dureau: Yes. I often tell people that because some people who are beautiful and sexy have a stump on one side doesn't mar their sexiness or their beauty. I often tell people who don't get it: "You don't say, 'Let's just throw out this little Roman sculpture because it's part broken.'" It's still there. We're still here.

Jack Fritscher: Do you feel that people respond to your pictures of missing parts because they feel not whole themselves?

George Dureau: Well, yes. Some people are really touched by them. I'm really thrilled when they ponder what they're going to buy. That's really profoundly interesting to me. I do drawings that are about life-size. They are usually 30x40-size drawings. They're torsos and sometimes they're torsos of people who are missing something. You can't quite tell what it is because the drawing is sort of ambiguous. Is that one arm off at the elbow? You can't quite tell.

When people come in to see my drawings and photographs, a man, very often with the wife, will ponder which one they're going to buy. Frequently it's a drawing that's going over their bed. Whatever that all means, I don't know. Very often they are very intellectual straight people like psychiatrists who worry and ponder such things. Very often with the photographs they will line up three amputees, and they'll talk about them, go home and ponder, and come back again.

For these reasons it's kind of delicious to sell things out of my home instead of a gallery. It's kind of a bother to have people come into my home, but it's kind of delicious because we have time to talk, no pressure, and it's interesting to hear their worrying and reasoning and help them choose the right one.

Robert loved the thrill of the sale in a different way. The thrill of the sale became the thrill of adulation. When he shot a scary picture, he saw it in the eyes of the beholders, rich people who would have to buy it, look at it, swallow it, live with it on their rich walls.

I look at my pictures from the point of view of the people I photograph. I get all nervous my models may not like their pictures. If there's a picture of them that's rude or shocking, I worry they won't like me anymore. Robert never cared about any of that.

Sometimes the buyer will not pick the prettiest picture. They'll say, "Oh, I know this isn't a beautiful picture, but for some reason I like it."

They're caught between classical and romantic art. Some of my work is more classical in the sense that the form dominates the subject, like Robert's. Others are more romantic in the sense that the subject is so important that it almost goes off balance, because it just has to, because you can't bend this boy around anymore. He is what he is.

You can't tell his story any differently than he tells it because I make contact with the person coming out of him. The engagement is that there's something coming out of him, emanating. He's lowering his head and staring at you funny, and he has his arm pushed at a funny angle. Sometimes I can change that. There are pictures in which I have directed things during a shoot, and others in which I have left the awkwardness in them. I just don't want to iron the person out of it.

Jack Fritscher: Robert did your ironing.

George Dureau: He cleaned my pictures up to make them respectable for respectable queers, especially queers with money. He wanted to give them something to talk about, bragging rights, like comparing the broken pottery of a boy to his perfect calla lilies. Baloney.

Jack Fritscher: Lucie-Smith told me, "A Mapplethorpe calla lily hanging in the dining room is only there because there's a Mapplethorpe fisting photo hanging in the bedroom."

George Dureau: Oops. Excuse me. I just had to turn down the stewing hen. I'm a very conscientious cook. I love to cook. So I got this hen and she turned out to be the Mother Courage of hens and I had to get a hammer and cleaver to break her thighs. I'm stewing her in what we call a *fricassee*, a dark brown *fricassee*. I love to cook with hens. They have so much flavor. Do you cook?

Jack Fritscher: I do. My home and studio are far out in the coastal hills north of the Golden Gage Bridge. I can't go running off to restaurants.

George Dureau: I go once in awhile to restaurants, but I cook every day. Sometimes it's a little meal. Sometimes it's big. Sometimes it's only a rice salad, but I love food. I cut down my eating a little because I was eating too much. I was eating healthy, but too much. Just because it's vegetarian doesn't mean it's not fattening. Five cups of bran a day is going to get you.

Jack Fritscher: I've been making tabbouleh lately.

George Dureau: You could be nice to me and send me a good tabbouleh recipe because I have one or two that I do and I would love to have one from somebody else.

Jack Fritscher: I never cook the same thing twice. I improvise as I go. I've added fruit as well as vegetables for a nice departure. Nice strawberries.

George Dureau: Do you put a lot of lemon in it?

Jack Fritscher: Yes. Tomatoes are basic and then build from there.

George Dureau: We do with tons of parsley and garlic.

Jack Fritscher: Yes. Garlic. Mint from the garden. Sometimes I add chicken or shrimp.

George Dureau: Are you healthy?

Jack Fritscher: Yes. I'm fifty-one. Are you?

George Dureau: Yes. Whatever that means at fifty-nine.

Jack Fritscher: The question usually means "What's your HIV status?" I'm negative. Because I knew Robert, people sometimes presume I have AIDS. You must know you are making me want to fly off to New Orleans to sit on your floor and look at your paintings and pictures.

George Dureau: What I have here is a 120-foot balcony with a roof over it wrapped around the corner of the block. It's the biggest and best balcony in the city. That's why I moved here. It's an ordinary 1840 house with guillotine windows, but 100 years ago it was gutted and made into a warehouse so [Laughs] it's Queen Anne front and Mary Anne behind.

It looks like the most wonderful, commodious house in the front with ironwork all over it and then you get inside and there are no walls. At one time it would have driven me crazy because I love details of architecture. I learned from the last house I lived in that you can go crazy walking around in beautiful old architecture that clashes with the new art I'm painting. So now I have these rooms that are 55-feet long. Two big warehouse rooms that are 55x30.

Jack Fritscher: That must suit your artist's perspective because you can stand back, put your thumb up, squint your eye...

George Dureau: It's wonderful. My drawings always want to be looked at from fifty feet away. I draw very big and bold. My contours are strong.

Jack Fritscher: As you probably know, Robert's studio on Bond Street was such a tiny place.

George Dureau: My God, what a terrible way to have to live when you're rich. He photographed me there.

Jack Fritscher: He photographed me there as well, and shots of the two of us together.

George Dureau: I photographed him there.

Jack Fritscher: It's so different from his designer apartment in the BBC documentary.

George Dureau: I didn't see that. You mean the one on 23rd Street?

Jack Fritscher: Yes.

George Dureau: I saw that apartment four years ago when I drove up there in my Jeep. [Laughs] You've got me going. Now I'm going to have to try to read your book in spite of all my reading problems.

Jack Fritscher: Perhaps Jonathan can read part of it to you.

George Dureau: Jonathan spends hours reading. I have to spend my time painting and photographing, but he sits and reads. I put him through "Art History" classes last year that almost drove me crazy. He had to read all this art history instead of helping me. He's not going to school this semester so I might get some use out of him.

Jack Fritscher: Did Robert ever seek advice from you or did he suck you up by osmosis?

George Dureau: We would compare notes. He already knew more about book photography and about printing. I had learned how to print from some local people. I know how to print, but I don't do it. I simply dictate to the printer what I want. I've had the same printer for about twelve years. So there's a kind of continuity and it all comes off exactly as I want because he does what I tell him to do. When he prints my work, it doesn't look like anything else he prints.

But technically Robert would ask me, "Why don't you use such and such? How did you get this?"

Sometimes he wouldn't like what I did because it wasn't slick looking enough. He knew my pictures were praised by people in the know. He was interested because sometimes I would shoot pictures that were muddy and heavy and dark, but you see there's an aesthetic input to it all. I'm not offering them something that is meant to be dangerous and scary. I'm being frank. If it's a one-legged man standing there naked and staring hard at you, that's a good reason that it should look a little muddy.

Jack Fritscher: Do you think Robert's work was dangerous and threatening?

George Dureau: No. Not really. When you say, "It's a Mapplethorpe," people expect to see something shocking, but how shocking can something be when it's so planned and expected?

A woman wrote in her thesis that Robert's art is speculative. His models are meant to be looked at. He pushed them all into a sort of come-hither calendar-boy pose that, even when they're looking menacingly at you, you're saying, "Oh, that's Robert's 'Mr. December.'"

His models are too available whereas mine look like something just dragged in off the street which they were. His were dragged off the street too, but he presented them in a way that every good faggot will know what it means. With mine every good faggot doesn't know what it means.

Jack Fritscher: So you had a sense he was after mainstream money?

George Dureau: I know it. He used to say, "George, how do you live off this? Who's going to buy these things?"

That was his big worry. He used to love some of the people in my pictures. He would fall in love with them. He was crazy about some of my models. And crazier about sales.

It was a big decision back then for people to spend $800 for a Mapplethorpe. Now it's jumped to $2,000 to spend on a picture that going to upset them and offend their guests.

My drawings do the same thing sometimes, but I'm so comfortable dealing with handicapped people that I don't offend the guests. I have lots of sophisticated, intellectual handicapped friends, and some who are lawyers for the disadvantaged, and they'll have me over to discuss sex, because I'm the only "normal" person they know who knows about having sex with handicapped people.

So all these handicapped people will get together and talk about sex. I almost died one time when there was this girl who had no arms, and a friend of mine was there and his wife, and they wanted to talk about what it was must be like to pick up a man who has shriveled legs, and what would it feel like if they put their arms around this girl with no arms. It almost drove me crazy.

You know, it was like the scene in the movie *Freaks* where the beautiful, "normal" girl has married into the freaks, and they surround her and chant, "Now you're one of us."

Jack Fritscher: I love Tod Browning. I often screened *Freaks* for my university film students. Speaking of films, is there a particular difficulty, that's the wrong word, in shooting blacks as far as lighting is concerned? Haskell Wexler made a major breakthrough in Hollywood when he figured out how to properly light black actors like Sidney Poitier for *In the Heat of the Night* [1967].

George Dureau: Well, here's the funny thing. Blacks are the first people I shot. Before the blacks, I never shot a white person. I was one of the peculiar people who get to the age of forty without knowing anything about cameras. I would hold up a camera and say, "What button do I push?" I never thought cameras or photographs were interesting.

Because I always painted and drew, I wasn't interested in the history of photography. I knew there were some nice-looking Avedon and Irving Penn photos in magazines. I knew those from when I was a queer teenager and once in awhile I would see a nice picture, but it would never occur to me to look up a person's name or to study photographs in any kind of way.

I was in my early forties when I picked up my first camera. I wonder if it is connected with my quitting drinking then? Just a "tittle bit." But I had drunk for forty years here in New Orleans. In New Orleans, you just drink. New Orleans is the drunkest city on earth. I used to sit on the bar when I was two years old, drinking my daddy's beer at the tennis club.

I picked up the camera as a kind of "proof" about my models. I discovered that for three or four years I had been showing these big torso-size drawings and sometimes they would have wings on them, or the people would have hooves. Dwarf friends of mine propped up on the pedestal. I discovered that because my style of drawing is rather classical, I have a real understanding of line, big long simplifying lines of contour. Because of that, people thought my models were my fantasy or something because I would put wings on them or leaves in their hair as a kind of commentary about what I saw in that person. People thought they were artificial people, fantasies, whereas they were in fact truly my garbage man, my mailman, my grocery boy.

Jack Fritscher: Kind of a "proof of life."

George Dureau: Exactly. I did it to make notes to myself and for posterity. I thought I should take some documentary pictures of these men that I draw. A photo also will keep me from having to have them in my house for the rest of my life, drawing what their ear looks like today and their eyebrow another day and how after the first pass, you go back again to see what the ears look like.

I asked a photographer friend what kind of camera to get, and he asked, "What do you want to do?"

I said, "Just black-and-white pictures, black men against a white wall."

He said, "Oh, your black friends, yes. What you need is a 2.25."

I said, "What's that?"

He said, "Oh, that's what stodgy old fucks like you photograph with."

"Oh, really? Where do I get one?"

I bought a $65-dollar Vermeer Lens and an eleven-year-old 2.25 camera. I photographed three years without a light meter. Some of them were wonderful. In the late 70s, Robert brought some of these dating back to my earliest days in 1971 and 72. The first one he bought [*Wilbert Hines*] was one he loved.

In 1972, I really started in photographing these blacks. It was a very black period. I've always had white lovers, maybe eight or nine great loves over the years, especially when spring is in the air. I should be dead now from all the sex. Oh, those lovers were such difficult numbers. They were all white, and I didn't photograph them much.

At first, I photographed black men standing against the neutral plaster walls in the two or three studies I had become accustomed to. Sometimes I would go off from my studio to the park on my bike with my camera over my shoulder to photograph somebody against a building. Because I didn't begin to photograph white people, the problem of how to photograph blacks presented itself immediately. I learned quickly from the start how to photograph black people in natural light because you frequently have a bleed-out background, the background just bleeds out, by the time you've adjusted the contrast to capture the tones of black or brown bodies in the foreground.

What Robert did to make up contrast was jump from natural lighting to studio lighting which was too MGM for me. He was using strobes, and lighting up the whole scene. I don't do that because I don't want to scare my darlings. I don't want to scare my trick to death. I want the sex and the shoot to remain sweet and tender and I want them to keep talking uninterrupted about their life. So

I never use strobe. But Robert would get everything illuminated in that magazine style.

Robert learned a trick from me early on. I think he got it from me. He must have. I told him how I grease my models with heavy Vaseline.

Jack Fritscher: I grease my muscle models with olive oil. A deeper sheen than baby oil.

George Dureau: I got the idea from my kickboxer friends because they always grease themselves for protection and to look good under the lights. I found out early on that the foreplay experience of greasing the person isn't a bad idea. You get to make them know how much you love them. Sometimes it's hard to keep a straight face while doing it.

Jack Fritscher: You make a visual experience tactile.

George Dureau: I always talk to my models. I explain my pictures. I let them know what I'm doing. I don't think Robert would do that.

I say to them, "I like the way your nose has a real straight inflection here. Cross your arms and lean forward on this pedestal here. Put your head down. Now look up a little."

If the result was close to what I wanted, but wasn't quite it, I would talk to them about what was nice in the picture and ask to re-shoot it. Film is cheap enough that you should shoot what they are presenting. So I'd re-set the shoot. There's a light shining down on their nose. So I'd move the light. I always like to talk to them about what's happening at the moment instead of leaving them sit there in a pose like a dead fish on the counter waiting to be cooked.

Jack Fritscher: Herb Ritts is so popular now. How does he fit in to all this?

George Dureau: Herb visited me down here. He was a jetsetter sort of person. He came to my house and was stunned by the environment which is really comfortable, big and wonderful, with tons of easels, and a piano and a four-poster bed, a big kitchen. It's a real live-in house, but also there are a hundred paintings of mine, giant ones all around the house.

He said, "Did you paint those? I didn't know you were a painter. They showed you at my gallery, but my director didn't tell me."

These gallery directors who sell photographs, but not paintings, don't mention I paint. They sell me as half a person.

There was a photograph that Herb wanted and he said, "Can we swap pictures? Would you select one from my show?"

So I gave him the photo he wanted, but I never did select one from him. I couldn't find one I really liked. I'd see a "Herb Ritts" in store windows and immediately get pangs of jealousy. "Oh, look at the big, fabulous, sexy picture." Then I'd look up close, and I'd say, "Why didn't he take the pants off more? Why didn't he do such and such?" They're real magazine pictures. There were one or two that I saw in the show that were alright. He also does a lot of celebrities. He's a friend of Richard Gere. He's photographed Richard. Do you know Richard?

Jack Fritscher: His movies. And, of course, his Ritts poster [*Richard Gere*, San Bernardino, 1977] hanging in every gay bar on the planet. If he'd sent it to me in 1977 when I was editor-in-chief of *Drummer* magazine, I'd have put it on the cover the way I did Mapplethorpe in 1978.

George Dureau: When Richard came to see me, I photographed him. He was nice enough. He reminds me of a nice, successful Jewish boy who owns the big department store. I think he manages himself in life like that, as if he's a department store. Robert managed himself like a department store.

I liked Richard. He invited me to stop and stay with him when he was making a movie in North Carolina at De Laurentiis Studios there. So I stopped on my way back from New York. Here in New Orleans, I went out with him to a couple of jazz clubs, but I don't know what he does, or what he's like. He's in a new movie with that Julia Roberts woman.

Jack Fritscher: *Pretty Woman.*

George Dureau: You said your last name is Fritscher. Do you know we have a dwarf here named Fritscher? I'll send you a picture of him. I'll be looking for Fritscher's photograph. He's built like a fireplug, a soft one. He's a little too heavy all the time and he's got a real "Grumpy" from *Snow White* kind of face, a real angry, middle-class-man look. He plays in a band standing on a box.

Jack Fritscher: [Laughs] I'm going to get a short story out of this. May I say I don't want to impose much more on your time. This is just a call out of the blue. So regarding my book, I'd like to interview you formally because what I'm trying to do with Robert is personalize him against all this censorship and give people a sense of who he was as the sweet person I knew for so many years.

George Dureau: You know, I think it's very important to realize that nothing could make him happier than to be the ultimate scandalous person. I was always a bit fascinated by his slightly repulsive taste in clothing and demeanor. All that leather-wear made him look like a boy groupie with a band. He tried to dress "dangerous." He used dangerous, bad-boy fashions to substitute for dick size as motorcyclists and gangstas do.

Jack Fritscher: He had a very nice dick. And a sweet body.

George Dureau: I mean, he brought all of this censorship down on our heads. I'm not blaming him, the victim, but he was really hard. He would look at some things I did, and it would be entirely too enlightened and noble and instructive and he would immediately think, "How can I do this and make it unacceptable."

I don't sit around and try to make things acceptable. I just have a sort of kind of lofty mind. I have an enlightened, noble, educated moralistic mind.

Robert would show me something of his and say, "Look! Don't you like to look at someone when they're sucking dick?"

And I'd say, "Uh huh."

He'd say, "Don't you want to make some cocksucking pictures?"

I said, "Well, I have one here."

I told him I met a sort of tough-looking guy once who always wanted me to photograph him sucking my dick which was hysterical.

"Is that what you mean, Robert?" I said. "Do you want me to photograph you sucking my dick?"

He went, "Ahh. You don't even want to talk about art. You're just being nasty. I want to tell you about art."

He was really possessed with how you can make a picture shocking.

My friend Edward Lucie-Smith as you know is an art historian from London, and he didn't like Robert much because Robert didn't like him much. Did you know that? Edward is a pudgy little English queer from Oxford and Robert just hated that sort.

"Oh, English queers, disgusting," he'd say.

Edward said, "You know Robert was playing a game of chicken with his gay following, wasn't he?"

And I said, "Yes, he was."

Robert would say to me, "Look! I'm showing a dick now. Did you blink yet? Look! I'm showing a dick with a mouth on it. Did you blink yet?"

He was playing a game with his gay mafia following. Their smart cocktail party talk was, "No. It didn't shock me a bit." That was their cool attitude in their well-kept apartments.

Jack Fritscher: I think I love you. Edward told me how he remembered Robert and Sam on a honeymoon trip to London sitting together on a roll-arm sofa in a drawing room showing everybody their portfolio of S&M Polaroids of bloody dicks tied down on bondage boards.

George Dureau: Scaring the horses. Will you be coming down for a few days?

Jack Fritscher: Yes. I would love to shoot you on video very soon. Your studio sounds beautiful and I'd love to see New Orleans.

George Dureau: It doesn't have the gorgeous style of San Francisco, but it has better buildings and it has this funny down-home warmth to it. People talk in the most Southern way, "Oh, honey, you look real cute" and "You fairies, you sure know how to dress." The old ladies like the queers. They'll help the queers get dressed for Mardi Gras. And everybody in every grocery store wants to tell you where to go to get your best beans. It's a really funny flash of southern Europe. It's accommodating. If you come down to see me, they'll say to you, "Honey, you going to have a good time here, and you won't want to go nowhere else."

Jack Fritscher: Sounds perfect. Things fall together in strange ways. I'm not saying this to bullshit you, but I so relate to you on this phone call. You've turned me on. I appreciate your candor. You've practically written a chapter of my book for me.

George Dureau: One would ordinarily be cautious and not talk so much to a total stranger. You don't know what they're going to write, and I have gotten my little ass in a vise doing that. On the other hand, I'm not an Episcopalian keeping my lips shut.

Jack Fritscher: I'm a Catholic. I hear confessions. I spent eleven years in a seminary.

George Dureau: [Laughs] I refused to make my First Communion and First Confession. Well, I'm going to go upstairs to the loft that I rent to my assistant. He's in Costa Rica right now. I'll see if your book is there.

Jack Fritscher: Look for the cover photo by George Mott. It's a picture of one of Mussolini's statues in the Foro Italico in Rome. It's plaster of paris, not marble. So it works metaphorically because the beloved bodybuilder in the book turns out to have feet of clay, just like the statue. This is one book you can judge by its cover.

George Dureau: It covers the halcyon time of gay lib, doesn't it?

Jack Fritscher: Yes.

George Dureau: The good old days that lasted for, what, ten years?

Jack Fritscher: Yes, from Stonewall in 1969 to AIDS in 1981. The book was writing itself at the time, I was running around with

Robert, and he said, "Why do you write for these gay rags? Why don't you cross over like I do?" Like you out collecting models, I was out in the streets collecting all the stories guys were telling in bars and baths and restaurants. I thought, "My God, take notes. Gay liberation is novel telling itself."

George Dureau: Robert never understood art as much as he loved the thrill of capturing someone or something. He loved the thrill of the kill, but the biggest thrill to him was the sale. I mean: the adulation. I think when he did a scary picture he was always thinking of the eyes of the beholders, the rich people who would buy it, look at it, and have to swallow it.

Jack Fritscher: Like Lucie-Smith said. Double-daring the British aristocrats in that London drawing room.

George Dureau: I'm inclined to see my pictures in the eyes of the people I photograph, not the buyers. I get all nervous and worried when a model asks, "Man, you got those pictures back yet?" I have to be careful. God, what if they don't like some shots that might be kind of rude and shocking? I don't want my models to stop liking me. Robert never understood any of that.

Jack Fritscher: He wasn't very involved except for models he was in love with.

George Dureau: Let's hang up and talk again some time. What's your phone number? Can you give me your address to send you a few pictures?

Jack Fritscher: I'd love to talk again. Here's my phone and address. May I have your address?

George Dureau: 1307 Dauphine Street, New Orleans, 70116.

Jack Fritscher: Can I ask you three final quick questions? What do you think will happen to Robert's future as far as his photography? You mentioned his fame will decline.

George Dureau: I think his reputation and sales may drop because he shot his wad. Who knows? This trial publicity should give him a bump. I don't think there's a lot more to say or think about his stuff. He had his glory on earth, so to speak. He shoved his work down everybody's throat so much, but I'm sure critics will be dining out on him forever.

One thing I'll give him. He was very good at editing his pictures, and figuring out what was the most bombastic and the best. He also cropped his frames. He has many cropped images that might not be so impressive if they weren't cropped.

So his work is already very edited, and what's edited is edited. What's not edited by him now he's dead must be edited by someone else. So it's not the same original as him doing it. Frankly, I don't think Robert was saying enough in his pictures to go on, presumably, as long as I think I'm going to go on because my work is just loaded with humanity and stories of people's lives, and my drawings. My drawings are my favorite things.

Jack Fritscher: Thank you so much for giving me so much time this afternoon.

George Dureau: You can tell I was doing just absolutely nothing this afternoon. Stewing this hen and watching *Zorba* on TV. I was amazed at how beautiful the movie is.

Jack Fritscher: Did you know that Alan Bates [bisexual star of *Zorba the Greek*] had twin boys, beautiful boys, and one of them died of a heart attack in Japan a few weeks ago?

George Dureau: He was quite beautiful young, but he got awfully sloppy, didn't he?

Jack Fritscher: Yes, but still I loved him. The second question is, I'm trying to put Mapplethorpe into a proper context. I've talked to my publisher and I'd like to include photographs of him by other photographers, especially you, because people have gotten the idea that Mapplethorpe is the only person who had a camera from 1970 to 1989.

George Dureau: Isn't that strange? But you know it's because of the power of that circle he operated in. All those people here and in Europe knew my work as much as his. I've heard people come back from some university in Belgium or from Paris and say, "Well, everyone over there knows that you were Mapplethorpe's master." And, "Oh, you know he had this master in New Orleans and he visited him like a pilgrim."

Jack Fritscher: That's how I heard of you and that's how I started this conversation, remember?

George Dureau: How?

Jack Fritscher: I said,"Were you Mapplethorpe's mentor?" He had studied with you.

George Dureau: Where did you hear that again?

Jack Fritscher: Keith Ardent, a model I've photographed for my video studio and for the cover of *Drummer.* ["Keith Ardent" born "Coleman Jones," 1954-1992, AIDS; *Drummer* 118, July 1988]

George Dureau: Oh, wait! Keith came here. He bought some photographs from me. Maybe he never came back to get them.

Jack Fritscher: That could be. He's quite the Lad.

George Dureau: The first thing he said to me was he was a porn star. I said, "Are you?"

Jack Fritscher: He is. And a good one.

George Dureau: I don't know if he came back and got the pictures. He spent a couple of hours with my assistant and me, but mostly with Jonathan, and he had some lady with him and he selected a couple of pictures and then was going away and come back and claim them and I don't know if he did or not. Keith Ardent. He didn't look like he would be particularly gorgeous.

Jack Fritscher: To me he has no particular personal sex appeal, but he knows how to work the camera. Guys worship him. He's a wonderful model because he's an actor who takes direction and improves on it.

George Dureau: I can give you pictures for your book.

Jack Fritscher: I'd love to include you. Thank you. You must be in it. The cover is yours.

George Dureau: What I think you should include are two or three pictures of mine that were Mapplethorpe's dream pictures. The two or three that he bought that he really adored.

Along with Wilbert and Oscar, there's another one he liked of my little friend Jeffrey [*Jeffrey Cook*, 1984] which is really funny because Jeffrey is a gorgeous little mulatto boy and is my protégé. He has an incredible stomach. One of these woven stomachs. Eight-pack abdominals. Washboard abs. He's little karate person with bowlegs that made him so bashful that he never took his pants off.

There's a real element of S&M in the pictures of Jeffrey posing with a long foundry tool. The picture is so sexy and so cute that Mapplethorpe didn't mind that he had his pants on. Robert loved Jeffrey so much that I think he bought four pictures of him to give to people over the years. It's so strange because it wasn't a totally lewd and sexy picture. He had these little underpants on. The picture was so hot looking. The boy was so wonderful with these bowed olive-colored legs. Robert and I both loved bowlegged boys. You can climb in and ride so much more easily. What I would do is give you the pictures that were obviously his favorites.

Jack Fritscher: Thank you.

George Dureau: I must say, Robert's work is synthetic in the sense of flattening models against geometry. His photography is distilled from other peoples's work. It's hysterical how many of Robert's photos of poses and attitudes and mock poetic postures are not real "Mapplethorpe" photos because they are really "George Platt Lynes" photos. They're more arty than sexual. Think of his strange angle of the boy lying back against a pedestal.

Robert, for all his creativity, seemed to have lifted everything. It's very strange. He wasn't comfortable with just the object or person in front of his camera. He had to frame it in terms of a style of someone else. Maybe I'm wrong, but there always seems to be reference in his work. I guess I might think that because I'm so styleless.

I've been drawing since I was ten the way I want. I just started intuitively. I once thought I should start drawing seriously, study art, go to art school. I was drawing one day and I thought, "Oh, my God, you've been drawing and you haven't thought about what one of these drawings look like. My God, maybe I'm a real artist."

I'm pretty much aware of art history with my camera. When I make a correction or a comment, I jump the bridge into history. I say, "This boy is through-and-through Velázquez." And, jumping the bridge, I'll make the light even stronger, or sometimes I make a comment to myself that will cross in from another medium.

There's one boy who has been my lover for years, named Troy, a beautiful blond with long curly hair.

[Meeting the handsome hustler Troy Brown in 1982, George found his white muse. Troy's profile portrait is *Troy Joshua Brown*, 1985.]

Troy's from North Carolina. When I draw him, he's a total Michelangelo. That's all he can be. His proportions are about the same proportions as Michelangelo's dream boys: a thick square body and big square shoulders and a head just a little too small. My Troy pictures were all Michelangelo because he had what his boys had. But I never think about other photographers.

Jack Fritscher: My third and last question. Is photography as good as painting?

George Dureau: As a painter I have to tell you, "No. It ain't." Photography is an editorial art. It's not a creative art in the sense that painting and drawing are in which you start with nothing. You're given a lot. The camera will give you too much so all you have to do is shut it up by editing it. The camera is just a mindless lunatic. You have to edit down what it's going to take in. You don't have to tell it, like you do a paint brush, how to make something look like a finger.

Jack Fritscher: Maybe like the last line in *Casablanca*, we're at the start of a beautiful something, if you don't mind me being personal.

George Dureau: Come by any time you like. You're a nice man.

Jack Fritscher: So are you.

George Dureau: I'm delighted you called.

Jack Fritscher: I'm so happy you received me.

George Dureau: We're lucky this wasn't one of my hectic days. I've tried to wind down this summer. I have bunches of projects. I'm doing sculpture now as well. I told everybody to go away.

[At that moment, George was working on designing bronze gates for the North Court at the New Orleans Museum of Art (1993). He then designed the pediment sculptures for Harrah's Casino in New Orleans (1999).]

Jack Fritscher: Keith said that perhaps a Sunday would be best to call. He just flew back from Bangkok and stayed with us a couple days. He said, "If you're working on Mapplethorpe, you have to talk to George."

George Dureau: Well, the boy can't be all bad. Call me next week if you want. If you have any more questions. I might just send you proof copies for now and better ones later.

Jack Fritscher: Even photocopies will do. My due date is October 1. I don't want you to have to go into the darkroom.

George Dureau: I can have copies made for $10 a print. I don't know how many prints you want, but I think I should give you something Robert really loved of mine, *Oscar*, who he fell for hook, line, and sinker. I think I mentioned that right before he died he had *Oscar* hanging in the hall right next to his bedroom which really surprised me.

Jack Fritscher: He kept a 1978 story I wrote about him [titled "Caro Ricardo" to protect his privacy back then] next to his bed and showed it to his biographer and told her, "This is about me."

George Dureau: He valued his past. I think you should have that one of Oscar which has all the redeeming social factors he didn't like in his work. There was nothing I could do about his "departures" of my work. Some of my pictures he wouldn't buy because they were too conspicuously my thing. I'm not going to get this to you till the middle or end of the week.

Jack Fritscher: That's fine.

George Dureau: Jonathan, the beloved assistant, just called and said he's not coming home for two weeks. The clerical aspect of my life is getting funnier and funnier. Give me a call around Thursday if you want to ask more questions. It was great talking to you. I hope we get together soon. Maybe New Orleans? You'll at least come to my show in LA?

Jack Fritscher: I'd like to. I'd certainly like to interview you on video in New Orleans.

George Dureau: [Laughs] I'm always at home to talk to posterity.

Jack Fritscher: I'll talk to you Thursday. Thanks, George, so much.

George Dureau: Thank you. It's been fun.

(Opposite page, top) George Dureau's longtime assistant Jonathan Webb (atop taller ladder) and Mark Hemry installing the unframed drape of George's ceiling-to-floor *Mars Descending* for the Contemporary Arts Center of New Orleans's *War Exhibition*, April 8, 1991. Video photo by © Jack Fritscher

(Bottom) George Dureau with *Mars Descending*, Contemporary Arts Center of New Orleans's *War Exhibition*, April 8, 1991. Video photo by © Jack Fritscher. Dureau, as a U.S. Army veteran from the 1950s, rarely spoke about his service, but he said, "I like to do things political, and I'm glad that today [1991] I'm just as happy to do that as I was in the 60s. I like to push people into a corner of social and political problems, but I always try to bring a broad universality to it. My gut politics guide my work. Does politics trivialize painting? Think of Picasso's *Guernica*, Delacroix's *Liberty Leading the People*, Jacques-Louis David's *Deathof Marat*."

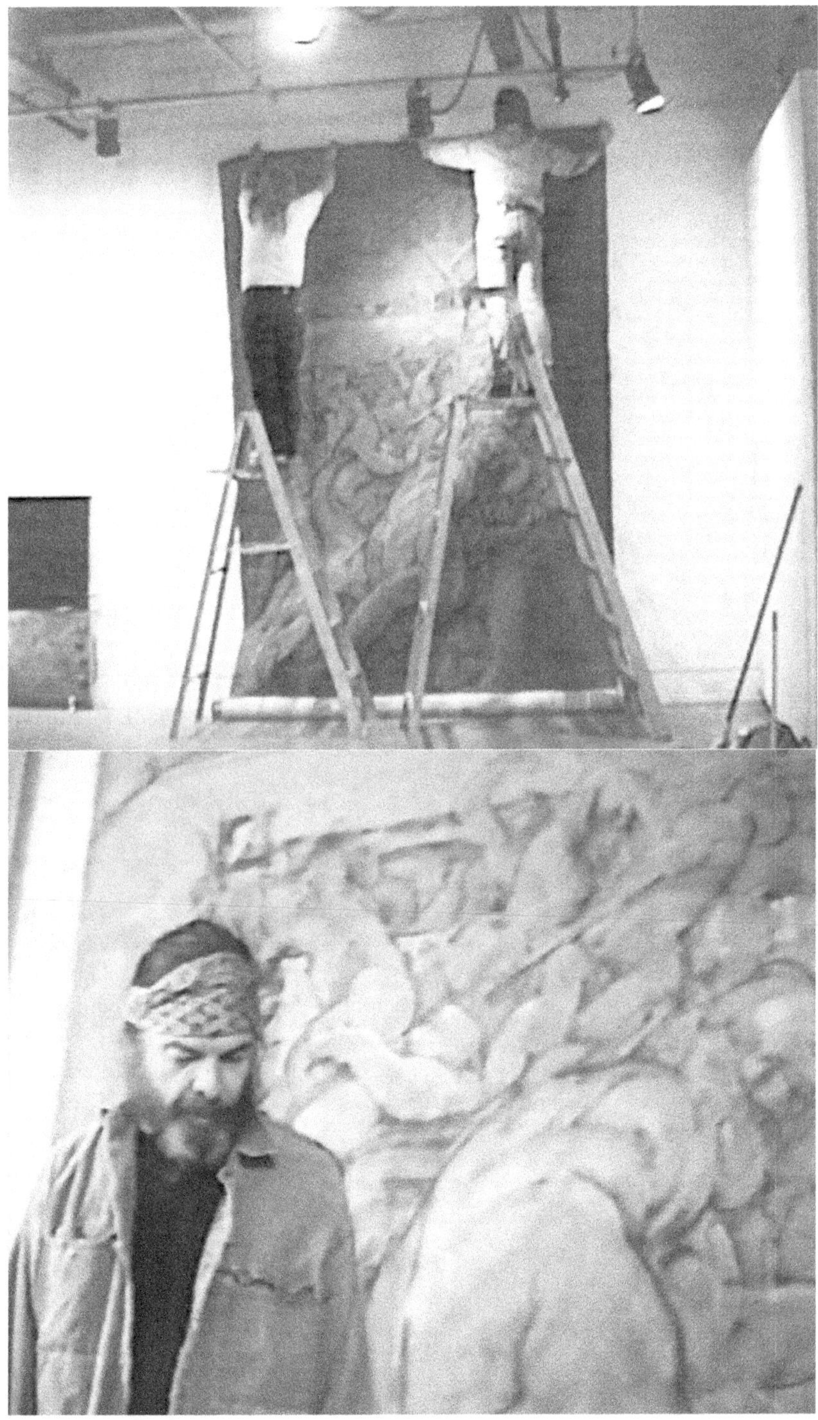

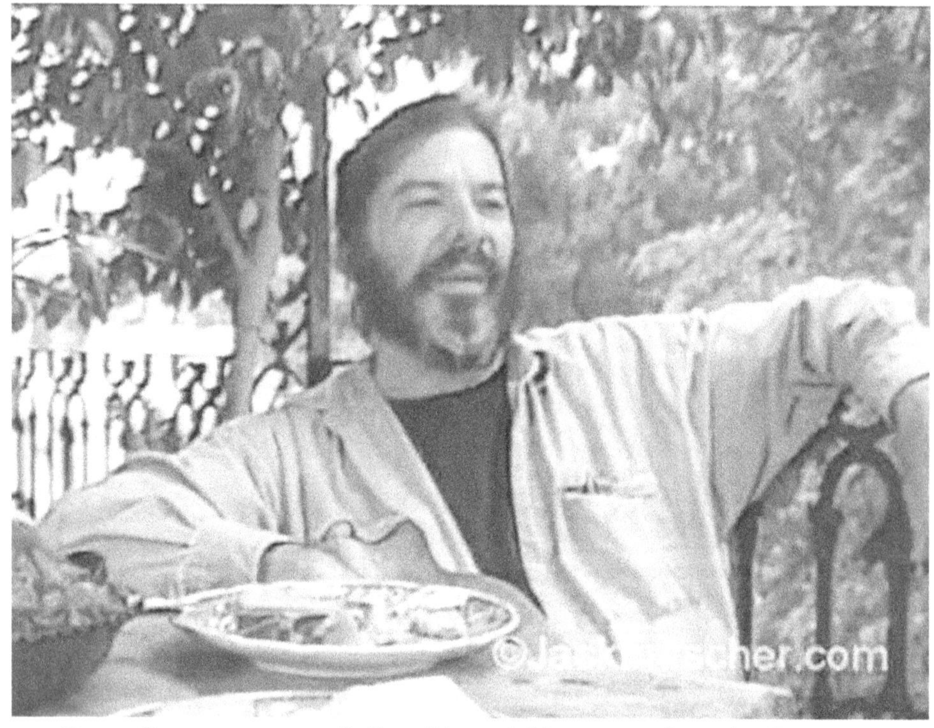

George Dureau on camera, "talking," he said, "for posterity" over his famous crawfish étouffée on his veranda, 1307 Dauphine, April 8, 1991. Asked if photography is as good as painting, he declared, "As a painter, I have to say, No. It ain't. Painting is a creative art. Photography is an editorial art. The camera is a mindless lunatic." Video photo by © Jack Fritscher from *Dureau on Dureau: Video Vérité* by Jack Fritscher and Mark Hemry

TAKE 3

DUREAU ON DUREAU
Video Vérité

Monday, April 8, 1991
6 PM-8:30 PM

EXT. NEW ORLEANS. TWILIGHT.
THE SECOND-FLOOR PORCH BALCONY
OF GEORGE DUREAU.
OVERLOOKING THE FRENCH QUARTER

Jack Fritscher: You are known as a photographer, but you began basically as a painter.

George Dureau: I've always been a painter. As a child, I drew things that children draw. My mother told me to draw courtyard scenes, magnolias, and I drew them. I didn't have any art training in high school at all. When I went to college, I studied all abstract things. I became an abstract painter. In the late 1940s and 1950s, I did very non-objective sort of Paul Klee, Miró things. Just when the whole world was convinced that's what they wanted, I was convinced I didn't want it. I was doing advertising and such like.

So in 1960, I just switched right over back to figurative work, still life and landscapes, aiming at doing figures. For the first five years of the 1960s, I, little by little, moved into figures by way of doing some landscapes and things to get my brush going on figurative expression. By the middle of the 60s, it was pretty obvious that the figures were going to take over as they moved up closer and closer, and became, I guess, what people call "Baroque."

Actually, it was just that I was so intense about the figures that I would articulate them and warp them, and try to make them

express what I was talking about, and so they got to look "Baroque."
I guess that's how "Baroque" gets to happen.

Fritscher: Isn't there a story about you out on location painting landscapes? There was a gentleman in your neighborhood who appeared
in the landscapes and all of a sudden…

Dureau: Yes. I had a house in the country that I shared with my
friend Chris. I would paint the levee in front of the house, the levee
on the river. And all of a sudden, my neighbor across the street, a
black man in this little country town, he came over and sat to watch
me. So I painted him into the picture and that was the end of that.
The figure took over the landscapes after that.

So by the late 60s, my paintings were almost always dominated
by figures. I realized by the end of the 60s that although the pictures were beautiful and decorative and even sumptuous sometimes,
I wanted the drawing to be more precise—not so much "tight precise," but explosive and expressive. And so I took up drawing again,
although I had not done drawing since my days in college.

When I was in college, they didn't teach drawing. Well, there
was a sketch class, but no one in it sketched as well as I did so it
wasn't doing me any good. I mean I already drew better than the
teachers did then. So I kind of had to invent how to do representa-
tional painting. The painting I did in college was abstract. I had to
invent what figurative painting was going to be for me.

I pretty well had a broadside, big slabby sort of, actually kind of
West-Coast-looking kind of painting. Big, buttery paint, a little like
Diebenkorn, I guess, if Diebenkorn were painting Edward-Hopper-
type street scenes. My street scenes, however, were always hotter and
more interested in the people than Edward Hopper would ever be,
so New England-y in his crispness. Mine were always a bit gushy. I
would jump into the ditches that people were digging.

So I took up drawing everybody in the late 60s, and it surprised people. It surprised people because drawing, although it was
respected, it was respected in a hushed kind of way. People would go
to museums and see beautiful drawings by someone who was dead,
right? And they never thought of drawing as it has turned out to be

for me: that is, my everyday thing, like writing notes to yourself, writing notes to anybody. I draw some pictures seriously and some more casually, but it's a handwriting.

But that way of looking at drawings isn't known to most people, even educated people who don't seem to know that the drawings are done with style most of the time. The reason Michelangelo's drawings, and Leonardo's and Raphael's and Rembrandt's and Rubens's, and all of those drawings seem to be related, one to the other? They are all so truthful. They seem to be talking about things that are real, more than the paintings do.

The paintings frequently drift away into some sort of novelty or operatic style whereas the drawings always are telling what the people are concerned about. My drawings always tell you more where I am at than the paintings. The paintings, frequently, because there is more money involved, have to go into a place, have to suit some thing, have to have a reason for getting sold. Although, as a rule, I don't paint a picture just because somebody tells me to paint such and such. Still you know you are creating this Big Opera, and it's going to have this style, and this bombastic effect.

In a drawing, because it is just paper and charcoal, in my case, you just do it, and if you have to throw it away, you just throw it away. And you don't think about that if you draw every day a lot. You just go and draw and if it's good, maybe you'll sell it, maybe you'll put it on the wall, but it's just like writing notes to yourself anyway.

Actually, it's my drawings that motivate everything. The drawings are at the middle of my career, and I go this way [through the drawings] into painting or that way into photographs.

It becomes more operatic and more involved with art elements when I take a subject and bring it into painting. If, on the other hand, I decide that I am fascinated by the person who I am drawing or thinking about, I'll turn to the camera because it provides a sort of clinical [take], [because of] the overwhelming talent that the camera has for capturing things. Now, I'm not particularly fond of sitting and capturing every detail of people, and sometimes you'll have a model who is fascinating in a lot of ways, although you don't care to sit and draw them all: the texture of skin or the hair or something like that.

So then I'll use the good offices of the camera and do that. That's the way I began photographing. I had absolutely no experience with cameras at all. I never even knew how to use Kodak. I was never interested in photographing anything. Anything! Because I drew and painted. I wasn't even interested in the history of photography. Nothing about it interested me.

I had models who were wonderful looking to me. They came out terrific in my drawings and paintings. And people didn't believe that they existed. They thought that I had just imagined these people. So I bought a cheap camera, two-and-a-quarter, very cheap one, and started making some pictures with just some advice like, "Oh, use such and such an f-stop when you shoot inside this window" and such like. I began making photographs that were almost exactly the compositions, the format and the attitude, that was already in my drawings. So I was just telling the camera how it was supposed to behave.

The camera, it seems to me, has the talent to capture any and everything. Therefore, photography, for me, anyway, is an "editorial art" or an "applied art" as opposed to the *total* creative art that drawing is. You don't have it if you don't make it. The camera just has to be throttled and controlled and made to do just those things that you want it to do, and not do anything else, otherwise you wipe it [creativity] out somehow.

Jack Fritscher: Once you set up the camera, sometimes it has to be told, "Just shut up."

George Dureau: Exactly. I spend all my time moving things out of the picture, it seems to me. I'm constantly—I'll start taking the picture, and then I'll start getting more out of it, or reducing the light so as to not see so much. Lately I've been cropping some pictures, but I used to not even crop them. So I spent a lot of time emptying out the frame because I wasn't going to crop them down as most photographers do.

Actually, I think it is a kind of nonsense about thinking that it's so pure to have used the entire frame. People used to rave on about, "Oh, he never crops." So what? I never cropped for fifteen years. Now I do crop sometimes when I want to. I think it's nice to have the knowledge and forethought and wisdom to be able to shoot without cropping. It's nice to be able to do that.

Sometimes, however, you capture something that's great and the whole composition is not that good, and so you might as well just crop it, even as you might as well crop a painting if that happens, if you have a gorgeous middle to it. Manet should have done that. In fact, he did, in *Dead Toreador*. He just cut the top off. He never could solve that. He couldn't solve anything more than this distance from the middle of the picture. I think he must have had a visual problem.

So photographs are just one way of seeing people for me whereas painting is another way, both of them just spinning off of drawing which for me is always the best.

I love line. I love the definitive, decisiveness of line, even though my lines are sometimes thick and thin, soft and smeared, but also, and maybe this is why drawing is not as popular anymore, now that photography is all over the place, there isn't that line in nature. You're creating that. There's a difference between this surface and that surface where this one ends and that one starts. But there's no such thing as line. It is a totally intellectual pursuit. So you might have some flourishes, some chiaroscuro, some effect in your drawing that makes it look a bit like real, but never looks real like a painting does or real like a photograph does. It's always an abstraction.

That may also explain my tremendous attraction to black-and-white photography, although I also do some color. I'm not that much interested in color. I'm more interested in the abstraction that black and white is. You're taking only line and form, and shapes between things, and negative shapes, and making them into your picture when you do black-and-white photography whereas once the color comes in, there's also festivity and distraction and other things happening, and there's an imitation of life, an exact imitation of life with color, and it's not so in black and white.

That's always been very strange that in movies, as in photography, we have this interest in black-and-white photography, and we think it is more realistic. We associate it with documentation. Black-and-white photographs that were very documentary. Black-and-white film seems very hardcore and documentary. It's very funny because it is missing one of the things, color, that makes it look like life. It's as though we want to believe what the author, the artist, the documentary director, whatever—we want to believe what they have found out.

It's an intellectual interest we have in seeing Humphrey Bogart with his gun shooting somebody in a dark alley. Instead of seeing it in color, we want to see it in black and white. And it seems more real to us. I don't know. Everybody didn't grow up at that [mid-century] time, but the people who learned black and white to be a documentary kind of hardcore picture found it very hard to see the thing in color, and believe it as much. That's very strange. Black and white 8x10 photographs of the way we saw criminals, or events in the 1940s and 50s…

Jack Fritscher: The movies of the 30s were black and white. German Expressionism. Leni Riefenstahl. Italian neorealism after the war, and Hollywood *film noir*. The dark beginning of the *Wizard of Oz*. The black and white of Tennessee Williams' kitchen-sink drama *A Streetcar Named Desire*.

George Dureau: I don't know why [Italian actress] Anna Magnani [who won an Academy Award starring in Tennessee Williams' dramatic black-and-white film *The Rose Tattoo*] stirring tomato gravy pasta sauce in black and white is more convincing to us than it is in color. I know I like it better, but I don't know why that is so convincing.

I know that in printing photographs you have a different latitude for printing. You can make more drastic changes, or, I can, because I don't know much about doing color. But you can make serious poetic and orchestral changes in black and white so that you're always dealing in a sort of abstraction. If you emphasize purple, it doesn't suddenly look like the flowers are a different color. If you darken something, it isn't giving an added meaning somehow. You can work with the poetry of what's already there without adding anymore elements into it. I don't know. That's a really hard one to resolve.

Jack Fritscher: I've always thought that black-and-white photography has the quality of moonlight. Just the way we believe our experience in the actual night, we believe black-and-white film because there is no color in the night, and yet it's all real, and somehow more magical.

George Dureau: But isn't it funny that black and white can be used—you said *moonlight*—and it made me think *romantic*—either in a beautiful seductive way, or it can also be harder than color.

In my photographs, my first photographs that I took of black men, they're not much different from the ones I take today, almost twenty years later. The first black-and-white pictures were so velvety. The people's flesh was so velvety and the backgrounds were white, maybe plaster, maybe dirty brick.

I tried a bunch of different papers, trying to decide what to do, and they were so prettified and yummy when they were warm like Portriga portrait papers.

> [George Dureau's assistant Jonathan Webb told me: "Agfa Portriga silver gelatin printing paper, which is no longer made, had a particularly warm finish to it. I got George to switch to Ilford Galerie which had rich deep neutral tones, but still gave very good blacks and whites and detailed contrast.]

I decided then that I needed the harshness of very white paper and very black printing to make the thing less romantic and less sentimental. So we have this kind of clinical printing of my pictures with a few yummy flourishes on it, but it's a sort of hard clinical thing. And then, by the lighting now, I make it happen. But I never let it happen in the darkroom. The picture becomes a soft romantic kind of thing. I'm a "camera photographer."

Mapplethorpe was too. We talked about that many times. We totally loved directing, nursing the people, wringing them out, getting out of them what we wanted, although I wanted much more humanist things and he wanted much more formalistic things.

But my formal training is always there and it never changes one way or another. I've been drawing and painting forever, and my drawings were always so classical, and my paintings were always so classical and fixed that that's a regular thing with me. So I assume that somewhere in my head is my predilection for shapes. I am inclined to orchestrate.

I imagine like a movie director does.

I make people do things that they didn't expect they were going to do. On a roll of film, I always try to get into it [the photograph] what they think of themselves, that *primarily*, or I should say *originally*. And then I move into what I think of them. And I hope I can pull the two of them together. Anyway, I'm crazy about working with the person and pulling something out of them that is unexpected to me and/or to them.

I don't like the darkroom at all. Robert didn't like the darkroom at all. He hated it. He thought it was really degrading.

Jack Fritscher: He always sent someone else in there with the film.

George Dureau: Exactly. Jonathan [Webb], a friend of mine and a photographer, prints my pictures with another photographer. They know what it is I want. The most I do is reject them, or say, "I didn't want that," or "I wanted to burn this a little more." I worked in the darkroom when I first did them, but now I hate the darkroom.

I like the distance. Other photographers will hate me for saying this, but I feel that the *distance* keeps you more an artist. Because *distance* keeps me more an idealist/artist who is doing photographic art with "art" in mind, not with "technique" in mind.

I think you can really lower your aims when you're thinking about what happens with chemicals and what not. I guess it makes a difference that I know what I want to say about people. I very seldom have been happily surprised about what happens in the darkroom.

I don't want to be surprised. I want the picture to say what I want the picture to say.

A friend of mine, Gene Thornton, a critic from the *Times* in New York, said he liked my photographs so much because I have something I want to say about everything, and I either say it with a pencil or a camera or a brush or whatever. But I already have the thing I want to say. And he says that most photographers study "photography" and then go out and photograph "photography." They don't photograph something that's in their head. They see something, "Oh, that would make a good picture."

I've never had that feeling. I see somebody, and I say, "Oh, I'm going to tell such and such about him." Or "I'm going to tell about his plight by doing this thing." Or "I'm going to show how absolutely seductive and overwhelming this person can be when I pull him up close. When I tickle him."

But I've always had my own individual, greedy, demanding things that I expect the camera to do, and if it doesn't, I'd just as soon hit it with a hammer.

I mean I really have no interaction with the machinery of it at all. I have two Hasselblads, two lenses and two bodies, and I only have that much because people have screamed at me because there is dust in my camera and it is about time that I get it cleaned. I had one lens and I used it for about eight years, a normal lens, until somebody convinced me that I would, really would, do better by having a portrait lens for some of this stuff.

I used to actually bend the people to make them not do "fisheye" kind of things. Everybody in my earlier pictures is sitting like this.

[George extends his arms and hands on the table, forward and wide toward the camera] in the picture to make them look like this [arms up close to the body]

Which is just crazy. I knew nothing about [the fact] that I could go get another lens.

It's funny where this advice came from. There is this really wacky photographer boy who just did journalistic stuff for one of the little trash papers. I said to him that I wanted to photograph my models, and they're just going to be, oh, they're velvety black figures against a white wall. The contours just like in my drawings, essentially silhouettes with some kind of detail in them. I said, "What kind of camera could I get?"

He said, "Oh, you go get a two-and-a-quarter."

I said, "What's that?"

He said, "That's what old farts like you like. Very stodgy."

So we went and bought a $68 Mamiya and I used it for a couple of years with no light meter even.

I asked people, "Should I do this a little darker?"

Some of my really good pictures, some people's real favorites, were done on that camera, as a matter of fact. When I first got the Hasselblad, it was so much better than my early one. It took months for me to get the pictures right. They were so hard looking and had so much more "depth," it seems to me, and I didn't want "depth." I'm not very fascinated by deep spaces.

My photographs and my paintings all sort of suggest a bit of Piero della Francesca [1415-1492]. Sort of four feet back there is a figure and then [he gestures farther back] a figure and [farther back from that] another figure sort of at the end of the architecture, or there will be another figure coming across, but there is a shallow stage, on props, sort of. They [the pictures] are like performances in front of a curtain.

I very seldom paint or draw very deeply. I can, but it doesn't intrigue me to pierce the surface very far. I like very often to do pictures that have the front in focus and the back to four or five feet all in focus, I like to do that, but I don't go beyond that.

I have a flat wall back there. I just have no interest in what we probably have going here right now [with the camera on him and not the trees behind him]. Behind me there are you things you can't read exactly. I like to read everything [foreground and background] in my pictures, I guess. If it's not worth reading—*wwww-wwwik!*—out it goes.

Jack Fritscher: Rather like peripheral vision fading away when the eye focuses on something distinct.

George Dureau: I like everything [I put] in the picture. It's so "left brain" of me to be telling a story. It can simply say that this is photography being done in the front room of my house on Esplanade and it says it's there because there's the corner of the mantelpiece, and then that mantelpiece appears in another picture as the main item, and then you're seeing just an edge of the mantelpiece in another photograph because there is the corner of the mantelpiece again. And the mantelpiece appears as a main item in another photograph.

Some of the earliest photographs I did were [set up] in front of the back of canvases, my painting canvases. And I thought that was keen because that showed [told the story] that I was a painter, right? And then I got some bigger canvases that I just hung down the wall.

I've never liked the surfaces of paper. Maybe because when I was younger, I was made to do display windows [at Kreeger's women's fashions department store on Canal Street] and there was that wretched seamless paper to deal with everyday. But I always have real canvas. I don't care if it is dirty or has fingerprints on it or grease or what. I love fabric.

At first, I would do these big canvases and there was a little space on the side and it became quite typical that my pictures would have a little lap space on the side where you see [I've included] pieces of my walls. You saw how tall were the baseboards or a little pipe coming up, a little gas pipe going to a gas heater sort of thing. Those little details were in the picture. I called them "Velázquez details" because, unless I'm mistaken, one of the coy things Velázquez did was to leave things in the picture that told that the picture was a lie, like the little prince on the horse, and then you have a rug on the bottom, or the backdrop stops suddenly, and you have a floor coming out.

I think that's fun to do. Maybe not in every picture. Sometimes you want to give the picture an illusion of something. But I love to give an illusion of something exotic or perfect or marvelous and then give it [the seriousness] away and say, "Oh, I'm just kidding. It's really my living room." I like to do that.

It's in most of my photographs. In this present series that I did, the photos were going to be very deceptive, very convincing illusions of people buried in the sand, or buried in water, such as that. When you first see them, they look like that. The printer thought they were very convincing.

People asked me, "How did you do that?"

In the pictures, you can see the canvas wrinkled up around the people because I didn't bother to hide it. I feel funny about being completely illusionistic. I'd rather just do what they call "telling the lie." I just like to tell that I'm "lying" here and there. I'm not interested in being a seamless illusion. I don't know why.

Maybe I'm not much into fantasy. I'm a real earth-sign person, I've been told. Even when I was a child, my idea of a divine and wonderful life would be going swimming in the bayou with the man who lives down the street or something.

And you know that in my drawings all of the angels have very big feet and hoofs. That's because they have to land [come in for a landing], I think. I'm very earthbound.

The other thing that has a big play in my art, I think, is my being so cerebrally ambivalent. I'm left brain, right brain, and there are some aspects of over-orderliness. Some of my things are just incredibly orderly. I'll peruse real tidiness and real explicit details of certain things or structures and then I'll bust it all up with a passion, a kind of romance. So there is always the classical-romantic always fighting each other.

I believe that's what good art is made of and I just have to go with that. I'm being Géricault [French painter Jean-Louis Géricault (1791-1824)] half the time and I'm being Ang [the Filipino painter and figurative expressionist Ang Kiukok (1931-2005)] another part of the time. I think that's why we like what we like in Michelangelo, and in Rembrandt and Rubens. I don't think you should have to have romance without classicism. You shouldn't have to give up all formality to have wonderful expressions of things, and vice versa, I don't think you should throw away all expression just to make things tidy.

How do you know your video sound is good?

Jack Fritscher: It'll be good. I'm trying to mask out a little bit of the wind when it blows in. You're doing very well with the traffic because when it goes by you kind of pause. Sound is really funny. When you shoot outside, you realize how much noise there is.

George Dureau: Here there really is a tremendous amount of noise. Saturday morning is much quieter. Sunday mornings are too. If this evening [Monday] were calmer, it would be less of a problem, but at the same time, it gives you a context that I think is worthwhile. Won't you eat something?

Jack Fritscher: Later, thanks.

George Dureau: I recently, just last summer, and then again just last month, I did a set of photographs which are different from what I am usually known for. My best work has always been, I think, those photographs which you might call "buttery portraits" in the sense that Manet's closeup, straight-on portraits were where the person is focused on you. They just invite you or challenge you to jump into their personality and see what they are about. Those photographs are very simple in composition, but hard to work out. Usually a head or shoulders, what is ordinarily called a bust, or else, which is much more complicated, going down to mid-thigh because then they become both a naked picture and a portrait.

If I have contributed something strong to photography, that is probably it, my ability to picture the model's sexuality and his brain, or his life as told through his face at the same time. So my photographs have almost always been the fact that there is this barbative back-at-you look of the people talking back to you, that the observer is observing you. Looking back at you and questioning you even as you are questioning him.

I recently departed from it, not for any particular reason except that I wanted to make some studies similar to my drawings and paintings of people that are just torsos. Just sort of sitting nowhere or sitting in the sand or somewhere like that. I thought I would express something you find more in my drawings and paintings than you do in my photographs. Probably just because I don't wish to involve myself in all that trickery of the arrangement.

But then there are the frustrating photographs of the vanquished or the dispossessed or the defeated, the abandoned, and the best way to do that for me was not to let them look back at you, because I usually in my liberal and generous spirit, invite the person to share the camera with me, even as I do in painting, and have them look back at you and tell them your story, as much as I get to tell mine, and probably more.

But in this case I did these frustrating, I thought, pictures of my models, Glen [Thompson], Troy [Brown], and other people, who are known for how wonderful they are, looking into the camera. I did them [laughs] as a piece of meat, just sitting there, being just torsos, just, just behinds, and torsos, just the two of them sitting there, sometimes with a strap on them, or something demoralizing. I think it was the war.

I *know* it was our recent war that brought that on. Then surprisingly and practically, something that doesn't happen all the time, those photographs became very important to that big painting I just finished against the Gulf War. [His epic twenty-foot-tall unframed canvas, *Mars Descending*, for the *War Exhibition* at the New Orleans Art Center, April 1991.] A big war painting, that canvas incorporated a lot of what I had done already in the photographs. It expanded and did things that photographs don't do for me because I'm not going to sit there [with the camera] and concoct the trickery [like the easier 3-dimensional effect in the painting] so you have people coming at you and such [out of the photo]. That's something [I could do in painting] that I could never have done in photography because I don't care to stage all of that.

Anyway, that series of photos is a very different series for me because it is frustrating, very unsatisfying. I guess most people would think the figures are *classic* in some kind of way. I think they are very limiting and frustrating, but I like them a lot because it's just another thing for me to do with the camera. I'm not very interested in doing a lot of things with the camera. I'm not very experimental. I don't care to see all the things the camera can do.

I'd like to do some video soon. I'd want it to look pretty much like my photographs. I guess I'd be pretty foolish if that's all they looked like, if I didn't do anything different [from my stills]; but maybe I'll [figure] some sort of thing where there is—what is video called? The hot medium?

> [He's thinking of Marshal McLuhan who said cool media require participation from users; hot media require low participation. Film director Haskell Wexler called his participatory film of the police riot at the 1968 Democratic Convention in Chicago, *Medium Cool*.]

Maybe it'll be hot on you and then go cold and settle down to [look like] my "still" kind of scenes, my "still" kind of portraiture, a fixed kind of pictures; but maybe I'll go through some active things to get to it. I don't know if that can work.

Jack Fritscher: I'll think you'll find video a very expansive and imaginative medium.

George Dureau: But I'm not...

Jack Fritscher: Go around and work with it. Find your own role.

George Dureau: It's funny how I resist that. I must say I'm not very open to influences or suggestions.

I have gathered some things from other painters in the last ten or fifteen years. But they probably hang around in my head for ten years before they ever find their way into my art. I'm just not much influenced by people. I'm not very interested in going to art shows. I never remember what I saw. But if I go to New York and just see a couple of Manets, I can be happy with that for five years. It's awfully stodgy of me, but I seem to have what I want to talk about in my painting.

I'm an artist. I grew up thinking what an artist is *supposed* to be, and, that is, I live a warm, involved, humanist sort of life. There are lots of people passing through my life. I have exciting experiences and learn things about people and they always go into my art. It is amazing; I cannot have an experience and not have it get into my art. Sometimes by the next morning, sometimes the same evening.

I had a friend. He's dead now. [New Orleans painter Robert Gordy, AIDS (1934-1986)]. He was a wonderful artist, but he went into a very dry period, and he said, "I just don't know what to do."

I said, "Well, just sit around and draw."

He said, "I don't draw."

I said, "Of course, you draw. You have wonderful looking drawings."

He said, "Those aren't drawings like *you* draw."

I said, "What are they?"

He said, "Those are pictures. Those aren't like you draw."

At the time, I hadn't clarified in my head what that difference was; and, about a year after, I realized what it amounted to was I draw from life and he drew from art.

So if he drew, it looked like a Léger or Léger-Picasso-Miró, and they were gorgeous, but they were concoctions. And when I've drawn over the last fifteen years, I don't know what it is going to look like. I'm looking at it, but I'm drawing from some process of going from real three-dimensional life, or some story that goes through my head, and comes out as line and shade. That's not the same as making pictures. It's not saying what the picture is supposed to look like. It's saying what the picture is supposed to tell. It's like writing. You don't picture what the page is going to look like or how many adjectives you're going to have on the page—unless you're a computer—when you're saying quickly what you did yesterday.

Jack Fritscher: I also think of writers who take writing classes that ruin them for writing because it interferes with their own natural expression.

George Dureau: You see that people don't understand that about my work because they think that I work in some style like the "Michelangelo style." And it's not so at all. I just draw that way. And if the person has a certain kind of boxy, heavy, or muscular look, it might come out *looking* like Michelangelo. If the person is a dwarf, it might look to them, not to me, like Velázquez. If a person is sinewy like a lot of the black people are around here, it looks "Signorelli" [Luca

Signorelli (1441-1523)]. I know it looks "Signorelli." They might not know that.

Drawings and paintings in their own time are done by an artist who knows what people look like and knows what particular people look like. It goes through him and it becomes an art, and it is done over and over again. Now it is being done by me, and if that looks like someone else's, it doesn't have anything to do with my looking like that artist. It has to do with us doing the same thing. I know how different my drawings are. They're not at all like the artists that people think they are like.

You know it's just it's Baroque or it's coming at you, or something, but I know that there are no tell-tale things that look like that person's art. My drawing of a hand like this [gestures with his hand] is very strange and awkward and a different kind of thing as I see them, not the way Michelangelo saw them, not the way Caravaggio saw them. Not at all. If I sit and try to do what Caravaggio did, it irritates me, even if it works, because it is not the way I see things. I see them much more chunky and bombastic, and I guess more *butch*. I see things that are sort of carved out of space and jerky. Even my sinewy things will end up as boxy and bombastic.

It's very strange. It's hard to influence the camera to do those things. To make a drawing, for example, one [simply] has to change the perspective of a leg. But, say I'm photographing someone from the top of their head to mid-thigh. To keep it from having the photographic verisimilitude of fading out at the bottom away from the lens, the way it looks to us, going down smaller, I have to make it look more like I've always seen it on paper: flattened out.

I then have to have the person bring his leg forward, his arm forward, or something such as that, so that it flattens the space. So my photographs are not half so naturalistic as they look. They are very posed as a rule. I get some startled or natural look on the face to make you think that the person is just caught there, but they are always very posed. I don't think I've ever done a photograph that wasn't very posed. Always posed. Sometimes the posing gets in the way and then you just don't print that.

Jack Fritscher: With your dual reputation as painter and photographer, do you find it difficult dealing with people confused about you and your work?

George Dureau: I find it very hard to deal with. People make assumptions that just aren't fact at all. They think I made photographs and then I learned to draw from the photographs which you can see is absolutely crazy. I've been drawing for fifty years or more, and painting that long almost.

I don't know if they should see the similarities between the things or not. I don't know. I think there is a very unnatural and uncomfortable interest in photography today. I'm certain that when I started making photographs I had absolutely no interest in becoming a famous photographer. No way! I was making some little records of those people because I was crazy about those people; and I knew that my drawings [of them] in their aesthetic delight and in their craziness were not [true] records of the people. And so I wanted to record the people, as well as the fact that I had expressed them in my drawing. I thought it would be fun to go back and look at them later.

It became interesting to me when people told me I made wonderful photographs because I couldn't imagine why photography or any art field could be in such bad shape that they would think that mine were good—when I didn't know how to do anything. What it amounted to is I transposed from my drawing and painting. All that knowledge came over and I put an overabundance of a kind of wisdom on top of the photographs. It wasn't photographic wisdom. It was art wisdom.

There were several classical things happening in my photographs that people didn't understand that the camera could be made to do because we had been through those wonderful photographs of the Farm Security Administration [with its pictorial record of American life between 1935 and 1944], and then the war and all the wonderful documentation that had been done. So people were astounded to see these "monumental" photographs, which is what they seemed to be.

I jammed the people up close [to the lens], but still I kept it all in repose, all in focus. So you had this monstrous person looking down your throat, telling you his story. But always seemingly classical and composed and held in.

It tremendously influenced Mapplethorpe. He was absolutely shocked by them, because until that time [we first met in person] in 1979, he had never seen compositions that he didn't understand, I think, at first. But it all came out of art history. It didn't come out of photography history. It came out of painting and drawing history, my photographs. Because that's what I brought to photography. I brought the knowledge of postures, of poses, of things that had happened in the Renaissance, etc.

Not that I'm such a careful student of art history. I'm not, but I am an observer of art history. So I brought to photography all these tried-and-true ideas of presentation of the person, and it had nothing at all to do with what the camera does well or what the camera does other than what I wanted it to do. Nothing to do with the various things the camera can do. It had only to do with how, if you want to tell about a person, you want them to come across, how to direct them, how do you frame the thing, how do you work out the negative and positive shapes so that positive shape looms at you, but the negative shape supports it.

Those are the things I had been doing in my paintings of heads and torsos all along. I didn't do anything different in my photographs than I had been doing for twenty years in my paintings. My paintings were buttery, close up, strong, carved-out portraits with very strong contours. Sometimes naked, sometimes just heads. The photographs were exactly that type of thing.

Jack Fritscher: That must have startled Robert when he first saw your work.

George Dureau: He always had scenarios, nasty scenarios, in mind. What kind of scenarios, what kind of hanky-pank will catch people's attention? As far as I know, up to that time, there was always some kind of activity that was unnerving or shocking or exciting in his pictures. There was sort of a "things-happening-in-a-room-sort-of-look" in the photographs that he showed me. We swapped some photographs then. In the ones I picked out, I was looking for ones more like mine—filled with space, contours important, shapes important, and them some presence in the person.

His photographs before that were more like slices out of an intimate movie. The ones of him with the whip [up his bum, *Self Portrait with Whip*, 1978], boys in the room doing different [S&M fetish] activities, and what not. His were more like figures in a space, and mine were more like the big figure occupying the space totally and just leaving small negative spaces parked around the thing.

He loved the ones that were close-ups of deformed arms, the boy looking at you. Things like that had strong lighting, but the bodies were always sculptural and immediate. The immediacy in my pictures was also kind of sociological, appealing, and solicitous. You were brought into the person's plight or his beauty or whatever. It was solicitous in the sense that I was saying that this person is wonderful and you're going to want to know about him, or this person is terrible and you're going to want to know about him.

That immediacy for him was a way of scaring people even more. So the early ones—in which I may have had some influence—would have been those in which he had his same scary subject matter, and he made it more scary by moving them in tighter and composing more tightly as I did.

Judging by the pictures that he bought from me at first, that's what he did. That is to say he bought my pictures which I immediately saw reflected [in his photographs shot immediately after]. Heads real close and leaning over, but the eyes still looking at you.

That [eye contact] was a funny thing. I never would have thought that art photography, even as I was turning to it, didn't do the same wonderful thing that candid photography does or painting did. That is, capture the person by looking straight into their face, right?

But art photography before that always seemed to be someone staring off somewhere into space being instructed not to look at the camera. The only instructions I ever gave were: "Stay looking at the camera" or "Look into the camera." That difference was very strange because my pictures had maybe the arty finish and the modeling, the shape and form, made from another kind of art, but they had the straight-on look of a [personal] photograph of your little boy or your wife. So they had that funny [hybrid] look about them.

Now the first ones [of my photographs] were mistakenly said to look like Diane Arbus when what they were was "anti-Arbus." They were so close-up, because all I had was a short lens, and I didn't know that. They were very close-up. So the very first pictures were thought to be scary like Diane Arbus. And since a lot of my friends were dwarfs or people with missing limbs, people who were handicapped in some way, because I've always known a lot of them, it was believed that my pictures were like hers in that way. It was absolutely opposite because mine are so solicitous and the people are presented always [kindly]. You want to know more about this person whereas she did the "Bang! Shoot One! Kill Him and Get Him out of Here" approach to people. Diane Arbus, um, Diane obviously, really and truly thought all those people she photographed were just freaks. I mean she really and truly believed that. Just freaks. Don't blame me. Susan Sontag said that to me. She said, "Arbus is a middle-class New York woman and those are freaks to her."

There's a real "Walt Whitman" air, I guess, to my photographs. [Whitman's famous inclusive line in *Leaves of Grass* is: "I am large, I contain multitudes."] I now allow myself the luxury of composing more, and making more prettified pictures, without the portraiture being so strong, and *that* may be Mapplethorpe's influence back on me, doing that sort of thing.

But I always did that in my paintings anyway. On the other hand, there are some people who are so wonderful to look at straight in the face, I find that I can't turn them away. There was a big difference in that Robert's orientation to people was so much, I'm afraid, shallower than mine. He had much less patience with people whereas the people you see in my photographs, you'll see them again ten years later. I have photographs of people, for instance, of Troy, over twenty years. You might see them again just six months later when you might see them in a different kind of way. But I don't think Robert had the patience to put up with people after he shot them dead once. It's very funny, isn't it, that you "shoot" people and you "shoot" pictures.

Jack Fritscher: And presidents.

George Dureau: The camera can be very mean, very disturbing, very dispassionate, really hateful, and it can be adoring.

Jack Fritscher: Don't you think that perhaps your romantic approach as opposed to his slick fashion photography…

George Dureau: What we now call his "slick fashion photography," I'm not so sure that he didn't develop that off me and Berenice Abbott and other people like that, and [Irving] Penn and [Richard] Avedon; but it wasn't there, I don't think, when I first met him in 1978 or 1979.

My photographs were never slick and fashionable, but they have a rich velvety air and careful composition. Sometimes they might have a false candor. A person might be coming at you like this.

> [George crosses his arms with left palm on right shoulder, and right palm on left, and leans forward on his elbows, ready for his close-up, tight into the video camera.]

George Dureau: Am I too close? [Laughs] I had been going through two rolls trying to get the arms into the right position for that, right? So there was a mock candor to mine, as there might be in a Manet portrait. You might say, "Oh, the candor in a Manet portrait!" Well, that candor took Manet six months or six years to get in that picture. So it ain't so goddamn candid. Well, that's how my candor is too. Sometimes you work at it, you build it, you get it there, and then you blow it all in an act of love of getting the eyes right.

Maybe it took you six months to get to that point. In my photographs, sometimes I keep moving the person [the protagonist in his photo narrative], nudging him into position. [Leaning into the video camera] Am I too close? [Laughs] And then trying to get the focus right. "Put your head a little bit higher, a little higher, a little lower."

I would take two, three, or four rolls of the very same pose because I *knew* the pose was right. I just had to *get* it right. But Robert was doing more scenarios [that were] kind of wacky. [It was as if Robert were saying,] "Didn't I surprise you with this?" Those weren't quite up to slick photography. Not that it should have been; but I think his slickness developed after taking the classicism from me and from some other people like me.

Hmm. Are there any other modern photographers, contemporaries that he seems to have shared something with? Because we know how influenced he was. [There are] the pictures of his that are definitely reminiscent of George Platt Lynes, and, certain muscle photographs that we all grew up on twenty-five years ago in cheap magazines [that he found in adult bookstores on 42nd Street]. But he's taken all of those things and given them a certain slick beauty.

Jack Fritscher: He liked 1950s physique photographs [in pocket magazines like *Tomorrow's Man*].

George Dureau: But I don't know any others [influences]. I'm trying to think. Are there any contemporaries of his? He knew, liked, and admired my photographs, right? Were there any others that were like that to him?

What he did with the others, he would take muscle photographs that would appear in leather magazines and he would improve them

> [To build his first collages at Pratt, Robert cut photos out of magazines featuring muscled leatherboys sold "for artists who can't afford models" shot by gay Chicago photographer Chuck Renslow at Kris Studio and published his pocket magazine, *Mars* and *Triumph*, both founded 1962. Influenced by Renslow, he was well steeped in leather when I assigned him to shoot the cover of the leather magazine *Drummer* in 1977.]

George Dureau: He would take the subject matter, just the funny wacky, sleazy style, and he would glorify it. What's funny is that in mine he would take [my], what I would have called "moral nudes," what Kenneth Clark calls "moral nudes," meaning nudes that are non-sexual. Those moral nudes talk about values—like a chorus, like Greek things do, like true classical art does.

He took those and made them more, I guess you could say, *contemporary*, but that's not so. By making them more *sleazy* or more *common* somehow. I would have details in mine that would maybe say *who* the person was, or *where* they were from. He would put details in perhaps that would say what *act* they were going to get engaged in or something. He put in cruel sorts of details that would speak sort of *using* that person. And mine would be details that would say where that person is from and what he's like: maybe a tattoo would say that, or some piece of luggage under an arm—but [my photographs are] not what I was going to do with him, or what you [the viewer] might do with him.

He made pictures that appealed to the rich, conservative, or fascist gay audience that he was appealing to. He would put [cast] anybody in his pictures if they looked like somebody you could buy, or use, or handle. And mine would not look like people you could buy, or use, or handle.

I know his friend Sam Wagstaff was offended by the fact that I liked my models so much and they were permanent underclass kind of people. He thought that was not right for Robert to be interested in; but it was alright for Robert to be interested in these people if they looked like they could be used by the people who would buy the pictures.

And knowing who buys the pictures, that's what worked. They were publicized. His whole career has been further publicized and bought by people who are usually well heeled, or look like they are, or wish to be well heeled. People who can buy and sell the stuff that's in those pictures.

Whereas there is always that look of "other" human beings that you have to tolerate in my pictures. I'm shamelessly humanist—and it's all over the pictures. It makes mine a lot less saleable and sometimes a little less bearable because my pictures flush you into a corner sometimes by being full of problems, social problems and political problems and such.

Jack Fritscher: Robert formalized those people, stylized them into something beyond themselves.

George Dureau: I think he bought people more than I did. I pay people a certain amount of money to pose for me, but I don't pay them enough so that [unlike Robert who paid too much] I'll never have to see them again. We discussed prices a lot; and there was the major difference that in New York people [models] know who you are and they know what they can get out of you. And they say, "$500." In New Orleans, somebody would say, [he smiles lovingly]: "Gee, ah'd like to be in yo pictures, oh yeah." So then I'd pay them for taking the picture, but I'd see them the next day and the next year and four years after that when their momma would tell them, "I have to pay the electric bill."

I paid less for the modeling fee; but I would pay more later in friendship or closeness or just our village co-existence. But Robert felt very threatened by the people that he photographed. He wanted them never to come back again. He would get furious. He would give them a signed photograph and they were supposed to go off and sell it, but [instead] they would say, "Oh, it rained, or it [the photo] went down the toilet," or something, and they would come back for another one and he was furious that they would keep bothering him because he just wanted them to go away.

Jack Fritscher: He wanted them, like his tricks, for the moment.

George Dureau: Do you know? I have a friend in New York who once talked about an early Louis Malle picture, *Lucien Lacombe*, I think. Anyway, the actor had been discovered—the star of that movie was a non-professional; he was a wonderful-looking peasant boy. Louis Malle discovered him. The boy got lots of money, got a convertible sports car, raced it down the street, went off the road, and was killed. And my friend said, "Oh, what a wonderful way! He [Malle] didn't have to put up with him making more movies." And it's true. I think Robert felt that way [wishing]: "I want them just to exist in this picture and don't want to see them again."

There were very few of his models he'd would get a crush on so much that he wanted to carry on with them. There were some, of course. Unfortunately, I'm capable of carrying on affairs with every-body on earth at the same time. Not successfully, but energetically.

I know the sons of people that I've photographed back in the 1970s. I've drawn people in the 1960s that I now draw the children of. It's a very strange thing. I'm not saying it's the only way to do it, but once you're doing that, especially if you're a sort of "classic art creature" which I am. I live my life and it's reflected in my art. My art tells what I've learned or failed to learn. It's very hard to give that up and say, "Oh, I'll just go someplace where I don't know the people and I'll see some different kinds of faces."

Jack Fritscher: He liked shooting new faces of leathermen in San Francisco.

George Dureau: I think New Orleans is about the size that Paris was when Paris was great, yeah, I mean for creating art, for know-ing your subject matter, for knowing the people you're dealing with, for reusing them and them being there when you need them for reconsidering things, for redrawing a picture and throwing it away and doing it another way. The people are there the way you know the grocer you've known for thirty years.

I don't know if it's insecurity on my part, but I really like the fathers of, the brothers of, the children of, the wives of [my models] to think of me as that nice artist who drew their daddy.

They don't have to like all the pictures, but they come in, some-times, people who I've photographed or drawn, they'll come in and say, "Man, you see me better than I do." Or "You just know how that kinda dude thinks."

To me it is somehow more comforting than having a critic say, "He did that well," when I know the critic doesn't know what I did well because he probably doesn't have the experience I have.

My pictures are frequently experienced and shared with the models. Only I know a lot about what they are and it goes into the pictures and only they can verify it. Not that I spend all my time getting it verified, but it's comforting that things regularly get veri-fied. You can move along knowing that you've done a human activ-ity which is attractive to yourself, that you're proud of.

Jack Fritscher: Some critics struggle to fit "what's new" into the traditional principles they studied years before in school.

George Dureau: We have an energetic and very serious—you met him the other night—critic here in town. But I don't really expect him to know all of what I'm doing. He's the one [local] critic and it's kind of hard for him to like all the things I do. It's very hard for a critic in a place like New Orleans who has been looking at the same artist for fifteen years to find something new to say. So all of a sudden critics get negative. Simply because they got tired of being *positive*. They can't keep saying the same thing year after year. They wish you would change, but I'm not going to. I want to improve, but I don't hope to change.

Jack Fritscher: A new set of critics is needed?

George Dureau: Change the critics, but keep the artists. That would be good. You could shift critics around from town to town.

Jack Fritscher: Many artists in many towns would be happy if that were to happen.

George Dureau: I really haven't been damned much. I've been praised a lot. I think my work is a great deal more sound than people know. We live in this age of novelty because of galleries and sales. Galleries cannot keep paying the rent if they don't have novelty.

It's the same as in the fashion industry. I once was a "window dresser" in the fashion industry and it's exactly the same thing. You have to convince window shoppers that this new thing is better than last year's. So you have to damn last year's wonders in order to convince people that they're going to want this year's horrors. I'm not going to change for those reasons. I doubt that I'd do the right thing for me and my talent and I just have to pursue it and improve it.

Jack Fritscher: What drove you initially to physical disability, to men with missing limbs?

George Dureau: Charcoal! [Laughter]. Since childhood I've been more than fascinated, just *drawn* to people who are handicapped, but particularly to people who are triumphant though being handicapped. I've always loved tough dwarfs. Always. I can remember "Long John Silver" kind of creatures. The buoyant, tough, or wild drunk on one leg. I've always thought that the pirate-y kind of person was always the most fascinating to me. I've explained it to myself, but it's too hard to explain in public. But I've always been attracted to little people who act strong and big. It's just super triumphs that I like: heroes!

I guess that's one of the things that made people like Sam Wagstaff un-attracted to my work. He kept saying how wonderful it was, but he wasn't about to buy any. I saw him a great deal. He would pick out the things that were all right for Robert to be influenced by, but…

Jack Fritscher: For Robert to build on.

George Dureau: Right. Exactly. Because Robert loved my stuff, and had already bought a number of things. Wagstaff picked out some things from one of my shows, but Robert just absorbed them. Wagstaff didn't buy them. Robert bought them, a lot of my stuff. So he had about sixteen pictures [before we met] because that's what he bought from me, but it turns out [George alleged] that the gallery we're both in, in New York, the Robert Samuel Gallery [in which, Frances Terpak and Michelle Brunnick reveal in their 2016 book *Robert Mapplethorpe: The Archive*, Mapplethorpe was an "active business partner"] must have paid off some debt to him or something with a bunch of my photographs because a whole lot of photographs that I never sold have gone through the auction houses and some of them have ended up on the West Coast. There's a gallery out there that Robert showed with, a big, very flashy gallery that had, apparently, a bunch of my photographs that were 8x10s that I never had sold. They were just proofs that the gallery in New York had.

I think something inexplicable happened in the 70s and early 80s and a lot of photographers' work got picked up by somebody mixed up in a, I don't know, some kind of shady deal, and then the pictures got spread out again. People were paid off. A lot of people got my work that they did not buy, as such, because they were kind of like reimbursed for investment in the gallery, or something like that. It's hard to make galleries work what with high overhead, and the gallery directors sometimes just turn bad. Although they may not have started off bad, they turn bad thinking that they're going to make it work for all of you, you know. "Oh, it's all going to be all right, darling. Just don't worry about it. We're going to pay you back eventually." And it goes down, down, down, and nobody gets paid for anything. But I didn't pursue that [West Coast] gallery. Mapplethorpe did pursue it, but I didn't. I wasn't going to be retaliatory about it.

Jack Fritscher: Where do you think you're going to go in the 1990s with your painting and photography? A balance between the two, or do you have a feel for...

George Dureau: I'll always do more paintings and drawings. I think. In terms of time, still photography takes so much less. Say, if I was doing two sessions a week, three or four hours each, I was just burnt out from doing it. First of all, because I don't make up a lot of stories that I want to do in photographs. I have a lot of stories already that I want to do in paintings—and photographs are almost always hinged on the presence of some person.

Even in these, where I've messed around with the people and used them in a sort of *repertory* way, turned them around and photographed their asses instead of their faces, even in those it's the person because [I ask myself] will Glen [Thompson] want to do that? Does he mind? Does he mind being used this [way] one time, knowing that the next time I'll do a wonderful job of looking into his eyes?

But anyway, it just exhausts me totally to do more than two afternoons of photography because we really work hard and intensely at it.

Jack Fritscher: How's your painting as far as timing goes? Do you find that you go on great binges of painting and then there's...

George Dureau: Sometimes I'll paint through a long time. But I paint in stops and starts. I'm painting a lot right now, and I'll get out of it for a while, and do photographs and drawings. [George effectively stopped shooting photographs in 1988.] Part of it is making a living.

I make the most out of small paintings and big drawings. But I just love drawing and I do it every day. So it is the link. Line and form as they are in my drawings are always going to hold the whip over everything else.

How I draw in the morning is going to influence how I pose someone in the afternoon. The contour from the head down to the leg as done in the drawing is probably going to come up in the pose somewhere, in my photographs, or in my paintings. Because drawing to me is always the backbone of what my head is doing.

Jack Fritscher: Your home is wonderful. How long have you lived here?

George Dureau: I've been here for about five-and-a-half years, almost six. Before that I lived in a house that was gigantic, but the rooms weren't as big as this. This [house and studio] is what we affectionately call "Queen Anne front" and "Mary Ann behind." It looks like a wonderful typical French Quarter house although it has a bigger balcony than all the others from the front. But when you go inside, it is relieved in a sort of Soho loft sort of way by the fact that it has always been a warehouse. It was gutted about one hundred years ago. I never would have gutted a house like this. They're too fragile, these little brick houses. I never would have dared to take out five or six walls, but since they did it and its still standing, I went ahead and kept it that way.

So I have two huge rooms with smaller rooms off them, and they function wonderfully because I learned in the other house that you need "back away" space.

In photographs, you have to back the stuff away from you.

In painting, you have to move the paintings away if you want to do another painting. You want to move them away if you want to work on something else. We didn't put walls in. We just left it. So it is a kind of family house with a huge porch wrapped around it and generous windows and comfortable furniture. But at the same time it has the flexibility of a little factory. So I can move my big bed and my little bed and my sofas to another spot if I want to as I'm going to do when we've changed that stair [stairway entrance]. We're going to change the orientation of the front room.

Jack Fritscher: You've lived in New Orleans all your life and you don't travel.

George Dureau: I lived in New York once for about nine months [in the 1960s]. I liked it while I was there. But as soon as I got home I thought, "Oh, thank God, I'm home." I'm not aggressive. I might be dominating, but I want to be told that I'm the one that dominates. I don't like to knock on doors and have to go tell someone that they're supposed to love my painting. I don't want to do any of those things.

If somebody invites me to go somewhere and do it, I'll do it. But I am not a traveling salesman. I cannot knock on the door.

I guess I'm kind of *grand* in that I expect to have a place in society that's comfortable. I expect to have a certain amount of respect, and I expect to work very, very, very hard all the time and not to have travel time, to be working all the time. So although I expect position and respect in my community, I work so hard for it, I don't feel bad about it. As Michelangelo said, "If they knew how hard I had to work to achieve my mastery, they wouldn't think it was so good."

Jack Fritscher: Since we're in the second year of the 1990s, the last decade of the century...

George Dureau: Yes, I'm the *fin de siecle* artist. *Fin de siecle*, here I am!

Jack Fritscher: Can we tie this up and can you project for me where you find art, painting, photography, you, what's expected of you. You've just joined this very political New Orleans exhibit in response to the Gulf War, a wonderful piece.

George Dureau: I like to do things political, and I'm glad that I'm just as happy to do that now as I was in the 1960s. When I do something political, it usually has a broad universal kind of aspect to it. I'm not very particular about things. I did all kinds of "integrated" pictures all through the 1960s and I also did pictures, if you wished to see them as "homosexual," yes, they were homosexual in that there was only one sex in the picture sometimes.

But I also did pictures that had women in them, and I also did pictures with just women in them.

But I like to make statements that I guess are political or sociological. Although most of my pictures in the house are not political, I'm not apolitical. There's always a certain politics to them, my own human politics, but I was once at a lecture and some critics and some art historians were talking, and my friend Edward Lucie-Smith asked them, "Now what is your favorite painting in the whole world?"

They went around this group and each came up with a painting that he thought the most wonderful painting ever painted.

And I said, from the audience, "May I have one question? Well, one statement? I think this is really strange because I never noticed it before, but every one of the paintings that you mentioned was a political painting, and we always think, 'Oh, painting is trivialized by bringing politics into it.'" They were *Guernica, Liberty Leading the People, Death of Marat.*

I mean, every one of the pictures, I can't think of them all, there were eight pictures, and they were all political pictures from their time. In their day, they were all some sort of a placard or banner.

All through the time I was in school in the 1940s and 1950s, we thought, "Political painting is trashy." You're supposed to be above that [because] that ruins you. But in truth it seems to raise the pictures above the ordinary. So I hope I paint a good political picture here and there.

Jack Fritscher: I think you do because of the consciousness raising you are bringing to the 1990s. Taking people who are physically disadvantaged and in a sense glamorizing them, helping them transcend stereotypes.

George Dureau: That's always going to be in my pictures. That's my gut politics. It's always going to guide what I paint. But it's nice too, and it gives you a nice *young* feeling to politically organize your thoughts behind a "Big Complaint." Once in a while a "Big Complaint."

Jack Fritscher: What would you see as the "Big Complaint" on the horizon as the century clanks to an end?

George Dureau: Unfortunately, I'm that artist who is content to paint the same pictures over and over, but better, he hopes. I'm sure that complaining against military police power, a police state, and police control in shaping of the world, is going to be something to continue to complain about and continue to chip away at over the next few years.

Because I have the feeling that we are getting into [government] controlling the way other countries do business. We are not just using "military might" to keep a peaceful order.

I'm afraid that we're on a tear now, that we've discovered where we've failed economically, and where we've failed politically and morally. We [think we] can clean all that [our national moral failure] up by using our guns and make "ourselves" like "ourselves." We really look like we're on that path.

Somebody said recently, "Oh, we Americans find it very easy somehow to turn success into moral right." Because we were successful in the Gulf War, we're bound to tell ourselves that "You see! We were morally correct.'" And unfortunately, I think we're going to do a lot of that [moralizing war] thing soon.

But my mainstay always will be painting pictures of particular people, of particular sets of people, or particular things that happen to people. bringing them to the fore so that they can be enjoyed and understood and shared.

Jack Fritscher: So you let the world go by while you continue with your art.

George Dureau: Well, presenting what is good about human beings is my particular talent. I know it is. It's why I sell. And I sell a lot! I don't sell pictures at New York prices, but I sell them at the top of New Orleans prices. The people who buy my pictures buy them in spite of themselves, half the time. That really makes you feel good because you know they bought it because they really had to have one of those. Even though it was going to be a bit unpleasant and they would have trouble explaining it to their teenage daughter or their own mother. They still had to buy the picture. And people would say, "I don't know why she bought that picture, but of course he's a wonderful artist; but I don't know why he paints those pictures either."

Jack Fritscher: Wasn't there a young couple who married, and all they had was a kitchen table, and a couple of chairs—and a Dureau?

George Dureau: Yes. That's one of the wonderful things. Wonderful collectors. I guess that's one of the things you give up when you enter a vicious—it's hard to think of "New York" as the mainstream, [more like] the "main eddy." I always think, I'm the mainstream in New Orleans and they're a serious eddy down the road over there.

One of the things you hate to give up [if you sell at New York prices] is selling pictures [cheaper] at not too terrible a price to wonderful people who share an intelligence with you, who share your beliefs or your humanity, people who are not necessarily very rich and people who don't necessarily follow art trends. But you say something in your painting that may be similar to what they think in their philosophy, or in their medical practice, or what they may be interested in, their poetry or story writing. I really like appealing to intellectuals other than art groups because you never really know why people who are art junkies are buying your pictures. Sometimes you go to their house and there's the one Dureau and the one so-and-so, and the one so-and-so, and the one so-and-so.

Jack Fritscher: The baseball collection card approach.

George Dureau: Yes. The full set. But I like my customers a lot. That really makes me happy.

Jack Fritscher: You mentioned you like your clients to come to your studio to look through your work because you get a chance to…

George Dureau: It's exhausting sometimes. It draws you away from your work and keeps you from doing things. But, on the other hand, I've met some of my very best friends by being patient and letting people visit me because they wanted to see my studio and see what it is I'm up to, to see why they like my photographs or my paintings.

It is kind of a problem to have someone want to come and see your work, and want to meet the people that you draw and paint. I find it very hard to not say, "Thank you. I'm glad you like me," when somebody really is devoted to my art.

Jack Fritscher: You also get a chance to watch the psychology at work as they make a decision between painting A and painting B.

George Dureau: Yes, and it's amazing. Not that one should paint according to that, but you learn some really interesting things about your own work when you do this. Some people pick tougher [photographs], and sometimes people make rougher and braver choices than I would make.

It's the reverse of what most people would think. The people who swim the moat, so to speak, the people who pick up the telephone and call you and say, "I didn't know I could get you on the phone. I would love to see your work, but I don't want to disturb you."

If you have them over, sometimes it is very strange. You can find out, in some sense, that they have better taste than I have. I might average out or normalize my work in my head. I'll be thinking that they're going to buy down-the-middle, something that is not too wild and disturbing and something that is not too sweet and gentle. Not so. They might fool me completely. They might like the unfinished drawing that is really tough and scary and I never would have shown it in a gallery.

Frequently, pictures that are bought from my home are pictures that never would have made it to the gallery. Not that my gallery doesn't have good taste, because he [gallery owner, Arthur Roger, who preserved Dureau's archives for posterity] certainly does, but in talking with him like a marriage where we talk things out, we might drop a photo. And it might not be his fault. It's me thinking it's not slick enough or pretty enough or frameable enough. When people come to my house, they sometimes buy something that is a lot closer to my roots, a lot closer to my bloodstream than I would have shown in a gallery.

Jack Fritscher: What's your lifetime estimate of how many paintings and photographs you've done?

George Dureau: I've done thousands and thousands of drawings. I've done little thumbnail drawings. I do drawings like storyboards for my photographs now. I didn't do that at first, but if I know I'm photographing two guys and doing them together, which isn't too frequent, I'll do a bunch of drawings, just so I don't forget what I was thinking about when we get into the heat and craziness of doing the shoot.

Some of those drawings I love, and I'll do little sketches like that. Regularly I do charcoal on rag paper. Every day I keep a couple of easels about and I draw faces, poses of several graceful women's bodies together. I'll do some fornication scene. I have all these things going all the time, and I begin an immense number of things and then finish them slowly over a period of time when I get an another idea of what to do next.

I work very fast so there are literally thousands of sketches lying around. And the photographs? I have them neatly filed away because you have to do that. It's the only way. You have to have negatives put away neatly and archivally. I guess there are hundreds of thousands. I don't know. If someone is worth shooting, I will do ten rolls of twelve. So there are 100 to 150 sometimes of very similar exposures of anybody I find worth photographing.

Jack Fritscher: We mentioned movies earlier, and since you are including storyboarding as a procedure, and since you mentioned video as an interest, might you take up shooting moving pictures as the century draws to a close? Perhaps a new dimension of Dureau's photography?

George Dureau: Storyboarding is just visual note making. I'm what they call them a natural-born adult note-maker. If I'm going to call somebody, I don't want to waste their time. So I make a list of things I want to talk about. That's hysterically boring, but that's what I do. And that's what you do in drawing too. You make some little sketches of what you're going to do. I draw them real fast. It's very easy for me to draw quickly to a certain satisfaction. Finishing something to make it elegant, poetic, and wonderful to look at, that's something else. But I draw well and fast. So why not draw all the time? Drawing is something you get nothing but better at the more you do it. Better!

Jack Fritscher: Can you summarize your own career at this point?

George Dureau: I may have said it in that [last] line. It's funny. I would have thought when I was in college, and right after, that my art was going to be this exquisite, somewhat austere, magnificent stuff out there, and that's happened, although it's big and Baroque and operatic, and it is to me exactly like my life. It's an extension of my life!

I don't know if anyone told me that's what I was supposed to do: live a life and reflect it in my art. But I think the paintings are a lot like I live. Although I live a conservative life, in its safety, I don't do drugs and lie around in the street, which I may have come close to in the 1960s, but I'm fairly self-preserving about how I live and what trouble I don't get into.

But there is a lot of warmth and passion, a lot of dinners and candles in my life.

I think it is in the art. When I get to the end of this century and look at my work, I will always know exactly what was going on when I look at a picture. It's not like looking at some abstraction. I mean I look at my pictures and I know all the people I've painted and I say, "Oh, that's Troy," but I had to use so-and-so's hand. Oh, wait, that's my hand. I know that hand. I painted my own hand in there. So everything in my art is something chopped out of my life and put into paintings. And some things that I put into my paintings, I then go ahead and live them out. Some stuff starts in my drawings, but then I make them come true.

I did drawings in the 1950s that I then made come true in the 1960s. And things I drew in the 1960s I know I made come true in the 1970s. That's a funny idea, but I know it's true. I guess it's the same brain, both sides of the brain are always thinking all the time both in the way I live my life and the way I do my art.

Jack Fritscher: So to young artists you might say what?

George Dureau: I don't know how they do it today. Life looks so dangerous. I'm glad I lived earlier. I don't know how I made it through the 1940s and 1950s. I really miss the 1960s though I don't go around acting like a 60s person, I suppose. But I really miss all the commitment and all the nerve endings hanging out in the 1960s.

And that's why I say it's fun, more than fun—great!—to once in awhile get really mad at something and put all your talents together and do a painting. I do it in drawings too, of things that I'm really mad at or really concerned about. I think it's wonderful to work with a great deal of concern.

Jack Fritscher: Are you frustrated by concerns sometimes? [Referencing a rumor in which Dureau vented discontent in front of witensses] Do you throw pots? Pre-Columbian pots?

George Dureau: No. If I get angry nowadays, it's because I'm frustrated about not having enough time in a day to get done all the things I want to. Too many careers going on, I think sometimes. And that gets me mad. I used to get drunk and frustrated back in the 1960s, but I don't do that anymore. I'm very controlled about eating and drinking.

Jack Fritscher: How old are you now? I'm fifty-one.

George Dureau: I'm sixty. I'll be sixty-one in December

Jack Fritscher: Do you think you're going backwards in time in terms of your youthful energy? Your energy level seems incredibly high.

George Dureau: I'm getting a lot cuter.

Jack Fritscher: That helps.

George Dureau: I'm in good shape, very healthy. It takes a certain amount of taking care of oneself.

Jack Fritscher: So that "self-destructive artist syndrome" is not part of your personality?

George Dureau: I outlived that. It's funny. I turned my Scots/Welsh/French and German [genes] in the right direction. I started out being drunk all the time. I just turned it around and decided to get mean in my own behalf. I'm very well controlled. I just wish the rest of the world weren't so boring.

Jack Fritscher: It's the decade. It's the end of the century.

George Dureau: Don't you think that we've said everything?

Jack Fritscher: If you think so, I think so.

George Dureau: Thank you. It was wonderful.

Jack Fritscher: Thank you. It was wonderful.

DUREAU IN STUDIO

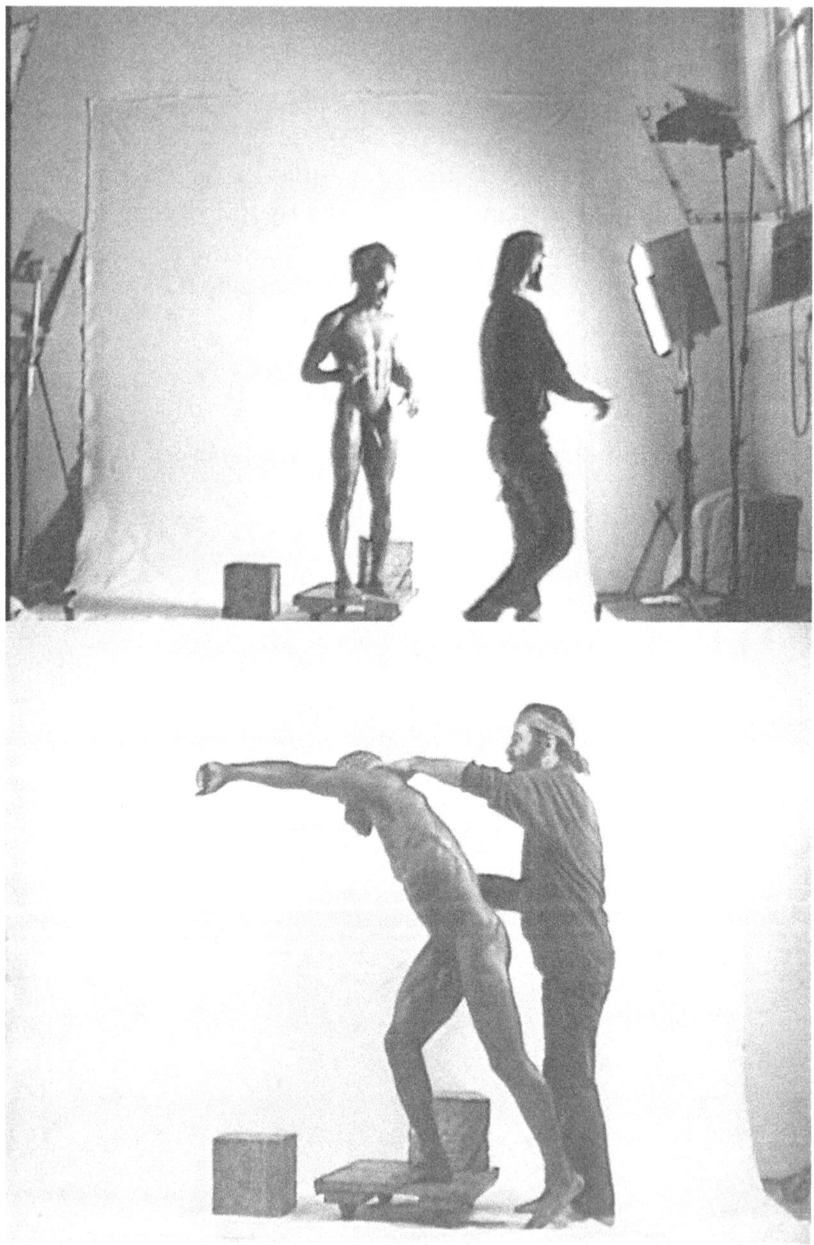

George Dureau, who choreographed all his pictures, directing Glen Thompson in his Dauphine Street studio for the documentary *Dureau in Studio*, April 10, 1991. Six video photos by © Jack Fritscher

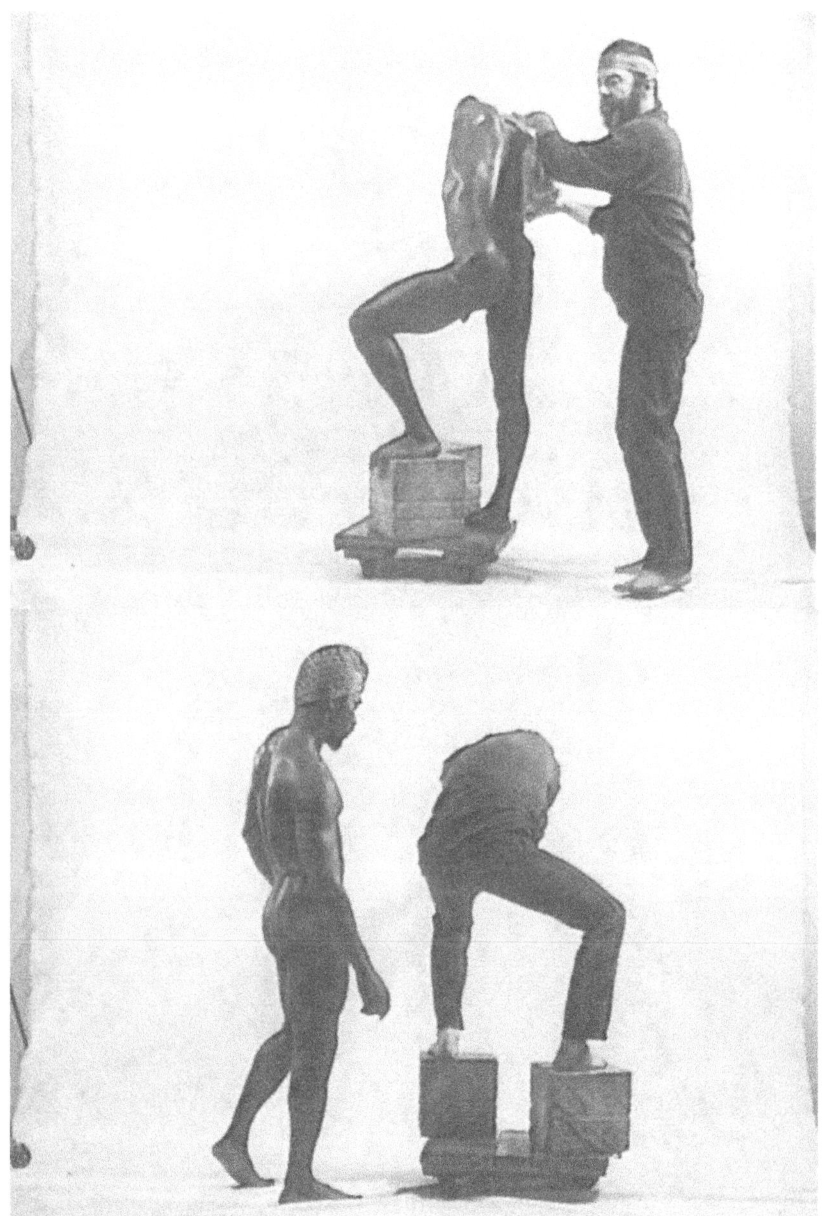

(Bottom) Dureau mounting two moveable dais blocks to demonstrate the basic pose he wanted Thompson to build upon in the photo they were creating together. "My camera gives my models voice. I frequently, always, let them do a couple of their own poses because they seem to crave something that they've been saving up for years. I give them space, step back, and kind of rearrange their ideas and hope for a compromise between my idea and their idea."

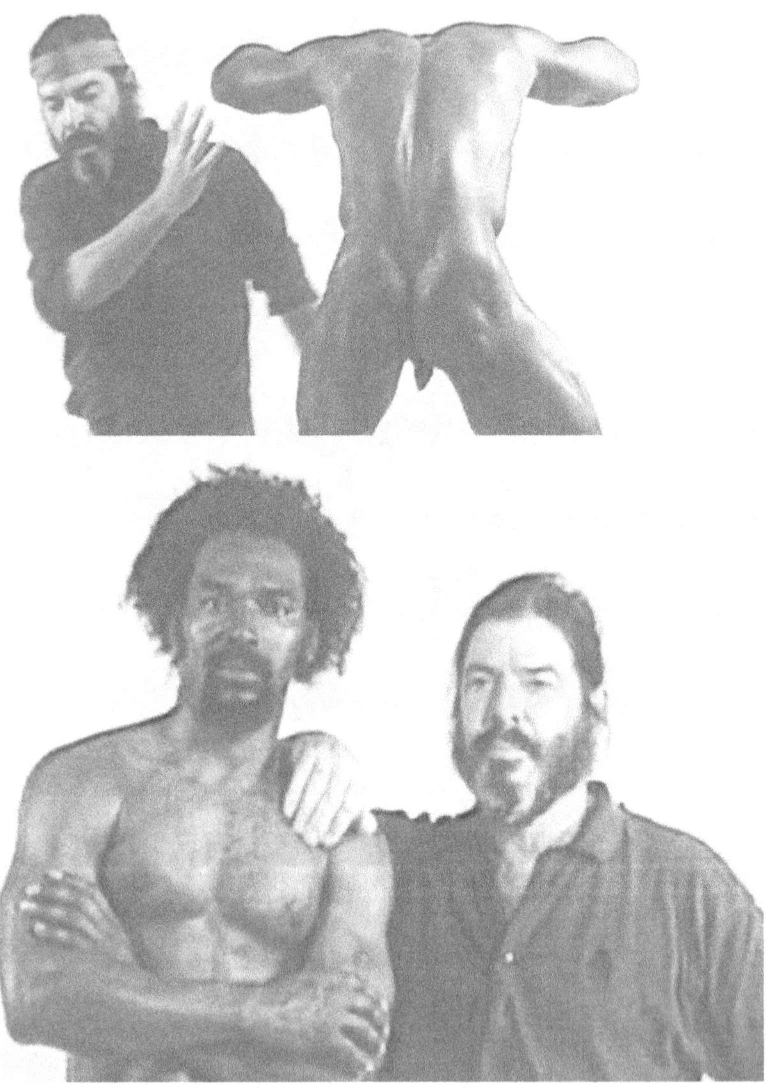

(Top) Dureau was a master of Optical Illusion. When shooting whole-bodied men, he often posed models with their healthy limbs folded away from view to evoke the beauty of broken Greek statues.

(Bottom) Glen Thompson, with George's hand on his shoulder, was an experienced figure model who responded patiently and creatively to George's gentle direction by holding physically strenuous poses until his muscles quivered. Glen Thompson was the first model George shot on video.

TAKE 4

DUREAU IN STUDIO

A Rainy Afternoon in the French Quarter
George Shoots His First Video
Wednesday, April 10, 1991

The documentary video *Dureau in Studio* opens with George Dureau shooting the black whole-bodied Glen Thompson in his *atelier* where the video picks up the moody soundtrack of early spring rain on the roof of his home on Dauphine Street. Dureau's careful lighting of his longtime model and friend Thompson illuminates the video dramatically in the theater of his studio. The effect is stunning. Thompson's muscular body glows incandescent in this solo shoot that reminds me of George's lovely dual shot, *Glen Thompson and Troy Brown*, which turns the eight limbs of the nude black-and-white pair leaning into each like dancers into an ascending array of at least nine perfect triangles.

Glen is an experienced figure model working as hard as Dureau to collaborate symbiotically on the shoot George is staging for our eyewitness camera. With voice and touch, George directs Glen. Speaking quietly to him, he arranges him, nude, greased, sweating, and shining under the heat of the key lights that present him standing on a low platform in a down-spout of light in the dark studio. Mark Hemry helps George set the lights because the overcast afternoon means George cannot shoot with the natural light he prefers. Unfazed by the four cameras in the room, Glen responds patiently to George's gentle direction by holding the physically strenuous poses until his muscles quiver.

From another room, the scent of fresh cut flowers mixes with the damp smell of our jackets worn in from the rain after lunch.

"Glen, drop your head and move your arms to your right….Can you please bend your left leg…That's it…Hold it…."

Dureau shoots carefully. He never clicks his shutter until model and light and framing turn the fleeting moment into a perfect moment. I watch the spark of that co-creation happen through my viewfinder as George backs away from Glen frozen stock still and steps behind his camera to take his shot. Again and again, he arranges Glen to shoot more frames.

Outside, distant thunder rumbles under the long breathy silences of the shoot as Thompson holds steady while Dureau continues to ponder the human sculpture.

When George is satisfied with directing Glen, as well as his own nonchalant performance for our camera, he puts down his still camera, walks to look at our color monitor, and announces he's never held a video camera in his hands.

"Here's one of our cameras," Mark says. He knows this is a significant moment. "Try it."

When George picks up our camera and asks Glen if he is okay with more shots, I begin to shoot George on video shooting Glen on video. That layered moment caught on camera documents George directing his first-ever video segment. The painter who became a photographer touches videography.

No one need wonder at the choreography of a Dureau shoot.

Just before George picks up the video camera, a miracle happens. The rain stops and he quickly turns the studio lights down because an amazing blue light from a skylight shafts down on the set lighting Glen.

Our video camera, condensing real time with a time-lapse strobe effect, catches Dureau on screen carefully positioning Thompson the way an artist moves a co-conspirator in the high crime of art.

I lament that video cameras were not available in the 1970s when I watched Robert Mapplethorpe shoot his photographs.

When George was satisfied with directing his own on-screen video performance from the inside out, he asked if I would like to shoot Glen with my still camera. As a longtime photographer for gay magazines, I appreciated his thoughtful generosity in sharing his model and his space with me—as he had with Robert who, sweet as he was, would never countenance another photographer's camera in his studio. When Glen agreed, I experienced the luxury of shooting a powerful man who was being directed and posed by the powerful George Dureau himself.

Dureau Documentaries

Dureau in Studio, a Jack Fritscher and Mark Hemry Documentary, 1991. Includes thirty Dureau photographs, drawings, and paintings. 33 minutes. Contains nudity. Not suitable for Youtube.

Dureau Speaks, a Jack Fritscher and Mark Hemry Documentary, 1991. 110 minutes. Available on Youtube.

George Dureau on His Bicycle (Age 75, Outside Faubourg Marigny Arts and Bookstore), a David Zalkind Documentary, 2015, 9 minutes. Available on Youtube.

New Orleans Artists John Burton Harter and George Dureau, Film Tribute, Jarret Lofstead, editor/producer, The Bend Media + Production for Saints+Sinners LBGTQ Literary Festival, 2021.

George Dureau: New Orleans Artist, a Sergio Andres Lovbo-Navia and Jarret Lofstead Documentary, 2024. 65 minutes.

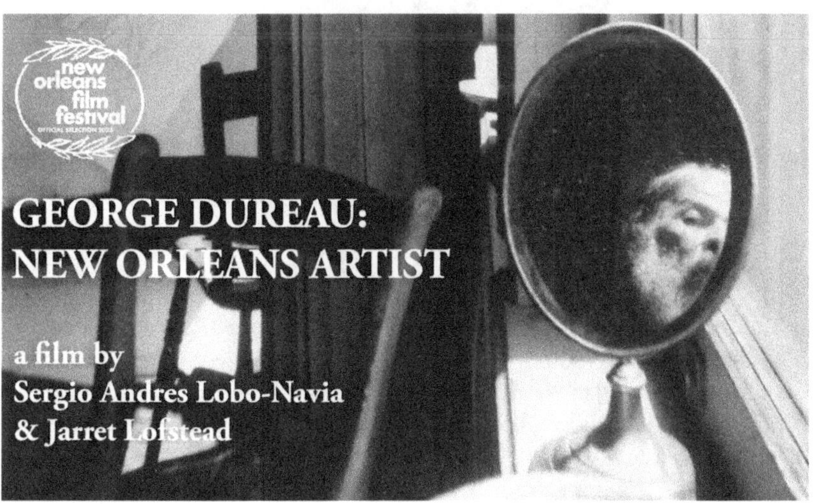

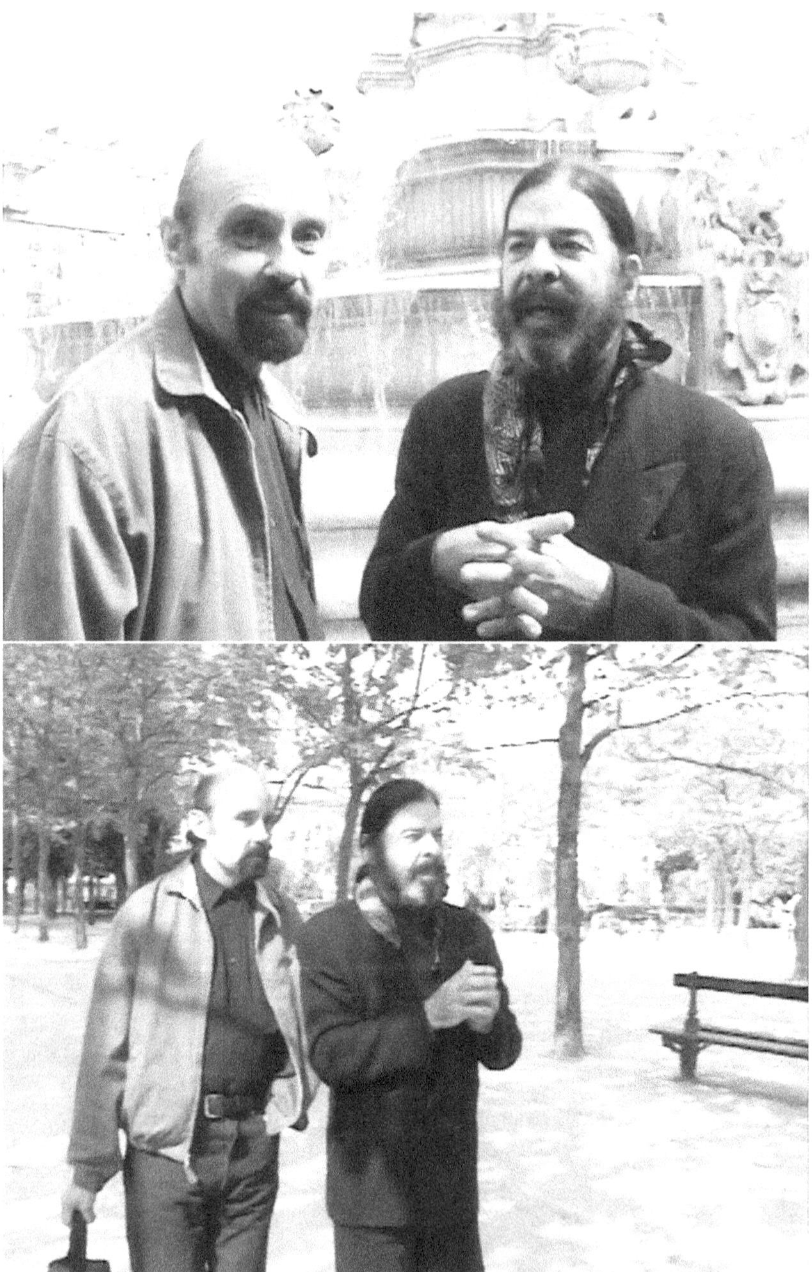

George Dureau and Jack Fritscher strolling the Grande Allée, the Tuileries, Paris, May 3, 1996. Video photos by © Mark Hemry from his unpublished footage of Dureau in Paris

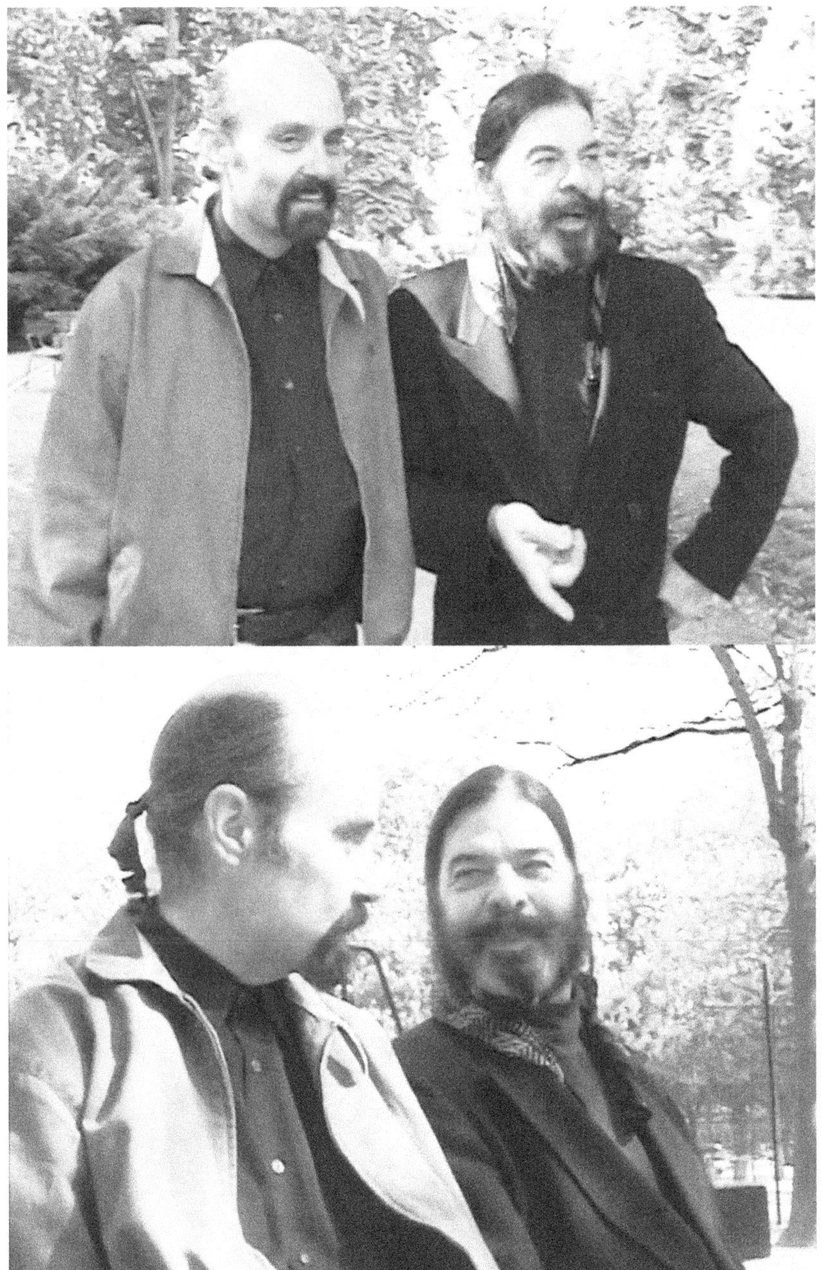

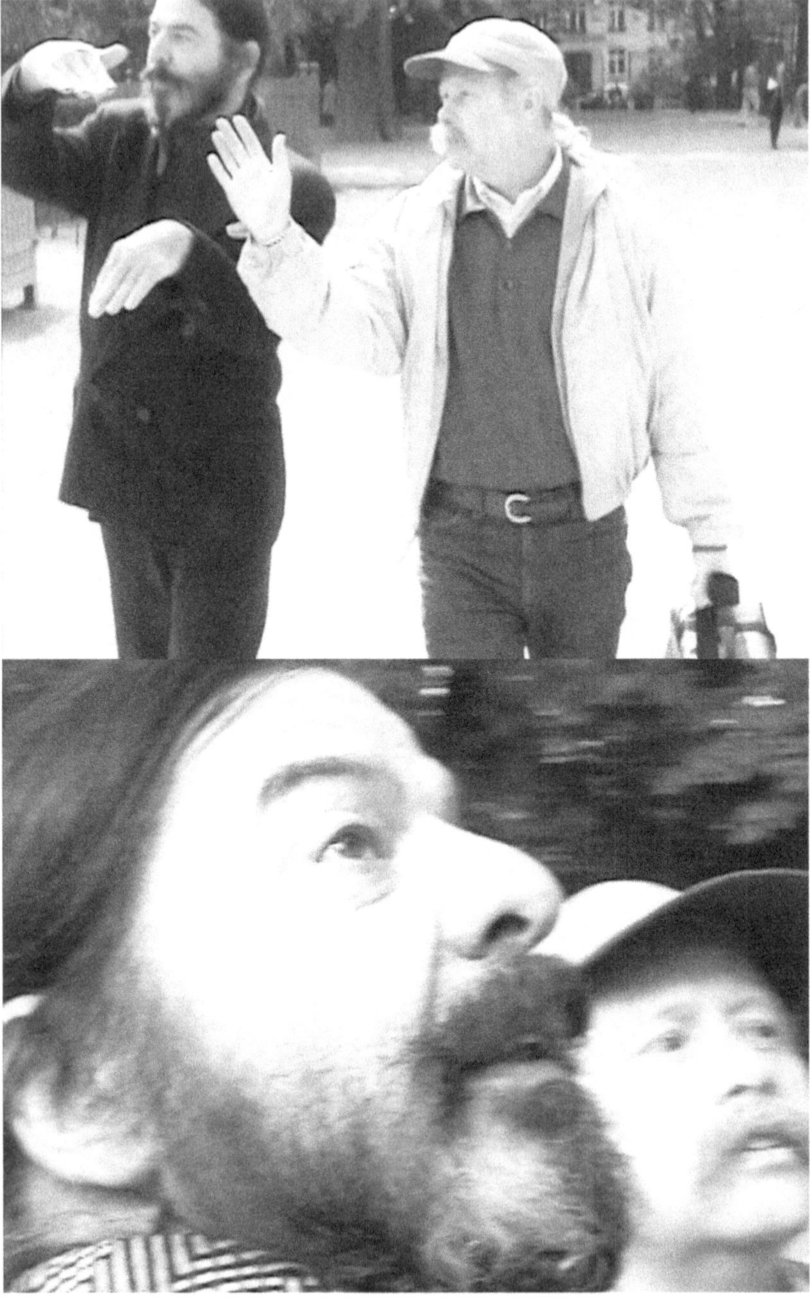

George Dureau and Mark Hemry strolling the Grande Allée, the Tuileries, Paris, May 3, 1996. Video photos by © Jack Fritscher from his unpublished footage of Dureau in Paris

TAKE 5

HELLO, GEORGE DUREAU:
San Francisco Calling

Telephone Conversation

**with Jack Fritscher
Six Weeks After a Week Together in New Orleans
Audiotape
May 28, 1991**

**"Give me the five pictures
that you absolutely want to be seen forever."**

Jack Fritscher: Hello, is this Mr. Dureau? This is Jack Fritscher calling. How are you?

George Dureau: Jack Fritscher! This *is* "the Jack Fritscher" who went to New Orleans, isn't it?

Jack Fritscher: Yes, who had a wonderful time with you in New Orleans.

George Dureau: Listen, dear heart, how are yez? How are you?

Jack Fritscher: I meant to call you all weekend, but I figured that you'd be out running around town.

George Dureau: I'm watching [gossip columnist] Kitty Kelly. She's doing rather well, actually, making everybody else look like a liar. She's blushing, saying, "Oh, I'm not a Washington insider." I think she's right about that. She's telling now where the Frank Sinatra thing started. She really knows her stuff. Oh my God, wait a minute!

I just kicked my wine over. When your bed is higher than your table, there's no telling what will happen to your beverage.

Jack Fritscher: I can picture where you are.

George Dureau: You *know* where I'm at.

Jack Fritscher: Yep.

George Dureau: I was sitting with my bare feet up on the post, right? And I flopped one foot down. It went onto the little round table in front, the ice cream table with all the pots on it, and kicked my ugly glass of white wine. Your model Glen Thompson just left.

Jack Fritscher: Your wonderful model.

George Dureau: He came by to visit. He seemed to enjoy the video shoot when you were here. He's fine. I'm always worried about him. When you were here, I was worried about his partying too much in this party town and not showing up. He always has to ask for money. It makes me crazy because I know he makes enough money to cover everything. It makes me worried…. He gets about $30 a day and he pays $55 a week for rent with utilities included, and every single day, because we're all friends, he calls somebody wanting money. When he doesn't get it, he calls somebody else.

"Could you give me $15 on tomorrow's money?'"

The other night he came over because I had withheld $10 from him last Thursday and when he would call over the weekend, I would say, "Oh no. I don't have it. I'm still broke." I thought I would play broke on him for a change.

To tell the truth, it was a reflection of the way I had actually been stretched for cash for days before when I suddenly had to pay up to the IRS and come up with $4,000 and some dollars to cover my debt. That left me with ten round dollars in the bank.

Jonathan [Webb, his assistant] said, "Well, what did you expect with all these guys wanting money?"

I told Jonathan, "Listen, sweetheart, I've been here before. This here sixty-year-old gentleman went through the 60s and the 70s, not to mention the 30s and the late 50s. I know how to manage by eating everything edible in the house."

Jonathan couldn't believe that. He always thinks I'm supposed to be so luxurious. Actually, he and I didn't do any serious starving. I'd say, "Now let's see. I want you to go buy a $2.50 chicken and from the leftovers of that chicken I'm going to make a chicken broth which will be made into a chicken soup." He was amazed. It was so funny that Jonathan, who comes from a much less pretentious background than I, doesn't understand this kind of self denial, a kind of postponed gratification.

I'm very good at tightening my belt and saying, "Direct your strong winds at me—for here I am."

I can really do a tight belt and stiff upper lip.

Jack Fritscher: As God is my witness, you are so Scarlett O'Hara.

George Dureau: Ha. So, we went through about a week of extreme frugality. A couple of checks arrived and Jonathan just went, "Whew! That was close."

I don't intend to change my ways too much. I say, "Jonathan, you have to remember that I'm the guy who pays some $1,500 or $1,800 of rent and expenses every month." God, it costs me about $3,500 a month just to open the door on my gorgeous rental. With the goddamn credit cards.

Jack Fritscher: People don't realize the overhead to keep a home going.

George Dureau: Enough of my money talk. You may remember that anecdote I told you about the *New York Times*. That peculiar incident when Gene Thornton wrote a major piece on me and it was pulled. At the time I didn't get particularly hysterical. I thought, "Oh, isn't that a shame."

But now that I look back and look at the hegemony of Wagstaff and Mapplethorpe, now I understand that there may have been something else than the *Times* saying, "Oh, we don't want to do a piece on photographs on men. And Dureau wouldn't be the person that we would do it on if we were going to do it." That was just the opposite of what Gene Thornton had told me.

He said, "I've never wanted to do a piece about men photographing men before."

Jack Fritscher: Homophobia is sexism.

George Drueau: Well, he tried to overcome it. He said, "Yours is the first time I've seen a noble kind of photography and so I felt I had to write this piece."

He raved on and raved on and the next day he called me and took me to lunch and explained to me that "I never show anybody what I've written about them before it's published, but I have to show you because I was so thrilled with your photos. I've never done that before and the paper has never pulled anything of mine before."

Jack Fritscher: Someone's thumb was on the scale.

George Dureau: Well, it *was* very strange because in the catalog that was coming out, there is a very large, beautiful, respectful photograph of Earl [*Earl Leavell*, 1977] with his crooked arms [possibly from Thalidomide] shot from the side. A very noble looking photograph. Everybody in the catalog is black. I don't know how aware you are of the fascism of most of the people in photography, but Mapplethorpe-Wagstaff and most of the other people who like homo kind of stuff are rather fascist. There's not many liberals around anymore. I have the feeling many gallery owners and a lot of others just let this high-handed attitude go by because they have to stay on the good side of the clients. Do you know what I mean?

Jack Fritscher: Gatekeepers laying down the law about art?

George Dureau: Not that they necessarily are fascists themselves, but they tell me, "It's okay, darling. We'll do the right thing because we want all these rich people to like us." By the way, I'm having a show this summer at the Fahey/Klein Gallery in Los Angeles.

Jack Fritscher: I remember you said so and I wanted to check with you on the dates [June 28-August 3, 1991 in tandem with Joel-Peter Witkin] .

George Dureau: Nice as all the people are at that gallery, I find that they don't really know who I am. They treat me like this person who one time did some photographs. That's so funny because I don't think that's who I am. I'm not just photographs. I mean, one guy at that gallery didn't know that I made paintings. He didn't know that I drew. Yet he insisted he was going to do a book on me.

I said, "You know, I think it would be wonderful if you learned more about me before we do a book."

He said, "Oh? Anyway, I can't do it right now. I hope you understand."

I said, "Well, I can't do it with you right now either. You don't have any idea who I am or what I'm about. I think you have to learn more about me."

[In this little petulant scene from a Dureau movie, George using third-person pronouns rather than a name expresses his emotional point of view about David Fahey who, in full disclosure, I found to be a most cordial expert whom I interviewed August 31. 1990, for my work on Robert Mapplethorpe. David Fahey is founding co-owner of the Fahey/Klein Gallery in Los Angeles. He has represented over 500 photographers, collaborated on nearly fifty fine art photography books, and was the West Coast editor of Warhol's *Interview* magazine. He is the co-vice president of the Herb Ritts Foundation and serves on the Photography Advisory Council for the J. Paul Getty Museum.]

I think he expects to come from LA to New Orleans at some point, but he insists on having a show first. So it turns out that the show is to be with [Joel-Peter] Witkin, and since Witkin and I started together, and Witkin has already become famous, I'm not going to play second fiddle by being there.

Plus I told him that I wanted a cohesive display, not a smattering of photos with a little o' this and a little o' that. I said. "If the purpose of this exhibit is to introduce me because you say I'm not known to many people, well, then, I think you should introduce the very, very best of me."

I convinced him to dig into all my vintage stuff and offer for sale some new prints, gorgeous new prints of all that earlier stuff plus prints of newer images that fit into the introductory theme. What I mean by that is this. I asked him, and he agreed, to introduce me with the warmest of my very humanist pictures. I didn't want to create the wrong impression of my work by starting out with the armless, headless torso pictures. I want the warmth of my personal relationships to come forth in the exhibit. So I want to do all the heads that show face. I wouldn't mind if some of his selections can be from my vintage work before I even met Mapplethorpe. Some of the prints are even that old. I'd like him to hang my amputee and black photos next to Witkin and Mapplethorpe so people can see what they lifted from me. Wouldn't you do that?

Jack Fritscher: Yes.

George Dureau: The thing is, Witkin is going to have a good turn out, but I don't want to be there and have people ask, "Now who are you, dear?" I'm not going to take that. I'm giving him an absolutely exquisite show, these gorgeous images.

He said about my idea of juxtaposing my work with Witkin and Mapplethorpe: "I wouldn't worry about that. I think your images speak for themselves."

The thing is I *was* letting them speak for themselves.

And then he said: "Oh, would you like me to do a book of your paintings, your drawings, and your photographs?"

What do you think? Would you do that?

Jack Fritscher: Well, he *is* David Fahey. He *is* a great arts writer. So yes. Work with him. He will get you the book you want.

George Dureau: I'd like it to be like a big two-part book: *Paintings. Photographs.* Apparently he is being very successful with books.

Jack Fritscher: Yes. David told me he's got eight in progress right now.

George Dureau: I know. He's working three of them, seriously, right now.

Jack Fritscher: What would you think if I duped a copy of our taped interview and sent it to him?

George Dureau: I told him that already. I told him that you had done a video that might enable him to know me more. I'm sending him the slides and transparencies that you saw, and lots of printed material, all kinds of stuff. After he studies that, then he can come and meet me down here in my environment and actually see, the way you did, what it is that I'm doing. I mean, I don't want him to be doing a book if he doesn't know anything about me. I don't want to be represented as yet another photographer who happened to have done certain images before Mapplethorpe. That doesn't say anything about me.

Jack Fritscher: So you want him to encounter you and your personality and your art world in New Orleans to get a take on you.

George Dureau: I told him I would ask you to send him the tape.

Jack Fritscher: Sure, I'd be glad to.

George Dureau: I think that would be good for him.

Jack Fritscher: Yes, I think so. Get him up to speed with a good introduction because you are really "you" on the tape.

George Dureau: Yes. Otherwise, he would never be able to say who I am. He wouldn't know how to say that I am somebody who has known and lived with and loved black people. He wouldn't know how to say it.

Jack Fritscher: Well, he's a smart man. I like him very much. I think he gives artists a fair shake.

George Dureau: I may not be the artist he himself prefers, but if he's going to do a book about me, he needs to do his homework.

Jack Fritscher: He definitely will. I 'll make a copy and send it off to him.

George Dureau: Is it edited enough so that one can sit through it?

Jack Fritscher: I haven't edited the tape because it's two hours long and I haven't thought how to cut it. I don't want to cut a single word. It's too rich to reduce to an arbitrary sixty-minute documentary. I love the rush of the raw footage with you talking a mile a minute. I think it's a wonderful long authentic take. You were so ready for your close up. He should immerse himself in the footage. I'll just send him the whole shoot. In fact. if you'd like a copy for your own files, I can send one to you.

George Dureau: Yes, I'd love to. I don't know anything about editing. I mean I might look at the tape and say, "Oh, I don't think we should mention such and such. I think we should leave out this and I think this could be shorter."

Jack Fritscher: Of course. You can just look at it and have the footage as shot for you own personal use. Then what gets made out of it gets made.

George Dureau: I could make notes on what I think is embarrassing. I would not be doing aesthetic editing. I'd just do self-preservation editing.

Jack Fritscher: Fine by me.

George Dureau: You know the thing that hurts me the most? I'm looking at some photo books right now. The thing that hurts me most of all is when I'm published in one of these photo anthologies, like the *History of Male Photography*, and almost inevitably, there's a Mapplethorpe on the cover, right? And inevitably it is one of the ones he lifted from me. It drives me nuts. It wouldn't matter to me that there is some Mapplethorpe on the cover, but that it should be one of the images that he got from me!

It just says something to me because that "Mapplethorpe filter" is used to create status in male photography.

And those photos? They're not him doing his "number." It's him doing my "number." What a pisser!

There is this guy from Austria, Peter somebody, who was wonderful. [Possibly Peter Weibel (1944-2023)] He did a photo-collection book that has five photos by each of us contributors. He did a show at the same time and all the images from the book are in the show.

He told me, "Just give me the five pictures that you absolutely want to be seen forever."

But what's on the cover? A Mapplethorpe which is absolutely reminiscent of something Robert saw in my house. It's a photo of a boy shot from the back. He's leaning forward with his two arms turned up in such a way that his arms sort of disappear. I could have killed him for that one.

Jack Fritscher: That's a bit much.

George Dureau: I'm tired of telling all these stories.

Jack Fritscher: So what's happening with you?

George Dureau: Oh, my painting show that I just did here is beautiful. Did you see the ones that were going to be drawings with varnish on them?

Jack Fritscher: The partial torsos? Mark is so in love with the javelin-thrower torso.

George Dureau: Those are the ones. I also did some male and female figures jammed together. I've done six of them now. Those are the hetero ones that sell all the time. Those javelins haven't sold. I can't believe it. Jonathan thought those would be the immediate sale.

Jack Fritscher: Because they're gay.

George Dureau: There's an Ajax, the *Dead Ajax* drawing you saw. I did a big one of that, a really big long one that flows down the wall. Then I did another one for the show *Drawing Monuments II*, a tall drawing of a statuesque guy—with the head of a dwarf snuggled up under him with the dwarf's hand wrapped around the perfect leg and the dwarf's arm pointing up directing this big beautiful Indian-looking creature.

It's this dwarf directing this big gorgeous monster to look at the stars. I've always been drawn to people who are handicapped, particularly to people who are triumphant though handicapped. I've always loved tough dwarfs. [*Roosevelt Singleton*, 1974] I've always been attracted to little people who act strong and big—like the triumphs of superheroes."

Jack Fritscher: With the Olympics coming up, your athletic figure paintings [like *Gymnast Crouching*, 1987-1988] should be a great tie-in.

George Dureau: Yes, maybe with tourists, because the tryouts are going to be in New Orleans in a stadium we're remodeling. I'm going to try to do a poster or something for it. [The 1992 U.S. Olympic trials for track and field were held at Tad Gormley Stadium in New Orleans.]

Jack Fritscher: Speaking of really big paintings flowing down the wall, how did the *War* show go?

George Dureau: It went well. The painting was just gorgeous. Everybody loved it. Unfortunately it had to be jammed in between all those other exhibit things. It's back at the house now and I just had publishing people photographing me with it. There's a book coming out by a photographer from Atlanta. It's called *Classic New Orleans Homes*. Believe it or not, I'm one of them.

I staged the shoot by hanging that *War* painting on the long wall in the studio the way you saw it so it falls down the wall and spreads out on the floor where I just scattered everything around it, easels, brushes, palettes, paints. My set decoration made it really easy for the photographer to create something. He shot it in my front room where you arrive at the top of the stairs.

We have not had sun since you've been here. It's rained for thirty days or more. The most rain you have ever seen forever. New Orleans has the highest rainfall in the states. We have had more rain than we have in a whole year.

Jack Fritscher: To a Californian living in drought that's a deluge.

George Dureau: We had a higher rainfall in January than you had in ten years. It got so wet here that the brick walls on the inner side of the house just have not dried. The water just runs down them. I've never seen it like this before. I'm glad I'm not the landlord.

Jack Fritscher: It's not damaged anything, has it?

George Dureau: No. It's funny because there are a lot of drips from the ceiling, every day another spot drips, but it always drips about a foot and a half out from the walls. Anyway, enough of the water.

Get this. I was talking to this woman [Rosemary James] who has this beautiful little house, something called "Faulkner House Books" here in the Quarter, and she had also been photographed for this *Homes* book.

She said, "Did he photograph your bed properly?'"

"It's a great angle," I said. "The bed's only about three quarters of the way into the picture."

She said, "Oh, the bed from the front."

"Yes" I said. "It looks like a Federalist bed that I draped sort of like Manet's *Olympia*." It had this Federalist appearance about the bed. It really describes my nature, I guess. Like *Olympia* with her come-hither stare, I'm forthright, upright, but you *could* get to me if you tried.

She said, "Did he catch that?"

I said, "I'm afraid it didn't come out as well as I thought he could have done." But he must have liked it because he asked if they could shoot a few photos for *Southern Accents* [a home, antiques, and luxury magazine].

He said, "Do you mind if we do you in *Southern Accents?*"

I said, "OK! *Southern Accents*, here we come!"

All the magazines get a notion to do me, but some of them drop out because they decide there's just not enough "precious stuff" in the house.

Jack Fritscher: Speaking of your precious stuff, I've sent the publisher of my book on Robert a photocopy of your portrait of him which I think captures his winsomeness.

George Dureau: Oh, the cute one that I took up at his house in New York in 1979?

Jack Fritscher: You printed him inside a circle.

George Dureau: Yes. I shot that one at his place in 1979 when I first met him.

Jack Fritscher: It's a great nominee for a cover. As far as I have anything to say about my book. [In 1994, that Dureau portrait of Robert was the cover of my *Mapplethorpe* book, and George said, "Turnabout is fair play."]

George Dureau: Really? It is a very good picture. What I like about it is it's very much the style that comes from my drawing that I've been doing since the 60s, the way it's posed and put into the circle. It wasn't until that time that Robert started doing this, what I would call *amplitude*. Amply filling the space. He learned how important it is to shape the negative spaces around people, but he had never done that before.

When he saw how I did my drawings and transposed my drawing technique into my photography, he realized that you could be classical and ample in the way the figure sits in the picture. You can give a sort of Greek nobility to the figures. A sort of classic look. So that one particular photograph of him really does show how he learned *amplitude* from me.

Jack Fritscher: Your portrait represents him perfectly during the period I knew him best.

George Dureau: Right then [1977-1980] he was achieving fame and feeling cool strutting down the street pretending he hated the people recognizing him, you know?

Jack Fritscher: Peter Berlin told me when he and Robert walked out together, Robert was jealous because Peter had a famous face from his movies and people said hello to him, but not to Robert.

George Dureau: Robert was bossy.

Jack Fritscher: He could be petulant. I remember he hated meeting people at exhibits where he'd sparkle even while he was shining them on.

George Dureau: Wait a minute! I've got to turn off the chicken stock! I'm getting the most out of my chicken. I'm a really thrifty food person. Even if I'm spending a little money or a lot, I cook up a bunch of different things and get my money's worth. I was a boy during the Depression in the 1930s.

Jack Fritscher: I was born during the Depression. I don't think I'll ever forget arriving for supper at your house and finding you in the kitchen with all your grocery bags filled with, what were they, crawfish?

George Dureau: I think we've finished those off by now. I said to the man when I was buying them, "There will be five adult men eating."

So he said, "You'll need this many."

He was that very fat black man I told you about.

I gave him a piece of my mouth. I said, "Do I look as large as you?"

He said, "Oh, honey, if it was for me, I would eat…"

I said, "Don't tell me what you would eat!'"

Jack Fritscher: That afternoon of our shoot, Jonathan was so helpful. How is he? Nice guy. Great photographer. We bonded.

George Dureau: I'm getting him out of town as fast as possible, as soon as I can get some money to send him on vacation. I love him, but I'm tired of looking at his face and he's tired of looking at mine.

Jack Fritscher: Where does he go?

George Dureau: He goes to Costa Rica every year. People like him. Every place I go people ask, "Has Jonathan left yet? When is he leaving?" Then I look like an ogre because I haven't sent the boy on vacation. I went through a lot of years and never managed to have three months of vacation. Did you?

Jack Fritscher: I did when I taught university, but I spent the luxury of that time working writing books and articles.

George Dureau: The only people who get three-months vacation are students and teachers.

Jack Fritscher: I'm sure people think my trip to New Orleans was a vacation. That was no vacation. It was a lot of fun, but it was no vacation. It was work.

George Dureau: Jonathan doesn't realize that if I send him down to Costa Rica with money while I keep his house here for him, that it's the best of all possible worlds. I'll just get the money and help him get out of here for a while.

I just love being alone. I love being an artist.

Jonathan is finally becoming an artist instead of just being someone who does arty things.

When I'm alone, I do this wonderful thing where I just go and ride and ride around the city until I can't ride anymore and then I come home and I just lie on the floor and beat my meat or let the air blow over me and just lie there until a thought comes in my head.

I think, "God, I'm alone." No house mate is going to come down the stairs saying, "I'm an artist. I'm an artist. I'm hungry and I'm an artist. I'll have a glass of wine."

Jack Fritscher: So you'll be staying home alone? You won't be coming to California?

George Dureau: Here's what I'm going to try to do. Since Arthur Roger is opening his gallery in New York in October, and I have a show tentatively scheduled for around April, it would be great if your book was out because he could coordinate my New York show with your *Mapplethorpe* book.

Jack Fritscher: My book won't be out for a year or more.

George Dureau: Oh. Books really help gallery sales, I'm told. I think I may also be in a group show in Los Angeles next year.

Jack Fritscher: We told you we'd drive down from San Francisco to hang out if you come to LA.

George Dureau: But I don't think I want a show in LA next year. I don't want another disappointment. I do not want to go out there, and have to put up with movie stars and celebrities like Madonna who will probably show up.

When I was talking with Russell Albright [art collector Dr. H. Russell Albright (1934-2017), who introduced Dureau to Mapplethorpe, bequeathed his photography collection to the New Orleans Museum of Art], he said, "You must do the LA show."

And I said, "Madonna can come back next year to see me because this year she's going to be coming to see Witkin."

They can discover me if they want to, but I don't like being patronized. It's true. I don't like playing a beggar's game. I don't like explaining to people supposedly in the know that my name is such and such, and I do such and such. Oh, I'm too old for that.

Jack Fritscher: I've reached a point of independence myself especially with all the competing books about Robert that have been announced and have yet to be written. I'm an independent West Coast writer which rather upsets New York writers who raise an eyebrow about a San Franciscan writing about a New York artist. One of Robert's Manhattan models threatened to kill me because he heard I'm writing a book and he fears I'm telling his story. I never met him. I never heard of him. Robert never mentioned him. When he sent threats to my publishers, they reported him to the NYPD where he's now on file. Art is a savage game.

George Dureau: There's angles on everything, yours, his, mine, especially around the politics of male photography.

Jack Fritscher: Kurosawa was right. Everything is *Rashomon*.

George Dureau: The photos I shot in a kind of liberal way, Robert re-shot in a dominant way which changes the politics from free to fascist. He was all over the map trying to conquer the world. He had to do one picture of everything in the world. It was really funny because he wanted the appearance of being the man of all the world.

Jack Fritscher: He *was* a man of the world.

George Dureau: He dominated his models. He could make people, and his models, and magazines do scandalous things.

Jack Fritscher: When I called Roger Koch [*Roger Koch in Fishnet Stockings*, 1983], he said posing for Robert was not a pleasant experience.

> [Bodybuilder Roger Koch whom I first photographed in 1981 soon became famous as Colt model "Frank Vickers." His muscularity and see-through vascularity landed him on-going work as a nude anatomical model at medical school classes where the professor would touch his splendid body parts with a long pointer stick. He was just days away from succumbing to AIDS.]

On his deathbed, he said, "I have nothing good to say about Robert Mapplethorpe."

George Dureau: I hope you have success in discussing those unwholesome practices in your book.

Jack Fritscher: Yes, Robert as dominant male. I do wonder about public receptivity to words like *fistfucking* and *shit*. I try to write *handballing* and *scatology* to soften reality a bit.

George Dureau: Handballing!

Jack Fritscher: Yes, it sounds more like a sport than a sex act. I've kept you so long. I must let you get back to your chicken soup.

George Dureau: Oh my God, you are running up some phone bill.

Jack Fritscher: I wanted to talk to you all weekend.

George Dureau: By the way, do you remember my friend Byron Robinson? Do your remember his face that looks at you so ferociously in my head-and-shoulders picture? [*Byron Robinson*, 1985]

Jack Fritscher: Yes, he looks like a lean pro-football player.

George Dureau: Byron's a kickboxer and has really intense eyes, tight mouthed. He wanted to be photographed again. After eight years. So I said I would, but I decided I'd already done such a good first picture of him that I was always going to haunted by it being better than anything I've done since.

So I said, "Jonathan, we're going to set the picture up exactly like we did before. We're going to shoot that picture again."

I wanted to make it different. I set up artificial lights because the first was shot by natural light. I greased him up, got him all gorgeous, black skin gleaming.

I said to him, "We have to make this as good as the one we did eight years ago."

He looked beautiful.

I told him, "We'll start with that set up, and then we'll already be at that level to build on the first version with the new light and the quality and the sexiness."

He loved the idea. Then when we got in there, the first thing he said was, "Don't you want me to take my pants off?"

He's never done nude shots before, and he has this large dick that goes out two inches, turns, and goes south for nine more or something. So I photographed him nude that way and I photographed him in a sort of John L. Sullivan antique-lighting sort of thing, a fighting pose. [John L. Sullivan 1858-1918, first heavyweight gloved boxing champion.]

He said, "I like the old-fashioned poses like this."

He hit the famous bare-knuckle "fisticuffs pose." And he did it beautifully. The prints are coming back tomorrow from the developer and I've got eight rolls of him. So that's going to be inserted into my next show and I'll send you something from that.

Jack Fritscher: That sounds wonderful.

George Dureau: They're going to be beautiful. I've always wished before that I could have shot him nekkid because he's never posed nekkid. They're just gorgeous.

It's very easy for me to absorb turn-of-the-century things and earlier, because, being a painter and a drawer, I'm used to that sort of static look. That frozen-in-time moment in antique pictures when people had to hold still, very stiff, because the shot had to be a time-exposure before cameras could shoot fast photographs.

If you look at my photographs, you can tell from the stillness that as a painter I'm used to someone having to sit for two hours, not just three seconds. If the model has the patience to pose, I have the patience to shoot that look.

Jack Fritscher: Many of the pictures of athletes in magazines you saw as a child were of that vintage era.

George Dureau: Yes. And when I direct people, I direct them at a slower turn-of-the-last-century pace because I'm a painter.

When I woo people I woo them to stay wooed. I don't woo them into something they're going to regret.

I'm not a fascist photographer. I do the long paragraph on them, with them, when I direct them.

Ohh, goodbye, darling. I have to go to work. And so do you.

Jack Fritscher: Take care, George.

George Dureau: Thank you for calling.

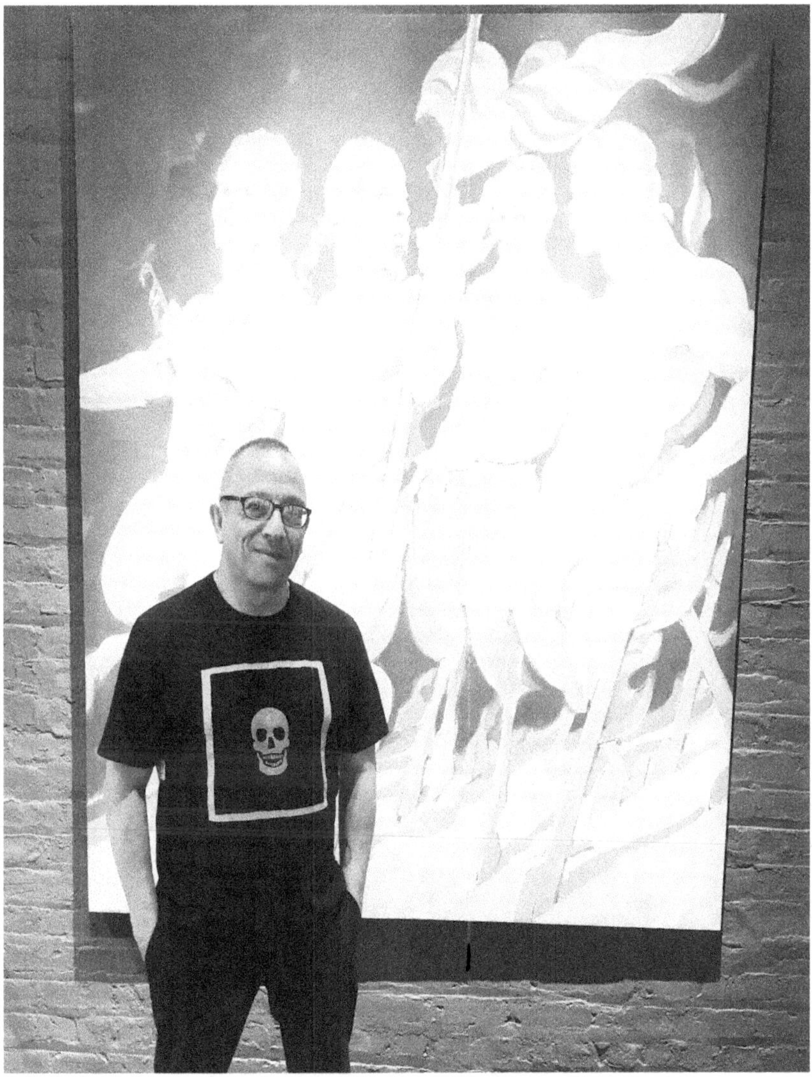

The large painting, *George and His Closest Friends*, 1997, pictured with Dureau's friend photographer Michael Alago, Arthur Roger Gallery, New Orleans, 2023. Photo by © Jarret Lofstead. George's Mardi Gras parade figure—second goat-footed Satyr from the left—is a self-portrait.

Other Works by Jack Fritscher

Novels

Some Dance to Remember:
A Memoir-Novel of San Francisco 1970-1982

Castro Street Blues
The Geography of Women
What They Did to the Kid
Leather Blues

Short Fiction

Rainbow County
Corporal in Charge of Taking Care of Captain O'Malley
Stand by Your Man
TITANIC: Forbidden Stories Hollywood Forgot
Stonewall: Stories of Gay Liberation
Sweet Embraceable You: Coffee House Stories

Non-Fiction

The Life and Times of the Legendary Larry Townsend
Gay Pioneers: How "Drummer" Shaped Gay Pop Culture 1965-1999
Gay San Francisco: Eyewitness Drummer
Mapplethorpe: Assault with a Deadly Camera
Popular Witchcraft: Straight from the Witch's Mouth
Anton LaVey Speaks: The Canonical Interview
Love and Death in Tennessee Williams
When Malory Met Arthur: Camelot
Television Today

www.JackFritscher.com